MEDICAL EXPENSE INSURANCE

The Health Insurance Association of America
Washington, DC 20004-1109

©1997 by the Health Insurance Association of America
All rights reserved. Published 1997
Printed in the United States of America

ISBN 1-879143-40-2

TABLE OF CONTENTS

TABLES v

FOREWORD vii

PREFACE ix

ACKNOWLEDGMENTS xi

ABOUT THE AUTHORS xiii

Chapter 1
GROUP MAJOR MEDICAL EXPENSE INSURANCE 1

Chapter 2
INDIVIDUAL HOSPITAL-SURGICAL INSURANCE 19

Chapter 3
MARKETING AND SELLING MEDICAL EXPENSE INSURANCE 37

Chapter 4
PRICING MEDICAL EXPENSE INSURANCE 53

Chapter 5
MEDICAL EXPENSE CONTRACT PROVISIONS 79

Chapter 6
UNDERWRITING MEDICAL EXPENSE INSURANCE 103

Chapter 7
MEDICAL EXPENSE POLICY ADMINISTRATION 133

Chapter 8
MEDICAL EXPENSE CLAIM ADMINISTRATION 157

Chapter 9
MEDICAL EXPENSE INDUSTRY ISSUES 189

Appendix A
SUMMARY OF P.L. 104-191, THE HEALTH INSURANCE PORTABILITY AND
ACCOUNTABILITY ACT OF 1996 199

Appendix B
COMPLYING WITH THE HEALTH INSURANCE PORTABILITY AND
ACCOUNTABILITY ACT OF 1996: A GUIDE FOR EMPLOYERS AND
HEALTH INSURERS 211

Appendix C
GROUP COORDINATION OF BENEFITS MODEL REGULATION 239

Appendix D
GROUP COVERAGE DISCONTINUANCE AND REPLACEMENT MODEL
REGULATION 257

Appendix E
RULES GOVERNING ADVERTISEMENTS OF ACCIDENT AND SICKNESS
INSURANCE WITH INTERPRETIVE GUIDELINES............................ 261

NOTES 275

GLOSSARY 277

INDEX... 297

TABLES

CHAPTER 1

Table 1.1 .... Reimbursement under a Comprehensive Plan
Table 1.2 .... Reimbursement under a Supplemental Plan
Table 1.3 .... Reimbursement with First-Dollar Coverage under a Comprehensive Plan
Table 1.4 .... Reimbursement with an Integrated Deductible under a Supplemental Plan (where the basic plan paid more than $500)
Table 1.5 .... Reimbursement with an Integrated Deductible under a Supplemental Plan (where the basic plan paid less than $500)
Table 1.6 .... Timing of Incurred Charges on the Deductible

CHAPTER 2

Table 2.1 .... Room and Board Charges for a 5-Day Confinement at $350 a Day: $1,750
Table 2.2 .... Miscellaneous Inpatient Hospital Expenses Incurred for a 5-Day Confinement: $6,148.55
Table 2.3 .... Maximum Surgical Expense Benefit: $8,000
Table 2.4 .... Payment for Multiple Surgical Procedures Performed at the Same Time
Table 2.5 .... Physician Inhospital Expense Benefits: 5-Day Confinement

CHAPTER 3

Table 3.1 .... Individual and Group Medical Expense Insurance Product Designs
Table 3.2 .... Sample HIPC Menu

CHAPTER 4

Table 4.1 .... Components of the Premium Rate
Table 4.2 .... Pricing a Medical Expense Policy with Five Benefits (for a 35-year-old male)
Table 4.3 .... Sample Expenses on an Individual Medical Expense Policy with a $1,500 Average Annual Premium and 70 Percent Anticipated Loss Ratio

Table 4.4 .... Example of the Development Method of Estimating Claims

CHAPTER 5

Table 5.1 .... Table of Continuance
Table 5.2 .... Examples of a Basic Hospital-Surgical Plan and Supplemental Major Medical Expense Plan Features and Dollar Limits

CHAPTER 6

Table 6.1 .... Average Charges for Inpatient Services
Table 6.2 .... Inpatient Utilization Statistics

CHAPTER 7

Table 7.1 .... A Training Model for Improving Customer Service Skills

CHAPTER 8

Table 8.1 .... Current Procedural Terminology (CPT) Codes
Table 8.2 .... International Classification of Diseases (ICD) Codes by Disease
Table 8.3 .... International Classification of Diseases (ICD) Codes by Health Status and Health Service Use
Table 8.4 .... International Classification of Diseases (ICD) Codes by External Causes of Injury and Poisoning
Table 8.5 .... HIAA Surgical Prevailing Healthcare Charges System

CHAPTER 9

Table 9.1 .... Pro/Con: Can Managed Care Keep Medical Spending under Control?

FOREWORD

The HIAA Insurance Education Program aims to be the leader in providing the highest quality educational material and service to the health insurance industry and other related health care fields.

To accomplish this mission, the Program seeks to fulfill the following goals:

1. Provide a tool for use by member company personnel to enhance quality and efficiency of services to the public;
2. Provide a career development vehicle for employees and other health care industry personnel; and
3. Further general understanding of the role and contribution of the health insurance industry to the financing, administration, and delivery of health care services.

The Insurance Education Program provides the following services:

1. A comprehensive course of study in the Fundamentals of Health Insurance, Long-Term Care Insurance, Disability Income Insurance, Managed Care, Medical Expense Insurance, and Health Care Fraud;
2. Certificate by examination of educational achievement for all courses;
3. Programs to recognize accomplishment in the industry and academic communities through course evaluation and certification, which enables participants to obtain academic or continuing education credits; and
4. Development of educational, instructional, training, and informational materials related to the health insurance and health care industries.

PREFACE

More than 184 million Americans have private medical expense insurance, which offers broad and substantial coverage for necessary medical care. As the health care system in the United States changes with the times, so too do medical expense insurance products. To help control health care costs, for example, the insurance industry has instituted managed care components in virtually all medical expense insurance products.

Students of Health Insurance Association of America (HIAA) courses were introduced to the concepts underlying medical expense insurance in *Fundamentals of Health Insurance: Part A* and *Fundamentals of Health Insurance: Part B,* which cover a wide array of health insurance products, including medical expense, supplemental coverages, accident, disability, and long-term care. The purpose of this text is to provide more specific information on medical expense insurance—the most popular kind of health insurance in America.

Medical Expense Insurance begins by describing the two coverages that provide health insurance to most Americans: group major medical insurance and individual hospital-surgical insurance. Subsequent chapters discuss organizational functions and other areas of importance to medical expense insurance products.

The contents of this book are educational, not a statement of policy. The views expressed or suggested in this and all other HIAA textbooks are those of the contributing authors or editors. They are not necessarily the opinions of HIAA or of its member companies.

ACKNOWLEDGMENTS

Chapter 1: Group Major Medical Expense Insurance
Bruce Boyd
Bruce Boyd Associates

Chapter 2: Individual Hospital-Surgical Insurance
Terry R. Lowe
State Farm Mutual Automobile Insurance Company

Chapter 3: Marketing and Selling Medical Expense Insurance
Ann Treglia-Hess
Mutual of Omaha Insurance Company

Chapter 4: Pricing Medical Expense Insurance
Alex Bagby and Joy McDonald
American Fidelity Assurance Company

Chapter 5: Medical Expense Contract Provisions
Bernard E. Peskowitz
NYLCare Health Plans, Inc.

Chapter 6: Underwriting Medical Expense Insurance
Richard Valentour
Mutual of Omaha Insurance Company

Chapter 7: Medical Expense Policy Administration
Julie Clopper-Smith
The Principal Financial Group

Chapter 8: Medical Expense Claim Administration
John C. Garner and Gerti Reagan
Garner Consulting, Inc.

Chapter 9: Medical Expense Industry Issues
Marianne Miller
Health Insurance Association of America

Reviewers
Bruce Boyd
Bruce Boyd Associates

Terry R. Lowe
State Farm Mutual Automobile Insurance Company

Marianne Miller
Health Insurance Association of America

Editor
Jane J. Stein
The Stein Group

ABOUT THE AUTHORS

Alex Bagby currently serves as vice president and manager of individual health products for American Fidelity Assurance Company. Among Bagby's numerous responsibilities are design, development, and compliance for the company's portfolio of individual health policies. Bagby's educational background includes a degree in statistical mathematics, and he is an associate of the Society of Actuaries and a member of the American Academy of Actuaries.

Bruce Boyd has enjoyed a 35-year career in the health insurance industry. As an officer of Teachers Insurance and Annuity Association-College Retirement Equities Fund (TIAA-CREF), Boyd managed the group insurance division, the group product development and marketing division, and the long-term care division. He chaired several HIAA committees and received the association's Founder's Medal for his work in long-term care.

Julie Clopper-Smith is a communication technology coordinator for The Principal Financial Group where she previously oversaw underwriting and customer service functions for small group life and health insurance. Before beginning her career in the insurance industry, Clopper-Smith taught mathematics and computer science. She has completed numerous education courses with the Health Insurance Association of America and the Life Management Institute.

John C. Garner is president of Garner Consulting, an employee-benefits consulting firm that provides auditing and claims services. Before founding his company in 1987, Garner served as a principal with Towers, Perrin and, earlier, managed claims for Lincoln National Life and Prudential. Garner holds leadership positions in the Western Claim Conference and the Los Angeles Life and Accident Claim Association.

Terry R. Lowe has enjoyed a 20-year career in the health insurance industry with particular emphasis in the area of claims. Currently, he is superintendent of training for State Farm Insurance Companies' life and health claims and is chair of the Health Insurance of America's Insurance Education Curriculum Subcommittee. Lowe has written extensively and edited numerous health insurance industry publications.

Marianne Miller is a health economist specializing in health care cost and financing. She has been with the Health Insurance Association of America for six years, and is currently director of policy development. She analyzes federal and state market reform legislative proposals and assists member companies in developing alternative recommendations. Previously, Miller directed health policy studies at the Minnesota Department of Health.

Joy McDonald currently serves as the group pricing actuary for the association group division of American Fidelity Assurance Company. She has eight years experience pricing group medical policies (including small group), as well as group life, group disability, and accident only policies. McDonald is an associate of the Society of Actuaries and a member of the American Academy of Actuaries.

Bernard E. Peskowitz has enjoyed a long career in the insurance industry working primarily in underwriting, contracts, compliance, and contract development for several large companies. Currently, as administrative vice president of NYLCare Health Plans, Inc., he oversees compliance and contract development for large and small group life, accident and health, and managed indemnity products, as well as large group contracts.

Gerti Reagan has specialized in health care management and financing in the course of her long career in the health insurance industry. She is currently vice president of Garner Consulting where she specializes in claims auditing. Reagan is responsible for implementing reviews of the managed care system within the changing health care environment and for looking specifically at the claims process.

Ann Treglia-Hess is currently vice president of individual and small group planning and product development at Mutual of Omaha. A marketing professional who is well known in the industry for market and new business development, Treglia-Hess has designed and executed numerous proprietary customer research studies, has developed new lines of business and new distribution channels, and has added value to existing plans.

Richard Valentour is a first vice president of group underwriting at Mutual of Omaha. He is responsible for risk management in 21 states and accountable for the success of 12 regional offices. He provides risk management oversight in HMO planning and development, contracting strategies, and strategic alliances. He has 18 years experience in the insurance industry and is a certified employee benefit specialist.

Chapter 1

GROUP MAJOR MEDICAL EXPENSE INSURANCE

1 *Introduction*
2 *Availability of Employer-Sponsored Coverage*
4 *Reimbursement Methods*
6 *Key Features of a Major Medical Plan*
14 *Exclusions and Limitations*
16 *Summary*
17 *Key Terms*

■ Introduction

Medical expense insurance has grown dramatically in the breadth of coverage offered since its origins in the 19th century, and especially over the past 50 years. With advances in medical care and increased experience on the part of insurance companies at pricing catastrophic risks, medical expense insurance now affords insureds the opportunity to select care from a broad array of options, some of which otherwise would be unaffordable to most people, such as organ transplants. In addition, earlier plans covered expenses only for necessary medical care and treatment of an illness or injury, but today some plans even reimburse for the cost of some preventive care.

The size of the industry also has grown dramatically. In 1950 private health insurance claim payments were $1.3 billion. By 1994 they had risen to $263.4 billion, a more than 200-fold increase in claim payments.[1] This figure includes payments from all sources: insurance companies, Blue Cross-Blue Shield plans, and, increasingly, self-insured programs and health maintenance organizations (HMOs).

While there are many reasons for this phenomenal increase, one prominent reason was the development of group major medical expense insurance, which was designed to provide coverage of even the most serious and costly of illnesses or injuries. This type of insurance is in contrast to basic hospital-surgical insurance, which was designed to provide coverage of more routine illnesses

MEDICAL EXPENSE INSURANCE

and injuries. (For more information on hospital-surgical insurance, see Chapter 2: Individual Hospital-Surgical Insurance.)

There are two kinds of major medical expense plans. A comprehensive plan provides protection in one policy for both basic hospital expense and major medical expense coverage; a supplemental major medical plan is written to augment a plan that provides basic hospital-surgical coverage.

This chapter provides an overview of how group major medical expense insurance works, discussing reimbursement methods, covered charges, and exclusions and limitations. The focus is on employer-sponsored insurance, since it is the primary way that this insurance is offered. More detailed discussions of medical expense insurance follow in subsequent chapters.

■ Availability of Employer-Sponsored Coverage

Group major medical expense insurance is provided in a number of different ways, including through:

- single employers;
- creditors or credit unions;
- labor unions;
- multiple employer groups;
- trade associations; and
- professional and other individual membership associations.

By far the most prominent way coverage is offered is through single-employer-sponsored group major medical plans. Perhaps no factor has had a greater impact on the growth of employer-sponsored group major medical insurance than the tax-favored treatment it receives. The federal income tax law provides that employer contributions to such programs on behalf of an employee and his or her dependents are a tax-deductible business expense to the employer and not taxable as income to the employee. Thus, the expansion of benefits and increases in contributions to employer-sponsored group medical plans have become highly tax-efficient ways to compensate employees.

The portion of compensation that employers paid to employees in the form of contributions to medical insurance has increased dramatically, rising from representing 1.17 percent of compensation in 1959 to 8.07 percent by 1995, according to the U.S. Department of Commerce, Bureau of Economic Analysis. In fact, the cost of medical insurance for employees increased to such a high level and at such a fast rate that employers recognized the need to find ways to contain costs. This ultimately led to a number of changes in medical plans offered to employees and their dependents, including the introduction of self-insured plans, the adoption of HMOs, increases in employee contributions, and changes in benefits offered under employer-sponsored plans. All of these changes were directed toward containing costs.

Where offered, group major medical expense insurance generally is made available to employees, their spouses, children under age 19, and dependent children who are full-time students and under age 23. Some companies are voluntarily including nonmarital partners of employees as dependents. The employer usually pays a substantial portion of the cost of the employees' insurance and sometimes pays a portion of dependent coverage.

Often insurance is provided for retirees who meet certain minimum age and years of service requirements and their dependents. Full benefits generally are provided until age 65, when the individual becomes eligible for Medicare. Some employers offer retirees benefits to supplement Medicare at age 65 and after.

The federal government requires that where coverage is offered through employer-sponsored programs it be done on a nondiscriminatory basis. The following are the major nondiscrimination requirements:

- A plan that extends insurance to the wife of a male employee also must extend such coverage to the husband of a female employee.
- Charges for all pregnancies must be covered in the same manner as those for an illness or injury.
- The use of any maximum age for determining eligibility under an employer-sponsored plan is precluded.
- Individuals with a handicap cannot be excluded from coverage nor can they have more restrictive pre-existing condition exclusions imposed on them than do other employees.
- Plans cannot base eligibility, benefits, or premium on the health status of an individual.
- Employers must offer terminating employees an opportunity to purchase, at their own expense, up to 18 months of insurance that is the same as or substantially similar to the employer-sponsored plan under which they were insured. Others who have the right to purchase such insurance for up to 36 months include dependents whose insurance terminates because they no longer meet the definition of eligible dependent, the spouse of a deceased employee, or a former spouse in the case of divorce.

Table 1.1

Reimbursement under a Comprehensive Plan

Covered charges during a calendar year		$15,000
Deductible paid by individual		500
Remainder		14,500
Reimbursed by insurance at 80%		11,600
Coinsurance by individual at 20%		2,900
Total covered charges	$15,000	
Total paid by plan	$11,600	
Total paid by individual	$ 3,400 ($500 + $2,900)	

■ Reimbursement Methods

There are a number of ways that major medical plans are structured to provide reimbursement to an individual. Under major medical expense plans, most charges tend to be treated in the same way for purposes of the deductible, coinsurance, and benefit maximum. Under basic hospital-surgical plans, each kind of charge tends to have its own reimbursement percentages and maximums.

Reimbursement under Comprehensive Plans

Under a comprehensive major medical plan, when an insured incurs covered medical expenses during a specified period, the individual generally pays the amount of the deductible first. The plan then reimburses the insured a stated percent of the remaining charges, not to exceed the lifetime benefit maximum stated in the policy. (See Table 1.1.)

Reimbursement under Supplemental Plans

As with comprehensive plans, the primary purpose of supplemental major medical coverage is to provide broad coverage for necessary medical expenses in and out of the hospital and for even the most catastrophic of illnesses. Usually the basic plan was already being offered by the employer and the major medical plan was added at a later date. Because cost containment efforts are difficult to coordinate with two carriers, one insurance company most often provides both the basic hospital-surgical and major medical plan.

Under a supplemental major medical program, the insured first receives benefits under the basic portion of the plan, then pays a deductible out-of-pocket. This out-of-pocket payment is referred to as a corridor deductible. The insured

Table 1.2

Reimbursement under a Supplemental Plan

Covered charges during a calendar year		$15,000
Paid by basic plan		9,000
Remainder for supplemental major medical		6,000
Deductible paid by individual		500
Remainder		5,500
Reimbursed by insurance at 80%		4,400
Coinsurance by individual at 20%		1,100
Total covered charges	$15,000	
Total paid by plan	$13,400 ($9,000 + $4,400)	
Total paid by individual	$ 1,600 ($500 + $1,100)	

then receives reimbursement under the supplemental major medical plan. (See Table 1.2.)

In each of the above examples the cost to the individual is the sum of the deductible and the coinsurance.

Variations on Standard Reimbursement Methods

First-Dollar Coverage

Some comprehensive plans provide first-dollar coverage. This means that the plan reimburses some expenses, such as hospital expenses, at 100 percent without prior satisfaction of the deductible. For example, the first $5,000 of hospital expenses might be reimbursed at 100 percent. The individual then pays the amount of the deductible out-of-pocket before the plan reimburses the remainder at 80 percent. (See Table 1.3.)

Integrated Deductible

Some supplemental plans provide an integrated deductible. A plan with an integrated deductible provides that the deductible will equal a stated dollar amount ($500 in the examples used in this chapter) or the amount of benefits paid under the basic plan, whichever is greater.

If the basic hospital-surgical plan pays an amount equal to or greater than the deductible, the deductible is fully satisfied. If the basic hospital-surgical plan pays less than the amount of the deductible, the individual pays the difference between the deductible, in this case $500, and the amount paid by the basic plan.

Table 1.3

Reimbursement with First-Dollar Coverage under a Comprehensive Plan

Covered charges during a calendar year		$15,000
Hospital charges reimbursed at 100%		5,000
Remainder		10,000
Deductible paid by individual		500
Remainder		9,500
Reimbursed by plan at 80%		7,600
Coinsurance by individual at 20%		1,900
Total covered charges	$15,000	
Total paid by plan	12,600 ($5,000 + $7,600)	
Total paid by individual	2,400 ($500 + $1,900)	

Table 1.4

Reimbursement with an Integrated Deductible under a Supplemental Plan (where the basic plan paid more than $500)

Covered charges during a calendar year		$15,000
Reimbursed by basic plan		9,000
Remainder		6,000
Deductible (basic plan paid more than $500)		0
Remainder		6,000
Reimbursed by plan at 80%		4,800
Coinsurance by individual at 20%		1,200
Total covered charges	$15,000	
Total paid by plan	$13,800 ($9,000 + $4,800)	
Total paid by individual	$ 1,200	

With an integrated deductible plan, the deductible may be higher than for a plan with a corridor deductible. The example used here is $500 for comparison purposes. (See Table 1.4 and Table 1.5.)

■ Key Features of a Major Medical Plan

Common features of major medical expense insurance plans are the deductible, coinsurance, benefit maximums, covered charges, and exclusions and limitations.

Table 1.5

Reimbursement with an Integrated Deductible under a Supplemental Plan (where the basic plan paid less than $500)

Covered charges during a calendar year	$15,000
Reimbursed by basic plan	300
Remainder	14,700
Deductible (balance of $500 after basic plan paid $300)	200
Remainder	14,500
Reimbursed by plan at 80%	11,600
Coinsurance by individual at 20%	2,900
Total covered charges	$15,000
Total paid by plan	$11,900 ($300 + $11,600)
Total paid by individual	$ 3,100 ($200 + $2,900)

Deductible

The primary purpose of the deductible is to limit reimbursement of truly minor, budgetable expenses and the cost of processing claim payments for them. When employer-sponsored major medical plans first became prominent in the mid-1950s, a $100 deductible was common. This level remained, and in many instances decreased, well into the 1970s, when employers began to become concerned about the cost of their employer-sponsored major medical plans.

The value of the deductible is diluted over time by many factors. If the $100 deductible in 1955 had increased at the same rate as medical care costs, it would have been $260 in 1975 and about $1,200 in 1995. However, there are other factors that affect the size of the deductible under an employer-sponsored plan, including what the competition does and employees' ability to pay. Clearly, employees' ability to pay the out-of pocket deductible has not increased at the same rate as the cost of medical care. Using increases in the consumer price index as a proxy for the increase in employees' ability to pay, the deductible would need to have been $200 in 1975 and about $560 in 1995 to have kept pace with the CPI.

Variations in the Deductible

Many employer-sponsored plans offer employees a choice of deductibles, with the employee paying a greater percent of the cost for options with lower deductibles. In this way, the employer can provide a plan that allows the employee to select an option that best meets his or her needs and, at the same

MEDICAL EXPENSE INSURANCE

time, to define the amount that he or she wants to contribute to the plan. For example, the employer may pay the full cost for a major medical plan with a $500 deductible but give the employee the option of selecting a $200 deductible if the employee pays the additional cost of this option. This arrangement not only gives the employee an important option but also clearly shows the impact of the level of the deductible on the cost of insurance.

While not common in employer-sponsored major medical plans, some individual major medical plans offer extremely high deductibles—$5,000 and even higher—to provide coverage of truly catastrophic expenses while leaving more moderate expenses to the individual to pay. Obviously, the higher the deductible selected the greater the out-of-pocket expense and the lower the premium for insurance.

Variations in Applying the Deductible

Multiyear deductible. While most major medical plans provide that the deductible must be satisfied once in each calendar year, some plans, especially individual major medical plans with a high deductible ($5,000 or higher), may require that the deductible be satisfied only every two or three years.

All cause vs. per cause deductible. While in most instances all covered expenses regardless of the cause are used to satisfy the deductible, some plans have a separate deductible for each illness or injury, or per cause. For example, if an insured breaks his or her leg under an all cause deductible, once the deductible is satisfied all covered expenses incurred during the calendar year are eligible for reimbursement regardless of cause, severity, or cost. Under the per cause deductible, a separate deductible needs to be satisfied for each and every cause.

The all cause deductible is the one used in most employer-sponsored major medical plans. The insured is often better served under a plan where his or her share of medical costs is predictable and budgetable, no matter whether the charges are incurred for one, two, or several illnesses or injuries.

A per cause deductible can be difficult to administer since it is not always easy to determine which charges are for which cause. Also, it is not always possible to determine whether charges are for a continuing illness or separate episodes of illness.

Variable or sliding deductible. Another form of major medical expense deductible is the variable or sliding deductible. This approach provides that the deductible that applies to a particular sickness or injury will be the greater of either:

Table 1.6

Timing of Incurred Charges on the Deductible

Insured Person A		Insured Person B	
Month incurred	Covered charge	Month incurred	Covered charge
Jan.	$100	Oct.	$100
Feb.	100	Nov.	100
Mar.	100	Dec.	100
Apr.	100	Jan.	100
May	100	Feb.	100
June	100	Mar.	100

- the minimum deductible stated in the policy, or
- an amount equal to all benefit payments received from any other medical expense coverage for the same eligible medical expenses.

Usually, a policy with a variable deductible has a special provision increasing the maximum benefit for a sickness or injury whenever the deductible amount applied is higher than the minimum deductible. Generally, group plans do not have variable deductibles. They are a feature of individual plans that can help reduce the premium for major medical expense insurance.

Effect of timing of incurred charges on the deductible. Some plans modify the impact of the deductible by allowing charges incurred during the last three months of a calendar year to satisfy the deductible for that year and also to apply toward the deductible for the ensuing year. This provision recognizes that the timing of incurred charges can affect the amount reimbursed under a plan that requires a deductible each calendar year.

The examples in Table 1.6 of insured person A and insured person B illustrate how the timing of incurred charges affects the amount an individual pays for the deductible.

If the deductible for each calendar year was $200, insured person A would have paid a $200 deductible and the plan would have reimbursed the remaining $400 at 80 percent, or a $320 benefit. Insured person B would have to satisfy the $200 in each calendar year and would receive 80 percent of the remaining $100 in each calendar year, or a total of $160.

If the plan under which insured B had been insured included the three-month carryover provision, the $200 incurred during the last three months of the first calendar year would also be used to satisfy the deductible during the

9

MEDICAL EXPENSE INSURANCE

ensuing calendar year, so each individual would have to satisfy one $200 deductible and each would have received a $320 benefit from the plan.

Common accident provision. Another way in which the impact of the deductible is modified is through the common accident provision. Under this provision, if two or more insured members of the same family incur charges due to injuries resulting from the same accident only one deductible applies.

Maximum number of deductibles per family. Some plans reduce the impact of the deductible for a family by including a maximum number of deductibles—usually two or three—that must be incurred by insured members of the same family during a calendar year. As the family deductible approach has become more common under employer-sponsored plans, both the carry-over and common accident approaches have become less prominent.

Coinsurance

Most group medical expense plans reimburse only a portion of the covered charge, with the remaining percent, the coinsurance, paid by the insured individual. The most common reimbursement percentage in employer-sponsored major medical plans is 80 percent, with the individual paying the remaining 20 percent coinsurance.

There are two ways in which the use of a reimbursement percent reduces the cost of a plan for the insurer.

- Obviously, it is less expensive for the insurer to pay 80 percent of the cost rather than the full cost.
- It is believed that coinsurance promotes cost containment because when the insured shares in the cost of care, he or she is more likely to consider cost when deciding whether to seek care, what kind of care to seek, and how much care is necessary.

Maximum Coinsurance

For extremely costly episodes of care, the amount of money paid for coinsurance could become a financial burden to most people. For example, if someone incurred $150,000 of covered expenses in a calendar year, 20 percent of that amount—$30,000—would be a difficult amount to repay. As a result, insurance companies developed a provision that limits the amount of coinsurance for any one individual.

For example, the plan may provide that once the individual incurs $2,000 in coinsurance during a calendar year, the plan will reimburse 100 percent of subsequent covered charges incurred during that calendar year. Some plans include a maximum coinsurance for a family, which may be double the amount for the individual, or in the example used above, $4,000. In such plans, once that amount of coinsurance is paid on behalf of all insured family members during a calendar year, the plan will reimburse covered charges at 100 percent for subsequent covered charges incurred by all insured family members during the remainder of the calendar year.

Some plans have a maximum amount expressed in terms of out-of-pocket expenses. This amount includes both the deductible and the coinsurance. When the total of the deductible and coinsurance reaches a stated amount, such as $2,000 for an individual or $4,000 for a family, the plan will reimburse covered charges at 100 percent during the remainder of the calendar year.

The Role of Deductibles and Coinsurance in Cost Management

Insurers use deductibles and coinsurance to help influence their insureds' behavior in selecting benefits and in using care. This approach has been especially important under employer-sponsored plans.

HMOs do not require a deductible or coinsurance for receiving medical care in the plan, and more recently employer-sponsored major medical programs have incorporated reduced deductibles and coinsurance within some of their plans. Under such an arrangement, for example, either employees can select their own providers of care and pay the standard deductible and coinsurance or they can accept the providers of care approved by the plan and pay a reduced deductible and coinsurance or none at all. Costs for insurers as well as the insureds will be lower if the insureds select the approved providers.

Another approach is to waive the deductible and coinsurance when people seek certain, more cost-effective kinds of care, such as:

- second surgical opinions;
- prehospital-admission testing; and
- use of ambulatory surgical centers.

Cost management also is possible by encouraging employees to select higher deductibles and coinsurance maximums. Under such an arrangement an employer may pay the entire premium for an individual who selects a major medical plan with a $500 deductible and a $2,000 coinsurance maximum, but require a substantial contribution from an individual who selects a plan with a $200 deductible and a $1,000 coinsurance maximum.

In each of the above examples, incentives are used to encourage people to select more cost-effective benefits or care to help contain the costs of providing employer-sponsored major medical plans.

Benefit Maximums

The employer-sponsored major medical plans in the mid-1950s allowed lifetime benefit maximums of $5,000 or sometimes even as high as $10,000. Due to increases in the cost of medical care and new and advanced medical procedures, benefit maximums are considerably higher today. In fact, a $1 million lifetime maximum is quite common, and some plans even have no maximums. Although it may be hard to believe that there is a need for a maximum greater than $1 million, some people do incur expenses that exceed that amount.

As with the deductible, benefit maximums may be written on an all cause or a per cause basis. The all cause approach is by far more prevalent under employer-sponsored plans. With an all cause benefit maximum, all benefits paid are subject to the benefit maximum. With a per cause benefit maximum, a separate benefit maximum applies for each cause for which benefits are paid under the policy.

Covered Charges

Charges, services, and *expenses* are three interrelated terms used by the insurance industry.

- The term *charges* is used when talking about dollar amounts or fees.
- The term *services* is used when generally describing what is done.
- The term *expenses* is used when talking about categories of bills or charges that may or may not be covered. Frequently these terms are used interchangeably when describing covered benefits.

Employer-sponsored major medical plans are designed to cover a broad range of services provided in and out of the hospital. There tend to be fewer internal limits on charges for such services in major medical plans than in basic hospital-surgical plans. Because of federal regulations that affect employer-sponsored major medical plans, there are some additional required coverages that may not apply to individual basic hospital-surgical insurance.

Charges generally covered by an employer-sponsored major medical program are those that are:

- reasonable and customary (R&C);
- incurred on account of an illness, injury, or pregnancy; and/or
- recommended by a physician.

Under most employer-sponsored major medical plans, there is no specific daily limit on the room and board charge for a hospital stay. If a semiprivate room is

GROUP MAJOR MEDICAL EXPENSE INSURANCE

used, the entire charge is covered; if a private room is used, the covered charge is usually limited to the hospital's average semiprivate room rate. In instances where private room use is medically necessary, as when someone is hospitalized with an extremely contagious disease, the entire charge is covered. Generally the entire cost of intensive care is considered a covered charge.

Many employer-sponsored programs also cover less expensive alternatives to hospitalization. Some of these are ambulatory surgical centers, limited stays in a skilled nursing facility, or home health care by a licensed home health care agency where care is of a medical and not custodial nature and where hospitalization would otherwise be required.

The list of services covered is quite comprehensive. The following are the major categories:

- professional services of a physician, including a wide range of medical practitioners;
- nursing care services of a registered nurse or in some instances a licensed practical nurse;
- physical therapy;
- anesthesia and its administration;
- diagnostic X-rays and laboratory procedures;
- X-ray or radium treatments;
- mammography screening;
- oxygen and other medicinal or therapeutic gases and their administration;
- blood transfusions, including the cost of blood (when not replaced by blood donors);
- drugs and medicines requiring a written prescription;
- local ambulance use;
- rental of durable medical equipment required for therapeutic use;
- artificial limbs or other prosthetic appliances, but not replacement of such appliances;
- casts, splints, trusses, braces, and crutches; and
- rental of a wheel chair or hospital-type bed.

Most employer-sponsored plans do not use a schedule to determine the amount of payment for physicians but rather base payment on the reasonable and customary charge. The reasonable and customary charge is determined by each insurance company based on the prevailing fees in a given area. Reasonable and customary charges can vary significantly from one area of the country to another. Therefore, the use of reasonable and customary charges, as opposed to fixed-dollar amounts, is particularly effective in an employer-sponsored plan where employees are dispersed throughout the country.

■ Exclusions and Limitations

While group medical expense insurance covers a broad range of charges, certain expenses are generally excluded or limited. A comprehensive discussion of limitations and exclusions as they relate to basic hospital-surgical insurance will be found in the next chapter. The exclusions and limitations that affect employer-sponsored major medical plans are discussed here.

Generally, exclusions and limitations are designed for the following reasons:

- to avoid the possibility of an insured receiving reimbursement twice for the same charges or making a profit from his or her insurance;
- to avoid the reimbursement of charges that would not have been incurred in the absence of insurance;
- to more clearly define necessary medical care and treatment; and
- to eliminate or limit the reimbursement of charges that are difficult to price effectively or the cost of which could have a devastating impact on the plan.

No Double Payment

To prevent an individual from being reimbursed for the same charges twice, the following charges are either excluded or limited:

- charges for care received from any government or by any government agency, unless the individual is required to pay;
- charges for occupational illness or injury to the extent they are reimbursed under workers' compensation law or similar legislation; and
- charges for which benefits are payable under any other group insurance plans. (For more information on coordination of benefits provisions, see Chapter 5: Medical Expense Contract Provisions.)

Some plans incorporate a subrogation clause, which gives the insurance company the ability to pay benefits but to retain the right to seek reimbursement for benefits it has paid to an individual should that person receive reimbursement for these same charges from a third party. An example of this process might be where an individual incurs expenses on account of injuries received in an automobile accident. Benefits would be paid under the employer-sponsored major medical plan, but if the insured subsequently receives reimbursement for these same charges from an automobile insurer, the insurance company that provided the employer-sponsored plan would be repaid if the plan included a subrogation clause.

Common Exclusions

To further define what is and is not a charge for necessary medical care and treatment, most policies exclude reimbursement for specific items, including:

- cosmetic surgery;
- experimental medical treatment;
- custodial care;
- periodic physical examinations;
- flu shots and other vaccines;
- dental care and treatment (except for charges incurred to repair damage to normal teeth caused by an accident);
- eye refractions and the fitting of glasses; and
- charges for transportation, except a local ambulance to the nearest hospital.

In addition, most plans generally exclude self-inflicted injury or illness and illness or injury related to serving in the armed forces and/or incurred on account of war, declared or undeclared.

Charges incurred on account of pre-existing conditions often are excluded. Recent federal law prohibits group medical expense plans from excluding coverage for pre-existing conditions for more than one year (18 months for late entrants) or having a look-back period of greater than six months. This means that during the first year an individual is covered under employer-sponsored insurance, the plan can exclude charges incurred by that individual on account of an illness or injury that had been diagnosed or treated only within the six months prior to the person's becoming enrolled.

Common Limitations

Charges for certain kinds of treatment or for certain conditions are limited under many plans. The following are some of the common treatments with limitations.

MEDICAL EXPENSE INSURANCE

- Benefits for treatment of a mental or nervous disorder and alcohol or drug addiction generally are limited. Common ways of limiting benefits include establishing a lower lifetime benefit for these conditions, such as $50,000; limiting the number of outpatient visits covered during each calendar year for mental or nervous disorders, and/or limiting the number of days per calendar year or per lifetime for treatment in a facility designed to treat such illness. There can be either a separate limit for each cause or one that applies to all. The Health Insurance Portability and Accountability Act of 1996 prohibits plans sponsored by large employers from imposing a separate lower annual or lifetime maximum benefit under the policy for mental health coverage.
- Benefits for the treatment of certain skull and jaw disorders, such as temporomandibular joint disorder, often are limited to a specific amount each calendar year. Because some group dental plans provide benefits for such procedures, provisions are made to avoid duplicate coverage.
- Benefits for services to detect and correct body distortion and to provide body manipulation and subluxation of the spine generally are limited to a specific amount per calendar year.

What charges are covered and what charges are not covered can vary from policy to policy depending on the employer and the requirements of the state(s). State regulation of insurance has led to a number of requirements as to which medical providers must be covered and the minimum level of benefits that must be provided for certain illnesses. The specific requirements vary a good deal from one state to the next and can add significantly to the cost of an employer's plan. These variations can be particularly onerous when the employer has offices in locations throughout the country.

Summary

Group major medical expense insurance covers a wide range of medical services provided in and out of the hospital. It was designed to protect insureds in the case of even the most serious and costly illnesses and injuries. Group major medical coverage is primarily offered through employer-sponsored plans and is made available to all eligible employees and their dependents. There are numerous ways that insurers reimburse insureds for medical expenses incurred; most include a deductible and some level of coinsurance. Deductibles and coinsurance can help contain health care costs because they can influence how insureds use covered services.

■ Key Terms

All cause
Benefit maximum
Coinsurance
Coinsurance maximum
Common accident
  provision
Comprehensive
Covered expenses
Deductible
Deductible maximum

Employer contributions
Exclusions and
  limitations
First-dollar coverage
Group major medical
  expense insurance
Individual basic hospital-
  surgical insurance
Integrated deductible
Nondiscrimination

Per cause
Reasonable and
  customary (R&C)
Reimbursement
  percentages
Subrogation clause
Supplemental
Tax-favored treatment
Three-month carryover
  provision

Chapter 2

INDIVIDUAL HOSPITAL-SURGICAL INSURANCE

19 *Introduction*
20 *Covered Expenses and Benefits Payment Determination*
29 *Excluded or Limited Expenses*
36 *Summary*
36 *Key Terms*

■ Introduction

Many individuals are not eligible for group medical insurance plans because they are self-employed, work in a small business that does not offer group coverage, or are between jobs and have lost group medical coverage. Individual medical expense coverage is marketed to these people as a way for them to guard against large debts as a result of lack of medical insurance.

Individual hospital-surgical insurance is designed to cover major expenses incurred for hospital costs, inhospital surgeon and physician charges, and a variety of outpatient services. These policies tend to be somewhat more restrictive in types of charges covered than are group major medical expense insurance policies, and benefits tend to force the people covered to bear more of the expenses. In addition, the limits on total benefits payable for any one illness or period tend to be lower than those available in group coverages.

Individual hospital-surgical coverage is sold through private insurers. Policies vary depending on the amounts of coverage desired. Most individual hospital-surgical policies are issued to a single individual, who is called the policyholder. That person may elect to include a spouse and children under the policy. Benefits apply to all covered persons in the same manner and amounts unless specified otherwise.

This chapter discusses the basic expenses covered under individual hospital-surgical insurance policies and those that are either excluded from coverage or offered with specified limitations. It also explains how benefits are determined for different coverages.

Table 2.1

Room and Board Charges for a 5-Day Confinement at $350 a Day: $1,750

Daily benefit	Benefit payment
$150	$ 750
$300	$1,500

■ Covered Expenses and Benefits Payment Determination

Individual hospital-surgical policies tend to cover various classes or kinds of expenses differently. Following is a description of various expenses and how the typical policy reimburses each class of expense.

Daily Room and Board/Intensive Care

Most individual hospital-surgical policies contain a separate benefit for daily room and board charges. Policy benefits for room and board charges usually are expressed as a flat dollar benefit paid for each day an insured is confined as an inpatient, up to but not exceeding the amount actually charged by the hospital. However, some policies pay up to the most common semiprivate room rate charged by the facility.

Insurers typically offer insureds an opportunity to choose their own hospital daily benefit maximums within a specified range—for example, $50 to $500 per day—to reflect differences in cost by area and to meet the varying needs of individuals. The higher the daily maximum amounts, the higher the premiums.

Table 2.1 illustrates the difference in benefit payments for room and board charges resulting from the selection of higher or lower hospital daily benefit maximums. In the first example, the insured selected a $150 daily benefit; in the second, a $300 benefit was chosen.

Insureds need to weigh the premium savings realized with lower policy benefits against the risk of incurring inpatient expenses that could result in higher out-of-pocket expenses for room and board charges. It is useful for insureds to know the range of charges in the area where they live before selecting the room and board benefits.

Hospital expenses for intensive care, critical care, and cardiac care rooms are substantially higher than for standard care rooms. For this reason, many individual hospital-surgical policies provide a higher daily benefit for care received in this type of setting. Often, the additional benefit is expressed as a multiple of the standard daily benefit (usually 1.5 or 2 times the standard benefit). For example, with a policy providing a double benefit for intensive care, an insured with a $300 daily maximum would receive a benefit of $600 per day for incurring expenses of $630 a day for care in an intensive care unit.

Nursing care usually is considered a component of the hospital room and board expense. Some hospitals, however, charge separately for the costs of providing routine inpatient nursing care. If separate charges are made for routine nursing care, these charges are added to the room and board charges and the total is considered subject to the hospital daily benefit.

Many individual hospital-surgical policies contain a maximum benefit period for any one confinement. This is stated as a maximum number of days, ranging from 30 to 365 days. Typically, a second confinement for the same condition but not separated by a period of required months is considered the same confinement.

For example, assume a policy provides for a maximum benefit period of 60 days. In addition, in its definition of period of hospital confinement, the policy states that any subsequent confinement for the same condition that is not separated by a period of more than 30 days is to be considered the same confinement. If an insured is confined for a specific condition for 45 days, discharged, and rehospitalized for the same condition two weeks later, the two hospitalizations are considered one confinement. The insured then has only 15 days left of the maximum daily benefit for that confinement.

Miscellaneous Hospital Expense Benefit

The miscellaneous hospital expense benefit is designed to provide coverage for inpatient ancillary charges not considered under the daily room and board benefit. Examples of ancillary charges typically covered under this benefit are:

- medications;
- medical supplies;
- radiology services;
- laboratory and pathology services;
- operating room fees;
- surgical supplies; and
- equipment usage fees.

MEDICAL EXPENSE INSURANCE

Table 2.2

Miscellaneous Inpatient Hospital Expenses Incurred for a 5-Day Confinement: $6,148.55

Policy pays 80 percent of incurred expenses	Policy pays expenses incurred up to $10,000 per confinement	Policy pays up to 15 times the hospital room and board rate of $300 per day
Payment = $4,918.84 ($6148.55 x .80)	Payment = $6,148.55	Payment = $4,500.00 ($300 x 15)

In addition, the professional component of many physician services that are provided to inhospital patients are covered under this benefit. Examples include treatment by an emergency room physician prior to admission, charges made by hospital pathologists and radiologists to interpret test results, and charges made for hospital-based ambulance transportation fees.

There are a number of ways in which individual hospital-surgical policies express the maximum amount payable under the miscellaneous hospital expense benefit. In some cases, policies pay a stated percentage of expenses incurred—for example, 80 percent. Other policies specify a flat dollar amount payable. This may be stated either as a specific amount payable for an entire confinement or as a multiple of the hospital daily benefit—for example, 20 times the hospital daily benefit. Table 2.2 illustrates the level of benefits provided under three different policy provisions.

In addition to covering expenses incurred for inpatient hospital services, the miscellaneous medical expense benefit often provides coverage for limited and specific outpatient hospital treatment. Payment for these services is based either on the same type of provisions used for inpatient cases or on outpatient payment methods that are specified in the policy.

Outpatient expenses that typically fall under this provision are those that are incurred:

- on the same day as an outpatient surgical procedure;
- as a result of preadmission testing (typically limited to tests done within 7 to 14 days prior to hospital admission);
- as a result of chemotherapy, radiation therapy, and other similar cancer therapy;
- within a specified number of hours following an accidental injury (typically 48 to 72 hours); and
- for diagnostic testing such as laboratory tests, X-rays, or EKGs.

INDIVIDUAL HOSPITAL-SURGICAL INSURANCE

While the miscellaneous hospital expense benefit is included in most individual hospital-surgical insurance policies, some policies only offer this coverage on an optional basis for an additional premium. Some also offer an expansion of the benefits through the addition of a policy rider.

Outpatient, Diagnostic, Presurgical, and Laboratory Tests

In addition to the outpatient hospital coverage provided by the miscellaneous hospital expense benefit, many individual hospital-surgical policies provide at least minimum and limited coverage for specifically identified outpatient testing performed in other settings. These policy provisions are intended to encourage insureds to use less expensive outpatient facilities when possible. Coverage is provided for expenses incurred in physicians' offices, independent laboratories, and outpatient treatment clinics.

Typically, the outpatient testing benefit is limited to coverage under specified circumstances, such as outpatient testing prior to hospital admission or surgical procedures. To qualify for benefits under the provision, the testing must take place within a certain number of days prior to admission or surgery.

There are different ways of providing outpatient testing benefits. Some policies provide coverage with a separate provision that generally limits benefits to a flat-dollar amount paid for each illness or injury (typically $50 to $250). This flat-dollar amount cannot exceed the amount of actual expenses incurred.

Another method of providing outpatient testing coverage is through the policy's miscellaneous medical expense benefit. When outpatient testing is covered in this manner, benefits generally are provided up to the miscellaneous medical expense benefit policy limit.

Finally, some policies offer this type of coverage on an optional basis through the purchase of a policy rider. In these cases, coverage is typically more liberal than in the other two methods discussed.

Surgical Expense Benefit

The surgical expense benefit contained in individual hospital-surgical policies is designed to provide coverage for the fees charged by a physician or surgeon for performing a surgical operation. Most surgical expense benefit provisions are for surgery performed in a hospital, surgical center, or physician's office.

Some policies base surgical expense benefit payments on the calculated reasonable and customary charge in a geographic area for a specified surgical procedure. Under this arrangement, the policy pays a specified percentage of the

23

surgical expense charge (determined by the coinsurance provisions of the policy) up to a maximum charge for that procedure—for example, up to 80 percent of the reasonable and customary charge in that area. The insured pays the insured's corresponding coinsurance amount up to that maximum level. If the charge exceeds the maximum covered charge (here 80 percent of R&C), the insured pays 100 percent of the amount above that maximum.

Surgical expense reimbursement most often is made according to a surgical schedule attached to the policy. A surgical schedule provides a listing of the more commonly performed surgical procedures and attaches a ranking or value to each procedure according to its relative severity and complexity.

In many cases, insureds are given a choice (within a range) regarding their maximum surgical expense benefit amount. The levels chosen usually correspond with the maximum hospital daily benefit selected. Therefore, policies with higher hospital daily benefit maximums usually contain higher surgical expense benefit maximums.

A surgical schedule states the maximum amount payable under the policy's surgical expense benefit for procedures determined to be of the very highest complexity. Other, less complex procedures are ranked according to their perceived complexity compared to these most complex procedures. For example, a procedure determined to be one-half the complexity of the highest complexity procedure is reimbursed at 50 percent of the maximum surgical expense benefit. In no event can the benefit payable under the surgical expense benefit exceed the actual fee charged by the surgeon.

Some surgical schedules indicate the actual dollar amount to be paid for each procedure. Others express this value as a percentage of the policy's maximum surgical expense benefit. Table 2.3 shows the difference between these two types of schedules.

It is not possible for a surgical schedule to specify the exact amount payable for every surgical procedure. Most policies itemize only those procedures that are performed frequently. To determine the benefit payable when surgical charges are received that are not on the policy's surgical schedule, most policies provide that the procedure be evaluated in a manner consistent with other procedures of similar complexity.

Multiple Surgical Procedures

The surgical expense benefit often contains language that tells how the policy benefit is to be determined for cases where more than one surgical procedure

Table 2.3

Maximum Surgical Expense Benefit: $8,000

Procedure	Stated amount schedule	Percentage schedule	and dollar equivalent
Tonsillectomy	$ 440	7.5%	$ 600
Hysterectomy	1,700	22.0	1,760
Balloon angioplasty	1,900	25.0	2,000
Laminectomy	2,900	42.0	3,360
Craniectomy	3,600	48.5	3,880
Repair abdominal aneurysm	4,400	53.0	4,240
Coronary artery bypass, single	6,700	80.0	6,400

Table 2.4

Payment for Multiple Surgical Procedures Performed at the Same Time

Procedures	Charges	Benefit paid
Total hysterectomy	$2,500	$2,000 (80% of R&C)
Repair of enterocele (substantial, same incision)	750	375 (50% of R&C)
Appendectomy (incidental, same incision)	500	0

is performed during the same operative session. Examples include an appendectomy performed at the same time as another abdominal procedure, or a knee cartilage repair performed at the same time as a diagnostic arthroscopy of the knee.

Often the method of handling multiple surgical procedures performed at the same time depends on the nature and the severity of the secondary procedures. For example, a fairly simple secondary procedure performed through the same incision as the primary procedure may not merit additional surgical expense benefit payments. On the other hand, an unrelated, complex procedure performed through an entirely different incision might merit payment of 50 percent or 100 percent of the usual scheduled amount for that procedure. Table 2.4 illustrates how these payments are calculated.

Maternity Benefit

Many individual hospital-surgical insurance policies do not treat charges for routine pregnancy and delivery the same as those for an illness or injury.

MEDICAL EXPENSE INSURANCE

Instead, pregnancy is viewed as a personal choice, something that often can be planned for and budgeted, unlike the generally unforeseen and unpredictable expenses associated with illnesses and injuries. For these reasons, normal pregnancy and childbirth are often not covered under basic individual hospital-surgical policies.

In cases where coverage is provided for normal pregnancy, the coverage generally is expressed separately and is limited. It is covered under a maternity benefit. Often the maternity benefit is expressed as a multiple of the hospital daily benefit. For example, the maximum maternity benefit of a policy containing a maximum hospital daily benefit of $150 and a maternity benefit offering coverage at 10 times the maximum hospital daily benefit is $1,500. This is a flat amount payable regardless of the actual expenses incurred; it is not to exceed the actual expenses incurred.

Many policies offer an opportunity to purchase benefit riders to cover the normal expenses of pregnancy and delivery, rather than including benefits within the basic policy. An additional premium is charged for this coverage, which is selected mostly by females in the childbearing age group. The benefits offered under the rider can be similar to the coverage described above (a multiple of the maximum hospital daily benefit) or they can provide coverage for all expenses incurred up to the reasonable and customary allowance for each expense. In this situation, reimbursement typically is made on a percentage basis—for example, 80 percent of expenses incurred.

Complications of Pregnancy

Complications of pregnancy are not considered to be subject to typical maternity benefit limitations or exclusions. Rather, complications of pregnancy are handled the same as any other illness. Policies differ in their definitions of complications of pregnancy. For example, some policies consider a cesarean section delivery a complication of pregnancy, while others view it as standard and therefore subject to policy limitations or exclusions for a normal pregnancy.

Common complications of pregnancy include:

- ectopic pregnancies;
- severe toxemia;
- stillborn delivery;
- acute nephritis in pregnancy;
- severe gestational diabetes;
- nonelective missed, spontaneous, and therapeutic abortions; and
- severe phlebitis developed during pregnancy.

Table 2.5

Physician Inhospital Expense Benefits: 5-Day Confinement

	Actual charges	Policy 1 (80% coverage of R&C charges)	Policy 2 (up to $50 per visit)
Day 1	$150	$120	$50
Day 2	40	32	40
Day 3	40	32	40
Day 4	40	32	40
Day 5	100	80	50
Total	$370	$296	$220

Some states have passed legislation requiring health insurers to provide coverage of charges for pregnancy in the same manner as for an illness or injury. Policies sold in those states must be modified to provide this coverage.

Physician Inhospital Expense Benefit

Fees charged by attending physicians for providing medical care for patients in the hospital are covered under the physician inhospital expense benefit. Physician charges for surgery and postsurgical follow-up visits generally are covered under the surgical expense benefit rather than the physician inhospital expense benefit.

Most individual hospital-surgical policies contain a limit on the amount paid for each hospital visit by a physician. This limit may be expressed as a maximum amount per day, or it may provide reimbursement at a stated percentage of the reasonable and customary amount for the specific type of service provided. In addition, some policies contain a maximum physician inhospital expense benefit payable during a single confinement (usually a multiple of the daily maximum). Table 2.5 illustrates the two primary methods of benefit calculation under typical physician inhospital expense benefit provisions.

Some policies offer additional-coverage riders that extend the coverage provided for physician services to treatment received in an outpatient setting, including at home.

Extended Care and Home Health Care Benefits

Provisions for an extended care benefit and a home health care benefit are commonly found in individual hospital-surgical insurance policies for coverage of the care of patients recovering from a sickness or injury. Typically, these benefits provide coverage for care that is needed in lieu of continuing inpatient treatment. They are designed to encourage the use of less expensive facilities or services for people who no longer require the high level of professional care offered by hospital inpatient settings.

Extended Care

Charges for nursing homes are covered under the extended care benefit when certain criteria have been met. Most policies require that care in these facilities be received within a specified number of days following discharge from a hospital. Some policies require that the patient be transferred directly from the hospital to the extended care facility; other policies provide coverage as long as the admission takes place within a range of 14 to 30 days of a hospital discharge for the same illness or injury. Eligible facilities usually are required to be licensed as an extended care facility, must be supervised by a physician, and must maintain medical records for their patients.

Reimbursement of charges incurred in an extended care facility is limited in two ways.

- First, policies state the maximum number of days for which reimbursement is allowed. This period ranges from 30 to 90 days, and the maximum generally applies for all confinements in an extended care facility during the same calendar year and for the same illness or injury.
- Second, the daily rate of reimbursement usually is stated as one-half the policy's hospital daily benefit for regular inpatient care. For example, a policy containing a maximum hospital daily benefit of $350 per day provides an extended care benefit maximum of $175 per day.

Home Health Care

Home health care is intermittent nursing care received in a patient's home. Typical types of care provided include dispensing medications, monitoring vital signs (blood pressure, temperature, and pulse), intravenous and catheter care, physical or speech therapy, and other skilled services. Associated medical supplies, dressings, and medications generally are covered under this benefit.

Many individual hospital-surgical insurance policies provide some coverage for home health care when the attending physician certifies that the patient would otherwise need to be confined in a hospital or extended care facility. Reimbursement for home health care services generally is provided on a scheduled basis. The policy schedule indicates the maximum number of home health care visits that are considered eligible and how much is paid for each visit. The amount considered eligible for each visit can be a stated flat amount or can be expressed as the reasonable and customary amount for each specific type of home health care service provided. Full time, 24-hour nursing care is not considered eligible for reimbursement under most home health care benefit provisions.

Ambulance Benefit

Some hospital-expense policies provide coverage for necessary ambulance transportation to or from a hospital or for transfer from one hospital to another. Most policies require that eligible transportation services must be provided by licensed ambulance services. Medical vans and transportation services usually are not covered under this benefit.

The ambulance benefit often stipulates that coverage is only provided for transportation to the nearest hospital providing the type of care required for the patient's condition. Transfer charges incurred strictly for patient convenience purposes—for example, moving the patient to a hospital closer to home—usually are not covered.

Most policies limit the amount payable under the ambulance benefit. The maximum amount usually is expressed as a flat reimbursement as shown in the policy schedule. Typical maximum amounts range from $25 to $150. Charges made by a hospital for ambulance transportation resulting in inpatient care typically are reimbursed under the miscellaneous hospital expense benefit instead of the ambulance benefit.

■ Excluded or Limited Expenses

Certain types or kinds of expenses are not covered under individual hospital-surgical policies. Some policy provisions are very specific while others broadly state what will not be treated as a covered expense. The following are common exclusions and limited expenses.

Pre-existing Conditions

Historically, individual hospital-surgical policies either excluded or limited coverage for expenses incurred as a result of medical conditions that existed or became obvious to the applicant before the application date or the policy effective date. Typical pre-existing exclusions specify that no benefits are payable for any illness or injury for which treatment is received prior to the date the policy became effective. Less commonly, some policies only place a limit on the amount of benefits provided for a certain period of time—for example, payment is limited to $500 for the first two years a policy is in force.

The pre-existing conditions exclusion generally appears in the policy in one of two places:

- as a pre-existing statement within the exclusions, exceptions, and limitations section of the policy; or
- in the section of the policy where sickness and injury are defined.

Some states place limits on the length of time for excluding coverage for pre-existing conditions, and some preclude the use of any pre-existing conditions exclusion if prior coverage resulted in the satisfaction of a pre-existing exclusion period.

Federal legislation passed in 1996 has affected the administration of pre-existing conditions clauses in specific situations. The Health Insurance Portability and Accountability Act of 1996 (HIPAA) provides that individual hospital-surgical insurers cannot refuse to offer coverage to people who have lost group coverage due to career and similar transitions, and that pre-existing conditions limitations and exclusions cannot be applied for these individuals. Certain criteria must be met for individuals to qualify under the conditions of this legislation:

- Eligible participants must have had 18 months of coverage under an employer, government, or church plan.
- Applicants must not be eligible for a group health plan, Medicare, or Medicaid or be covered under any other health insurance.
- Applicants must not have lost prior coverage due to fraud or nonpayment of premiums.
- Eligible participants must have both elected and exhausted any continuation coverage available under COBRA or a similar state program.

Specified Common Conditions

There are certain ongoing conditions for which an insured is able to put off seeking medical treatment until hospital-surgical coverage has been secured. To avoid frequent, costly pre-existing investigations on first-year policies, individual policies generally exclude coverage for specified common conditions for a period of 180 or as many as 365 days after the effective date of coverage. Most exclusions of this type specify that coverage can be provided for these conditions if a physician certifies that the treatment was an emergency.

These conditions are typically:

- hernias;
- hemorrhoids;
- diseases of tonsils and adenoids;
- diseases of the middle ear; and
- diseases of the reproductive organs.

As with the pre-existing conditions exclusion, administration of this 365-day exclusion is affected by passage of the Health Insurance Portability and Accountability Act of 1996. Insureds who secure individual coverage under the terms of this act are not subject to this exclusion.

Attempted Suicide

Another common exclusion found in individual hospital-surgical insurance policies deals with suicide attempts and intentionally self-inflicted injuries. While this exclusion is found in most policies, insurers typically find it difficult to enforce due to the uncertainty that can surround events of this nature. To successfully enforce the exclusion, an insurer must prove that an insured intentionally sought to harm him- or herself. Police reports, witness testimony, suicide notes, medical records, and other similar documentation generally are needed to prove attempted suicide or intentionally self-inflicted injury.

It is often difficult to distinguish intent from accident. While some methods of attempted suicide are more obvious, others are very difficult to establish. Especially difficult cases include motor vehicle accidents, drug overdoses, and carbon monoxide poisoning. It is sometimes equally difficult to prove intent with intentionally self-inflicted injuries. Again, the insurer must establish proof that an insured actually intended to cause him- or herself physical harm.

Intentional actions that result in accidental injury usually are not excluded from coverage. For example, if an insured intentionally hits a wall in anger and accidentally fractures a bone in his or her hand, this would not technically fall under the category of an intentionally self-inflicted injury. The insured may have intended to hit the wall but probably did not intend to have this act result in a broken hand.

Military Duty and Military and Government Hospitals

Coverage is excluded in individual hospital-surgical insurance policies for illnesses or injuries that occur while an insured is an active member of the armed

MEDICAL EXPENSE INSURANCE

forces, either for the United States or any other country. Most policies temporarily suspend coverage for any length of time an insured is serving in the armed forces. Premiums are not collected during this period of time. Most policies allow coverage to automatically continue once the active duty terminates.

Some policies do not apply this exclusion for short-term military assignments or activities. For example, weekend or month-long training sessions provided by the National Guard, Army ROTC, and similar organizations established by the armed services of the United States do not fall under this exclusion. Other policies apply the exclusion only for conditions that are the direct result of military service while continuing to provide coverage for nonservice-related injuries or illnesses. For example, an injury sustained while practicing military exercises is excluded; treatment received for an upper-respiratory infection is covered.

Most policies also contain an exclusion for care received in a government, military, or Veterans Administration (VA) hospital. This exclusion generally is intended for treatment for which the insured does not normally incur an expense. If a facility does not typically charge the patient in the absence of insurance, then the exclusion applies. State laws, however, often require coverage when the patient is ultimately responsible for payment of medical expenses incurred while confined in one of these facilities. If the patient is billed and is responsible for payment of the bill, the exclusion does not apply.

Sometimes patients receive treatment for nonservice-related injuries or illnesses in a VA hospital. The Veterans Administration Amendment passed in 1986 requires private health insurance companies to provide coverage for these conditions. Care received in a VA hospital for service-related conditions is still subject to the exclusion.

War

The war exclusion is much broader than the one that applies to actual active duty military personnel. The war exclusion applies to any insured who suffers a loss that is the direct result of war or an act of war. The wording of this exclusion is intentionally broad to cover all acts of war, whether declared or undeclared, since many of the conflicts in recent history, such as in Vietnam and the Persian Gulf, have not resulted in actual declared war.

The war exclusion is necessary to prevent private insurers from suffering widespread, catastrophic losses as a result of a single event.

Workers' Compensation

Expenses incurred for the treatment of occupational illnesses or injuries that are covered under workers' compensation laws are excluded from individual hospital-surgical insurance policies. This exclusion is designed to prohibit insured workers from getting duplicate benefits or in any way profiting from a work-related injury.

Many potentially work-related conditions are difficult to link directly to an occupational cause. Among these conditions are:

- mental and nervous disorders and substance abuse;
- repetitive motion injury claims; and
- heart disease and high blood pressure.

In cases such as these, it can take months or even years for a workers' compensation carrier to establish liability and pay a claim. Many hospital-surgical insurance policies provide interim benefits in these cases and seek reimbursement from the workers' compensation carrier if the claimant is later determined to be eligible for workers' compensation benefits.

Occupational disease laws are treated in the same manner as workers' compensation laws. For example, eligible expenses under the Longshoreman's and Harbor Workers' Compensation Act or the Black Lung Benefits Reform Act are subject to this policy exclusion.

Dental Conditions and Treatment

Another standard exclusion applies to expenses for routine dental treatment of the teeth and gums. This exclusion is intended to cover any treatment that is strictly dental in nature, while still providing limited benefits for conditions that arise due to covered illness or injury. Routine dental cleaning, filling of cavities, denture work, root canals, and periodontal surgery are just a few examples of the types of dental treatment typically falling under this exclusion.

Examples of conditions that are covered in spite of a dental exclusion are:

- dental treatment needed as a result of an injury to natural teeth (coverage is not provided for injuries to dentures or bridgework);
- surgical correction of jaw deformities that interfere with normal bite and chewing ability;
- necessary inpatient hospital expenses for dental surgery.

Inpatient hospital expenses usually are the result of an underlying medical condition that necessitates special treatment during surgical procedures. For example, patients with severe mitral valve prolapse may need hospital treatment whenever dental surgery is performed. In these cases, hospital charges are covered while the charges for the actual dental procedure are subject to the exclusion language.

Mental and Nervous Conditions

Expenses for treatment of mental or nervous disorders are handled in many different ways by individual hospital-surgical insurers. Mental or nervous conditions can be long-term, recurring, and debilitating. They can result in confinements lasting months or even years. For these reasons, it is difficult for insurance policies to cover this treatment in full without substantially and negatively affecting premium rates.

Few policies completely exclude mental or nervous conditions. Instead, most policies address the problem by placing limitations on the coverage provided for mental or nervous disorders. Insurers, therefore, can provide some coverage while limiting their overall exposure to this risk. Many states require a specified minimum mental health benefit that must be included in all medical expense policies.

Various types of policy limitations are used by insurers, including the following:

- establishing a maximum benefit period stated as a yearly or lifetime benefit (e.g., 30, 60, or 90 days);
- establishing a maximum dollar amount to be paid over a specified period of time (e.g., $10,000 in any one calendar year);
- allowing benefits for inpatient treatment while excluding outpatient treatment;
- applying a different coinsurance amount for mental or nervous disorders than for other conditions (e.g., 50 percent rather than 75 percent or 80 percent); and
- excluding mental and nervous conditions under a base policy but offering an optional benefits rider to provide this coverage if the insured desires.

Some policies include a combination of two or more of the above variations. Similar limitations generally are placed on treatment for conditions related to alcohol and drug abuse.

Cosmetic Treatment and Surgery

Surgical procedures and treatment intended solely to improve appearance rather than serve a therapeutic purpose are considered cosmetic in nature and are subject to the standard cosmetic exclusion found in individual hospital-surgical insurance policies. Cosmetic and therapeutic surgery can be defined as follows:

Cosmetic surgery: That surgery done to alter the texture or configuration of the skin, or the configuration or relationship of contiguous structures of any feature of the human body, for primarily personal reasons.

Therapeutic surgery: That reparative or reconstructive surgery done to restore the patient's appearance to preinjury or presickness status, or to alleviate a severe condition that makes it impossible for the patient to function in school or in business.

Examples of commonly performed cosmetic procedures that are not covered are:

- blepharoplasty to correct droopy eyelids;
- rhinoplasty to correct or change appearance of the nose;
- abdominoplasty to tighten the muscles of abdomen and to remove excess skin;
- mentoplasty to correct a receding chin by inserting implant material;
- rhytidectomy or face lift to remove wrinkles and tighten skin;
- dermabrasion to remove scars on skin;
- sclerotherapy to remove superficial varicose veins;
- collagen implants to reduce wrinkles; and
- breast reduction to change the contour of the breast.

Surgical procedures performed to correct deformities resulting from accidental injuries or congenital defects generally are considered eligible as long as the event (e.g., birth or injury) occurred while the policy was in force. In addition, some primarily cosmetic procedures are needed to produce a therapeutic benefit. In these cases, coverage is provided. Examples include:

- blepharoplasty procedures when sagging eyelids obstruct normal vision;
- rhinoplasty procedures when bony structure abnormalities interfere with normal breathing; and
- abdominoplasty procedures when performed to correct back disorders or posture problems.

MEDICAL EXPENSE INSURANCE

■ Summary

Individual hospital-surgical insurance covers major hospital costs, surgeon and physician charges while a person is hospitalized, and a limited number of outpatient services. It is sold through private insurers to a single individual, who may include dependents under the policy. Policies, premiums, and benefits vary, depending on the amounts of coverage desired. The larger the proportion of expenses covered, the larger the premiums tend to be. To keep premium payments reasonable and affordable, some conditions and health risks are excluded or limited in coverage.

■ Key Terms

Ancillary charges
Ambulance transportation
Attempted suicide
Coinsurance
Complications of pregnancy
Cosmetic treatment and surgery
Covered expenses
Daily benefits
Daily maximums
Daily room and board
Dental conditions and treatment
Exclusions
Extended care
Health Insurance Portability and Accountability Act of 1996 (HIPAA)
Home health care
Hospital daily benefit
Ineligible expenses
Intensive care
Intentional self-inflicted injuries
Limitations
Maternity coverage
Maximum benefit period
Mental and nervous conditions
Military duty
Military/government hospitals
Miscellaneous hospital expenses
Occupational illnesses or injuries
Optional benefits rider
Outpatient tests
Physician inhospital expenses
Pre-existing conditions
Primary surgical procedures
Reasonable and customary (R&C)
Secondary surgical procedures
Surgical expenses
Surgical schedule
Therapeutic surgery
Time limit on certain defenses
War and acts of war
Workers' compensation laws

Chapter 3

MARKETING AND SELLING MEDICAL EXPENSE INSURANCE

37 *Introduction*
38 *Strategic Marketing*
39 *Products in the Marketplace*
42 *Price as a Marketing Concept*
45 *Sales and Distribution*

49 *After the Sale: Customer Service*
50 *Marketing in a Changing Marketplace*
51 *Summary*
51 *Key Terms*

■ Introduction

Marketing is the selling of products to customers. A customer is someone who buys the product or service being offered. Groups of customers are a market. Without a market, there is no business.

The U.S. health insurance industry developed largely in response to market needs for financial protection from unanticipated medical expenses. The following examples illustrate how the development of different medical expense insurance products was a direct outgrowth of customer needs.

- The group medical expense insurance market grew in response to employers' needs for products to attract and retain a labor force.

- Comprehensive major medical plans came into vogue because they provided a broad range of coverage and were easily administered plans that the average employee could understand.

- Individual medical expense products were designed to supplement Medicare coverage for people over age 65.

- A proliferation of health care delivery arrangements such as managed indemnity plans and health maintenance organizations (HMOs) were designed to control health care costs and improve utilization of services.

The result of these and other market-based solutions to customer needs has been a range of affordable and widely available medical expense insurance products. This chapter discusses the medical expense insurance market and how consumer needs, product design, and price affect marketability. It also covers traditional and innovative ways of selling and distributing medical expense products.

■ Strategic Marketing

To help sell and design insurance products, insurance companies analyze market needs and the existing and/or planned competition for that market. This analysis is called market research. An example of how health insurers use market research to sell products is the fact that some companies have print and television ads that intentionally appeal to women because market research shows that women often make the household's decision about purchasing health care products.

Marketing Mix

Based on market research, insurers develop a marketing plan to:

- identify targeted markets;
- outline what types of products are needed to satisfy the customers' needs;
- determine how to price the products in relation to the competition; and
- promote and distribute the products.

Together, the above components make up what is called the marketing mix. With this information, agents and brokers can target specific markets and meet the needs of group and individual customers.

Customer Know-How

From a marketing perspective, it is important for insurance companies to be aware of how knowledgeable customers are about their products and how involved they want to be in shaping the final plans offered. This information is useful for developing good relations with clients. It also can help agents and brokers sell the right products at the right price to customers. (Agents generally sell insurance products from one company; brokers sell insurance products from several companies.)

In the group market, the purchase decision and sale of a medical expense policy is a relatively formal process, with presentations made to key decision makers in the business, such as the president, human resources or benefits manager, or the comptroller. A growing number of employers—particularly large employers—have become sophisticated buyers of the group medical expense insurance plans they offer to employees. A large employer typically knows the demographic make-up of its employees and works with agents and brokers to design plans that fit the mix of employees' ages, income levels, and family needs. Large employers tend to shop for the best value since most of them pay a substantial portion of the premiums for their employees and often dependents, and they usually offer employees a choice of medical expense insurance products.

Small employers, in contrast, generally are not as sophisticated or do not have as many resources or options available to them in their purchase of employee benefit plans. While they know medical expense insurance is important to employees, many small companies cannot afford to offer it. Of those that do, only a few offer a choice of plans to employees.

The know-how of individual purchasers of medical expense insurance is very different from that of group purchasers. Individual purchasers generally have little knowledge about plan designs, an insurance company's reputation, or the level of expertise of the agent or broker with whom they are dealing. Their purchase decision is made primarily by comparing prices, much as they would when purchasing automobile or any other kind of insurance. An experienced agent or broker can help individual purchasers understand that not all medical expense insurance products are alike, even though they may appear to be.

■ Products in the Marketplace

Medical expense insurance is a product—a specific policy; but it also is a service—a means of transferring financial risk and ensuring access to health care that most people might not otherwise have. As a product and a service, medical expense insurance transfers the unknown risk of a possible financial burden from the person who is insured to the risk bearer (the insurance company). An insured person pays the insurance company a premium and, in return, the company assumes a portion of the insured's risk of having to pay large medical bills due to unavoidable circumstances such as illness or injury.

MEDICAL EXPENSE INSURANCE

Table 3.1

Individual and Group Medical Expense Insurance Product Designs

Plan features	Indemnity	Indemnity with cost containment provisions	Preferred provider organization (PPO)	Point of service (POS)	Health maintenance organization (HMO)
Copayment	no	maybe	yes	yes	yes
Coinsurance	yes	yes	yes	yes	no
Deductible	yes	yes	yes	yes*	no
Out-of-pocket maximum	yes	yes	yes	yes*	no
Policy maximum	yes	yes	yes	maybe*	no**
Prescription drugs	yes	yes	yes	yes***	yes***
Wellness	no	maybe	yes	yes	yes

*usually out of network only
**in certain markets there may be a policy maximum
***in certain markets coverage is in-network only

While the different medical expense insurance products sold to groups and individuals vary in detail, the basic coverage does not vary substantially. Whether it is an HMO, point-of-service (POS) plan, or preferred provider organization (PPO) (all of which involve medical provider networks) or an indemnity plan (which does not involve a network), medical expense insurance products provide coverage for hospital visits, doctor services, prescription drugs, nursing care, X-rays, diagnostic and laboratory tests, and other acute care services. Some plans also cover preventive or wellness visits to the doctor for routine exams and immunizations.

There are, however, significant differences in plan design that can influence the market's behavior and the health care purchase decision (see Table 3.1). Two variables of prime importance are how much money a person has to pay and how much freedom a person has to choose a doctor.

Generally, HMO and PPO participants have no deductibles or minimum copayments when they see a doctor. Indemnity plans tend to have up-front deductibles that must be satisfied every calendar year, and the plan reimburses 80 percent and the individual pays 20 percent coinsurance. Covered medical expenses are reimbursed at 100 percent once the individual incurs a given level of out-of-pocket deductibles and coinsurance, up to a policy maximum.

Regarding freedom of choice, as customers select plans along the spectrum from indemnity to HMO, the amount of freedom to choose a doctor becomes more restricted.

Managed Care vs. Indemnity Insurance

Managed care developed in response to market pressures to reduce health care costs and manage the demand for health care services. Under managed care, the financing and delivery of appropriate health care services to covered individuals are integrated by means of:

- arrangements with selected providers to furnish a comprehensive set of health care services to members;
- explicit criteria for the selection of health care providers;
- formal programs for ongoing quality assurance and utilization review; and
- significant financial incentives for members to use providers and procedures associated with the plan.

There are many levels of managed care and managed care medical expense insurance products in the market, but they all fit on a continuum that begins with indemnity or fee-for-service insurance and moves toward provider risk-sharing through capitation (being paid a flat fee per patient per year).

Managed Care Product Continuum

Fee-for-service .... Capitation

Indemnity	Indemnity with cost containment provisions	Preferred provider organization (PPO)	Point of service (POS)	Health maintenance organization (HMO)

- Insurance risk assumption
- Freedom of choice of providers
- Higher cost to customer
- Less customer education needed
- In the system when customer chooses
- Less differentiation in product/service
- National scope

- Provider risk sharing
- Network restrictions
- Lower cost to customer
- More customer education needed
- In the system early
- More differentiation in product/service
- Local scope

(continued on next page)

(continued from previous page)

Generally, people who select an indemnity product are more likely to have the freedom to choose their own doctor and hospital and to decide on their own course of treatment. At the other end of the spectrum, people who select an HMO have less freedom to choose their own doctor and hospital and to control what health care services they receive, and when. Indemnity plans usually cost more than managed care plans. The trade-off is freedom of choice and the extent of access to health care.

==Managed care products are marketed quite differently from indemnity products. Managed care markets a way to prevent illness; indemnity markets a way to transfer risk. The marketing of managed care products is both a sales process and an ongoing health education process.== Proponents of managed care say that the customer gains from this process, with improved health care at a lower cost.

Managed care plans operate under the marketing philosophy that it is important for the customer to "get in the system" early, through preventive health care services such as immunizations, prenatal care, and fitness and nutrition programs. The managed care approach literally and figuratively manages the customer's health care and lifestyle. Indemnity plans operate under the philosophy that it is the customers' responsibility to take care of those things at their own expense and on their own time.

Which are better: traditional indemnity plans or managed care plans? From a marketing perspective, the answer is not important because it differs by customer. What is important, however, is that the customer has the choice—the freedom to decide which are better based on his or her own particular circumstances. Insurance companies, PPOs, and HMOs develop and market their products to be responsive to customer needs.

■ Price as a Marketing Concept

To get a customer's attention, money, and loyalty, the price of the product being marketed is as important as the product itself. No matter how much the customer may understand the need for a product, if it is not priced right, it will not sell. If something is considered too expensive by the majority of potential customers in a targeted market, then few will buy the product. Similarly, if the price is too low, potential customers may not see the value in the product or they may feel that the product is of low quality—and again, few will buy it.

Price is very important in the marketing mix of medical expense insurance. Customers have to be able to afford it and insurers have to be able to make a profit selling it.

Price and Demand

Medical expense insurance is expensive. People with employer-sponsored insurance, however, are insulated from the true cost of the product because they pay only a portion of the premium. Large employers often pay most of the cost of medical expense insurance for employees and their dependents. Small employers often pay a reduced percentage of the cost or the cost of employee coverage only. However, individuals who purchase medical expense insurance on their own pay the entire cost and are not insulated from the true cost of the product.

There are many reasons why medical expense insurance is expensive, including the costs to develop, distribute, and administer the products; the high cost of health care itself; and regulatory requirements. But the chief reason has to do with demand. Most people recognize the need to have medical expense insurance as a way to get access to the health care system and to protect themselves from the costs of unanticipated medical expenses.

Moreover, employers' subsidization of health insurance and low-deductible plan designs (which minimize both the individual's premium payout and his or her financial risk) encourage high utilization of health care services. In effect, the current system encourages customers to disregard a basic rule of demand management, which is that you should shop for the best price when you want something. Some economists believe that until customers have to pay more out of their own pockets for insurance or care, they will not fully appreciate that they have the economic power to control the rise in health care costs.

Of course, shopping for a doctor is different from most other kinds of shopping because of the emotions involved. In an emergency situation, for example, the decision to see a doctor is made in a hurry and under great stress. Having to shop for a doctor under these conditions can make the health care purchase decision even more stressful. That is why some plans, such as HMOs, require that enrollees have a designated primary care physician whom they get to know.

Demographic Influences and High-Technology Medicine

Demographics, technological changes, and cultural expectations also are factors in the high price of medical expense insurance. The baby boom generation is causing dramatic changes in the health care system, just as it is in many other aspects of society. As the baby boomers age and move into their fifties, their health care needs will begin to increase and the cost of their care is likely to rise.

At the same time, expensive, high-technology medical procedures are becoming commonplace. For example, heart surgery and chemotherapy are available to treat heart disease and cancer, the two leading causes of death. Most Americans expect that they will have access to these procedures if they need them. High utilization of expensive services tends to inflate the price of medical expense insurance, which in turn affects its marketability.

Impact of Regulation on Price

Regulation also affects the price of medical expense insurance. For example, the costs for mandated benefits such as transplant coverage are built into the price of an insurance product. Even though only a small minority of the insured population will ever need to have a transplant, the requirement for including this benefit raises the cost of insurance for all. In addition, insurers build in administrative costs associated with overseeing compliance with mandated benefits and other regulations.

Many large employers provide employee benefit plans to their work force under a self-insurance arrangement, which exempts them from many state regulations. Individuals and most small employers generally do not have this option, and products sold in these markets must comply with state laws and regulations regarding both mandated benefits and pricing restrictions. Satisfying all these requirements adds to the price of products sold in these markets.

Participation in state reinsurance pools also influences the price of medical expense insurance. The pools allow insurance companies to spread the risk of providing coverage to certain individuals or groups who may have serious health conditions. Insurance companies that participate in these pools periodically receive a bill or assessment that spreads the cost of the pool among them. Risk pools are vehicles through which states help fund the cost of insurance for less-than-healthy individuals. Funding for risk pools differs by state.

■ Sales and Distribution

The traditional way of selling insurance is through agents or brokers. However, alternative ways of selling medical expense policies are emerging, including selling through the Internet.

Agents and Brokers

Group and individual medical expense insurance is sold most often by agents and brokers representing specific insurance companies. A few companies (called direct writers) sell their products directly to the customer.

Agents

Agents do the face-to-face selling to the customer. They are recruited and trained by the insurance company's sales management personnel, and receive office space, clerical support, and fringe benefits. Some agents are considered employees of the insurance company, but many are independent businesspeople not considered employees of an insurance company. They are paid a combination of salary, commission (usually a percentage of the premium paid by the customer), and sometimes bonuses for production, persistency, and/or profitability of their book of business. Agents are the customer's main tie to the insurance company, which provides customer service, public relations, and advertising support.

The agency sales management hierarchy begins in the insurance company's home office and extends into regions, using a field office system based on geography and market size. Typically, a field office has access to specific markets and is authorized by the company to sell its products that have been approved in the state for those markets. A typical sales management hierarchy is as follows:

Corporate Vice President, National Sales
(responsible for all sales offices)

Regional Vice President
(responsible for sales offices in specific states)

Regional Sales Manager
(responsible for several field offices in a state or region)

Field Office Sales Manager
(responsible for one field office)

MEDICAL EXPENSE INSURANCE

Agents must be licensed and be appointed by the insurance company in accordance with state laws to sell insurance. Many companies require medical expense insurance agents to have errors and omissions (E&O) insurance. This is similar to malpractice insurance that doctors and other professionals have.

Brokers

Brokers do face-to-face selling of a portfolio of products that they design from as many insurance companies and financial institutions as they wish to deal with. Like agents, they must be licensed and appointed by each insurance company for whom they sell in accordance with state laws, and may be required to have E&O insurance.

Brokers are not employees of an insurance company. They do not generally operate within a sales hierarchy, although many work through broker organizations called wholesalers or master general agents. Brokers are paid a commission and occasionally a bonus for production and persistency.

How Agents and Brokers Promote Products

Medical expense insurance products are promoted through television, radio, newspapers, and other print media, primarily by agents and brokers. Most agents and brokers place ads in the local yellow pages to promote themselves and their products, and they often send direct-mail pieces to targeted audiences in their immediate areas.

Printed promotional materials developed by insurance companies also help agents and brokers explain the products to the public. Although the materials emphasize features of plans that are likely to interest customers, they also provide information on the company itself, including financial ratings and the number of years in the business. Because of mergers and acquisitions in the health care market, some advertisements and promotional materials are designed to introduce a new entity to the public.

Alternative Distribution

In addition to agents and brokers, medical expense insurance is available through health insurance purchasing cooperatives (HIPCs), direct selling, employer-sponsored payroll deduction programs, associations, and banks and other financial institutions.

Table 3.2

Sample HIPC Menu

Plan feature	HMO 1	HMO 2	HMO 3	PPO 1	PPO 2	PPO 3
Copayment	$5	$10	$15	$10	$20	$25
Deductible	n/a	n/a	n/a	$250	$500	$1,000
Maximum	none	none	$5 million	$2 million	$5 million	$5 million
Out-of-pocket maximum	none	none	none	$1,250	$1,500	$2,000
Prescription drugs	$8 copay; generic	$5/10 copay; generic/brand	$15 copay; generic/brand	$5/10 copay; generic/brand	same	$10 copay; generic
Wellness	yes	yes	yes	yes	yes	no

Health Insurance Purchasing Cooperatives

A fairly recent development, HIPCs are privately or state-sponsored groups through which small businesses can offer their employees a choice of medical expense plans, the way large employers do. HIPCs allow the small employer to join a health insurance cooperative, which, like any other cooperative, has its members band together to purchase goods and/or services less expensively. HIPCs offer small-employer members a menu of plans, including PPOs and HMOs (see Table 3.2). Employers that are members of the HIPC offer these plans to their employees, who in turn select the one that best fits their needs. Many HMOs are not accustomed to offering their products to small employers, and HIPCs provide them access to a new market.

HIPCs sell their insurance offerings through agents and brokers, although some states originally made them available through direct selling.

Direct Selling

In certain markets and for certain limited products, HMOs and some insurance companies use direct selling. Direct selling means marketing directly to the end customer—the person who is a potential purchaser—without an agent or broker. Direct selling is often done by telephone or mail.

Medical expense health insurance rarely is sold to individuals or small businesses through direct selling, primarily because the product is medically underwritten and that process is difficult to complete accurately over the telephone or by mail. For example, an underwriter would have difficulty gauging a person's true height and weight by talking over the phone. There are, however, certain types of products that are not medically underwritten, or underwritten

MEDICAL EXPENSE INSURANCE

to the same extent as a comprehensive plan might be, that are sold via direct response, including hospital indemnity, specified disease (e.g., cancer), and other limited benefit policies.

Selling on the Internet. Recently there has been much interest in using the Internet to sell directly to the customer. Because the population is becoming more computer literate than ever before, many marketers feel that the Internet will be the first place potential customers go for information about all types of insurance, including medical expense products. Insurance companies, agents, brokers, and banks and other financial institutions that sell insurance products are putting up World Wide Web pages at a staggering rate.

The interactive capability of the Web shows real marketing promise in the following three areas:

- market research and lead generation programs for agents and brokers;
- recruiting agents and brokers to distribute products; and
- direct response sales of limited benefit policies and other products.

By encouraging certain segments of the population to use the Web for insurance information, insurers can target a segment of the population that tends to be younger, middle to upper-middle class, and well educated. On the other hand, some people feel that until privacy and confidentiality concerns are addressed, the Web will be merely an alternative to the sales brochure in an agent's office or to an advertisement on television.

Employer-Sponsored Payroll Deduction Programs

Some types of limited benefit policies—for example, hospital indemnity policies—are distributed through employer-sponsored payroll deduction programs. A payroll deduction program usually refers to the voluntary or nonemployer-pay insurance market. (While employers often deduct a portion of their employees' health insurance premiums from their employees' pay, employers are not considered to be the payroll deduction market.)

Products sold in payroll deduction programs usually are not part of the formal employee benefit program. They are offered as an enhancement to the employer's benefit program at little or no cost to the employer. These products usually are portable, which means that the employee can take the coverage when he or she leaves the employer.

The payroll deduction market for portable, individual comprehensive medical expense policies has fallen off considerably as a result of small group reform legislation. In some states, if an insurance company markets individual medical expense insurance through payroll deductions, it is considered a small group sale for purposes of risk selection and management. As a result, the regulatory restrictions regarding rating would increase the product's price, thus reducing its marketability. Because of this, many insurers no longer offer this payroll deduction option.

Associations

Trade and professional associations offer their members (employees of smaller firms or individuals) the opportunity to buy individual medical expense plans at a discount. If members leave the association, they most often can take the coverage, or something similar to it, with them. Association plans developed as a way for the organizations to attract members and to provide small employers and self-employed individuals some of the advantages of large-employer group insurance.

Banks and Other Financial Institutions

There are increasing opportunities for banks and other financial institutions to market health insurance via agents and brokers, the Internet, and direct sales to their customers. To that end, insurance companies are developing strategic partnerships with banks to ensure that customers can buy products that address their needs appropriately.

■ After the Sale: Customer Service

While much of the insurance industry is distribution driven (meaning that the focus is more on agents and brokers), there is an increasing appreciation of the importance of keeping customers. Focusing on the customer is not only the right thing for insurers to do, it is more profitable. Market research shows that the happier a customer is with a product, the more likely that he or she will buy again from the same company. And the more a customer buys from one company, the more loyal he or she is to that company.

Taking a cue from the mail order, automobile, and transportation industries, many insurance companies have increased their efforts at providing customer service. To help them learn how customers are being treated, many companies now track how long it takes for customer service representatives to answer the phone, how many days it takes for mail to be received and answered, and how many in-bound calls are made and from what parts of the country. Companies also are training customer service representatives in how to communicate effectively with the customer and satisfy his or her needs. Insurance companies use focus groups and telephone and mail surveys to understand customers' perceptions of their services. Some companies tie the employee compensation programs of customer service representatives directly to the results of these surveys. This market-driven approach is called performance-based management of customer service. (For more information on customer service, see Chapter 7: Medical Expense Policy Administration.)

Insurers also are enlisting the support of their customers to write to state legislators about health insurance issues. Just as other industries have discovered, the insurance industry has begun to see that its customers are not only its greatest asset; they also can be the industry's greatest ally.

■ Marketing in a Changing Marketplace

The future of the domestic medical expense insurance market is uncertain. While the employer-based system of providing employees and their families with coverage for illness or injury appears to be valued as a social good, there are those who feel that this system should be replaced by a governmental system, with insurance premiums replaced by taxes. Others feel that the current system is adequate for those employed by larger firms but that there are too many people who work in smaller firms and/or are self-employed who fall through the cracks, either because they cannot afford today's insurance products or cannot qualify for them. It is important that the insurance industry continually develop market-driven strategies and products to help address some of the problems of affordability and access and to ensure that customers will have choices.

The nondomestic market holds some promise for U.S. insurance carriers. As other countries struggle with similar problems of access and affordability, market needs for supplementary types of medical expense insurance products are becoming more apparent. Faced with an inability to see providers when they wish, for example, some Canadian consumers are seeking coverage in the United States as a backup. Mexicans, too, are looking to U.S. insurers for coverage of high-cost procedures such as transplants or coronary bypass surgery.

Two other potential markets for U.S. medical expense insurance are:

- foreign nationals traveling in the United States; and
- customers in Eastern Europe, Russia, and the Ukraine who can afford to pay for insurance that supplements or replaces their current system.

Medical expense insurance companies that see the nondomestic market as an opportunity will have increased access to growing markets around the globe.

■ Summary

Medical expense insurance products are designed to meet market needs for protection against the unanticipated health care costs associated with illnesses and injuries. Through market research, insurance companies analyze customer needs and are better able to develop products to meet those needs. In addition to marketing medical expense insurance through agents and brokers, insurance companies are reaching new customers through purchasing cooperatives, the Internet, and banks. Market-based solutions will continue to help make health insurance affordable and available to a broad base of customers.

■ Key Terms

Agent
Association sales
Broker
Copayment
Customers
Deductible
Direct selling
Distribution
Employee benefit plan
Errors and omissions (E&O) insurance
Fee-for-service
Field office system
Health insurance purchasing cooperative (HIPC)
Health maintenance organization (HMO)
Indemnity
Internet
Managed care
Market
Market research
Marketing mix
Nondomestic market
Out-of-pocket maximum
Payroll deduction programs
Point of sale (POS)
Preferred provider organization (PPO)
Price
Product
Promotion
Risk pools

Chapter 4

PRICING MEDICAL EXPENSE INSURANCE

53 *Introduction*
53 *Components of the Premium Rate*
59 *Estimating Claim Costs*
65 *Establishing Reserves*
66 *Rating Structures*
71 *Experience Rating*
73 *Funding Methods*
75 *Regulatory Issues*
78 *Summary*
78 *Key Terms*

■ Introduction

Appropriate rating is crucial for a medical expense insurance product. Rates that are too high will result in an unaffordable product. Rates that are too low will cause profitability problems for the insurer.

Unlike claims in other types of insurance, there is no standard table to determine medical claim costs. This is because there are wide variations in plan designs and costs as well as differences in health care practices from one region to another, and indeed from provider to provider. Therefore, an insurance company depends on its actuaries to develop a rate manual for the plans it offers. This chapter reviews how insurers estimate claim costs and set premium rates based on those estimates.

■ Components of the Premium Rate

The basic components of the premium rate are claim costs, claim reserves, expenses, and profit and contingency margins. Persistency and mortality also affect the premium rate. See Table 4.1.

Claim Costs

The most significant component of the premium rate is the claim cost. The term morbidity often is used to describe the measure of claim costs. The claim

53

Table 4.1

Components of the Premium Rate

```
                    Claim costs
   Claim reserves        ↑           Expenses
            ↖            |           ↗
              ┌─────────────────────┐
              │   Components of the │
              │    premium rate     │
              └─────────────────────┘
            ↙            |           ↘
   Persistency           ↓           Mortality
              Profit and contingency margins
```

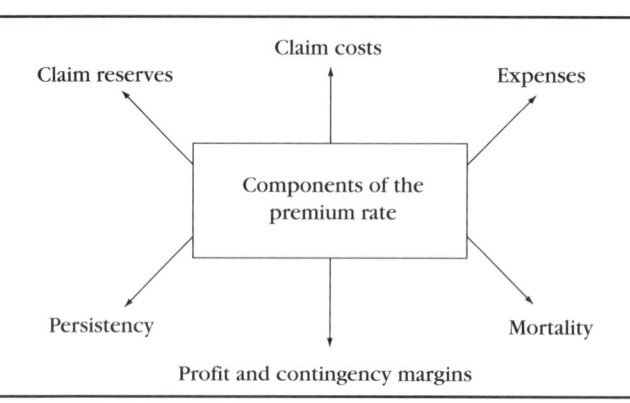

cost is the portion of the premium that pays the benefits provided by the policy. For medical expense insurance, the claim cost is a function of two variables: frequency and severity.

- Frequency is a measure of the number of times a claim occurs during a given period.
- Severity is a measure of the magnitude of the claim.

Frequency and severity often vary significantly by the type of benefit. For example, benefits for diagnostic tests, prescription drugs, and doctor's office visits often have a very high frequency of claim but the severity, or size, of the claim is relatively small. Conversely, benefits for hospitalization or surgery have a much lower frequency of claim but the size of these claims is much larger.

The overall claim cost for a policy is the sum of the claim costs for each specific benefit. Table 4.2 illustrates the pricing of a medical expense policy with five benefits for a male aged 35. In this example, the annual claim cost for a male aged 35 is $300 per policy. Insurers develop claim costs for each age (or groups of ages) and sex for each benefit offered in the policy.

Claim costs usually are incremented with a small contingency margin to account for higher-than-expected claims. The claim cost is just an estimate; no one can predict exactly how much money will be needed to pay claims. The contingency margin gives the company added protection against higher-than-expected claims.

Table 4.2

Pricing a Medical Expense Policy with Five Benefits (for a 35-year-old male)

Benefit	Maximum benefit	Annual claim frequency (per thousand)	Average claim size
Hospital confinement	$300/day	(.06)	$2,300
Surgery	$3,000/surgery	(.05)	$700
Diagnostic tests	$100/test	(.20)	$85
Office visits	$75/visit	(1.00)	$50
Prescription drugs	$50/prescription	(2.00)	$30

The annual claim cost per policy is calculated as follows:
$(.06 \times \$2{,}300) + (.05 \times \$700) + (.20 \times \$85) + (1 \times \$50) + (2 \times \$30) = \$138 + \$35 + \$17 + \$50 + \$60 = \$300$

Claim Reserves

The claim reserve is a mechanism that medical expense insurers use to fund claims that have been incurred but will be paid at a later date. Due to the nature of medical claims, it usually takes several weeks—and sometimes even a few months—to accumulate all the necessary information to process a claim. The actuary estimates the claim reserve to properly reflect the true claim liability and calculates the appropriate premium rate for the period. This estimate is especially important for group medical expense insurance products, which base the premium rate on historical experience and adjust it annually to reflect the actual experience and trend. Trend is the rate of growth of the premium needed to cover claims plus expenses. The following group medical expense example demonstrates the importance of the claim reserve in calculating the premium.

Experience period: 1996 calendar year

Renewal date: January 1, 1997

Premium earned during 1996: $1,000,000

Claims paid during 1996: $450,000

Outstanding reserve at the beginning of the period (BOP) (1/1/96):
  None (new group)

Outstanding reserve at the end of the period (EOP) (12/31/96): $250,000

MEDICAL EXPENSE INSURANCE

Since this is a new group, there is no experience on which to base the claim reserve. The claim reserve is estimated as some percentage (assumed here to be 25 percent) of earned premium based on the experience of other similar groups.

The loss ratio is the ratio of incurred claims to premiums (incurred claims divided by earned premiums). The loss ratio for the 1996 experience period is calculated as follows:

Loss Ratio = (Claims Paid − BOP Reserve + EOP Reserve) / Earned Premium
= ($450,000 − 0 + $250,000) / $1,000,00
= 70%

The renewal premium rate must take into account that the loss ratio in the previous period is estimated to be 70 percent. The estimated incurred claims of $700,000 during the period are much different from the paid claims of $450,000. The difference is the estimated liability for claims incurred during the period but not yet paid.

Expenses

Expenses are the costs incurred by the insurance company to market and service the policy. Medical expense insurance premiums must be sufficient to cover these expenses. There are six major types of expenses common to group and individual medical expense insurance policies. See Table 4.3 for an example of all expenses for a typical individual medical expense policy.

Sales Commissions

Sales commissions are paid to agents for soliciting and marketing medical expense insurance products. Commissions usually are allocated as a percentage of premium and may be a larger percentage of premium in the first year followed by a lower percentage in renewal years.

Acquisition Expenses

These are the costs incurred by the home office to underwrite and issue the business. They are allocated on a per policy issued basis or a per policy underwritten basis. Underwriting costs usually are significant for individual medical expense policies.

Table 4.3

Sample Expenses on an Individual Medical Expense Policy with a $1,500 Average Annual Premium and 70 Percent Anticipated Loss Ratio

Expenses	First year	Renewal
Sales commissions: 25% of premium first year; 10% renewal	$375.00	$150.00
Acquisition expenses: $75 per policy issued (first year only)	75.00	0.00
Policy administration expenses: $20 per policy per year	20.00	20.00
Claim administration expenses: 5% of claims paid	52.50	52.50
Company overhead expenses: 3% of premium	45.00	45.00
Premium taxes: 2% of premium	30.00	30.00
Total expenses	$597.50	$297.50
As a percentage of annual premium	39.83%	19.83%

A note about group insurance expenses: Some companies allocate all expenses for group medical expense insurance as a percentage of premium. In the example above, the company could have allocated expenses as 40 percent of first-year premium and 20 percent of renewal premium and produced roughly the same results, assuming the annual premium and loss ratio assumptions remained the same.

Policy Administration Expenses

The ongoing costs of maintaining a policy include billing, customer service, conservation (i.e., preventing the lapse of a policy or its transfer to another insurer), and reporting costs. These costs are allocated on a per policy basis or a per certificate basis on group insurance.

Claim Administration Expenses

Claim administration expenses cover the cost of investigating, processing, and administering the payment of claims. These expenses are allocated as a percentage of claims paid, a percent of premium basis, or a per policy basis.

Company Overhead Expenses

Overhead expenses are all other operating expenses not allocated above. They include management salaries, recruiting and training expenses, and sometimes office furniture and rent. Overhead is allocated as a percentage of premium.

Premium Taxes

These taxes, which are levied by the state, usually are allocated as a percentage of premium.

MEDICAL EXPENSE INSURANCE

Profit and Contingency Margins

Profit margin is the component of the premium rate that provides the company with a return on its investment and a reward for accepting the risk of insurance. For a company to develop insurance products, provide insurance services to its customers, and maintain a strong claims paying status, capital must be invested and products must provide an adequate return on this investment. Most medical expense insurance products are priced to return some measure of profit. The profit margin may include a contingency margin to help buffer the company from adverse claim experience.

Medical expense insurance products have produced relatively small profit margins in recent years. Regulatory pressures and high inflationary cost trends in regard to medical treatments have resulted in a steady increase in claim costs, and many insurance companies are finding it difficult to keep pace with these costs. Contingency margins and profit margins can erode quickly unless premiums are adjusted to the rising costs. In addition, companies writing traditional group and individual medical expense insurance are finding it increasingly difficult to charge a level of premium that is sufficient to maintain adequate profit margins while competing with managed care plans and self-funded plans.

Persistency and Mortality

Throughout the life of any medical expense plan, a certain amount of coverage will be terminated due to insureds voluntarily letting the policy lapse or to the death of insureds. Insurers use three measures to account for terminations:

- The *lapse rate* is a measure of the number of policies voluntarily canceled to the total number of policies issued.
- *Persistency* is a measure of the number of policies still in force to the total number of policies issued.
- *Mortality* is a measure of the number of policies involuntarily terminated due to death.

When pricing group and individual medical expense insurance, mortality is not usually as significant as lapsed policies and often the mortality assumption is included in the lapse assumption. For example, a typical first-year lapse rate might be 30 percent and a typical mortality rate might be 0.5 percent. The persistency rate would then be 69.5 percent (1−.30 −.005) indicating that 69.5 percent of the initial insureds are expected to persist to the second policy year.

Impact of Lapse Rates

Lapse rates can have a significant impact on the underlying demographics of the group or individual policy bases and on profitability, as the following examples illustrate.

Example #1. Lapse rates are typically higher with younger insureds than older insureds, except around the retirement ages. Younger and presumably healthier insureds lapse their policies more often than older and presumably less healthy insureds. This pattern causes the insured policyholder base to age quicker than normal, which in turn will affect the claims experience negatively.

Example #2. Lapse rates typically decrease by duration. The longer a policy is in force, the less likely a person is to lapse the policy. Individual lapse rates can be as high as 30 to 40 percent in the first policy year and grade down to 10 to 12 percent by the sixth policy year. Usually lapse rates level out after a period of time.

Example #3. Premium levels and rate increases also have a significant effect on lapse rates. A product that is rated too high is likely to have higher than normal lapse rates. Large or frequent rate increases also lead to high lapse rates. Such rate increases usually result in the healthier lives seeking more affordable coverage elsewhere and leaving the less healthy lives in the plan.

Example #4. Lapse rates differ by product type and renewability provision. Lapse rates on noncancellable policies are typically low since the premiums are guaranteed for the life of the policy.

■ Estimating Claim Costs

There are differences in the way that group and individual medical expense policy rates are determined. By and large, group policies develop rates for a group's coverage from the insurer's standard rate tables; individual policies use morbidity tables, which are statistical tables that show the average number of illnesses befalling a large group of persons.

Group Manual Rates

The largest portion of the premium for medical expense policies is the claim cost. For group policies the claim cost usually is estimated using a group rate manual.

A rate manual is compiled by actuaries and contains costs for the various benefits included in the plan, such as hospital stays or diagnostic tests. The manual also includes the average frequency for each particular benefit and adjustment factors for various aspects of the plan that affect the rate. Using this information, a group underwriter selects the appropriate benefits and calculates the manual rate for the plan.

Factors that may affect the manual rate for the group include demographics and plan design factors. Once the manual rate has been determined, it may be adjusted further based on a trend analysis or an experience study. As an example of such an adjustment, suppose a plan has a manual rate of $250, and all the manual rates are effective January 1, 1998. There is an annual trend of 10 percent, and this particular policy will not be effective until July 1, 1998. Accordingly, the manual rate will need a six-month trend adjustment. The adjusted manual rate would be:

$$(\$250) \times (1.10)^{1/2} = \$262.20$$

Individual Statistics

Actuaries use morbidity tables to construct manual rates for individual medical policies. Any source of population medical statistics is a good starting point. The best source of data comes from existing company experience on similar products. If the company is introducing a new product, however, company experience is not likely to be available. In these cases, actuaries turn to other sources of data to develop individual medical claim costs.

Popularly used sources include:

- intercompany studies compiled periodically and published in the *Transactions of the Society of Actuaries*;
- population medical statistics available from a number of government sources;
- industrywide statistics on insureds and population data from the Health Insurance Association of America;
- specialized statistics, such as accident data from the National Safety Council and annual cancer statistics from the American Cancer Society.

When using population data or intercompany studies, actuaries need to adjust the data to appropriately account for their company's underwriting and claim philosophy.

Variations from Rate Manuals

Several other factors affect group and individual rate manuals, and actuaries need to make adjustments for the following reasons: demographics affecting

PRICING MEDICAL EXPENSE INSURANCE

the group or individual, plan design, rate guarantees and renewability provisions, trend analysis, and company underwriting philosophy.

Demographic Factors

Demographic factors that affect manual rates include geographic area, age, sex, occupation, and industry.

Geographic area. Medical practices vary from one region to another, which affects the cost of services. Costs also are different in urban areas than in rural areas. Actuaries often use zip codes or area rating factors to account for variations in cost by geographic region. Other situations need to be taken into account, such as when an insured lives in a low-cost suburb but gets treatment in a high-cost downtown metropolitan area.

Age and sex. Age is a very important factor in developing claim costs since almost all medical claim statistics vary significantly by age. Medical claim costs also vary significantly by sex, and this variation often depends on age and the type of benefit. For example, hospital room and board benefits tend to be lower for females under age 30 and over age 50 and for males between ages 30 and 50.

Occupation and industry. Actuaries account for occupational factors in many ways. One may be as simple as considering the percentage of white-collar workers versus blue-collar workers in a group. If an industry classification is used, it is normally based on Standard Industrial Classification (SIC) codes. Certain industries, such as banking and financial services, may receive a discount from the manual rate. Other industries, such as mining or construction, may have a loading factor added to the manual rate. A loading factor is the amount added to the premium rate for a group to cover the possibility that losses will be greater than statistically expected because the employees work in a hazardous industry. (Loads also are added because of older average age, a large percentage of unskilled employees, and adverse experience.) These discounts and loads might range from 5 percent to 50 percent of the claim cost.

Plan Design Factors

Plan design features affecting the rate include deductibles and coinsurance, services covered, conditions covered, cost containment features, and limitations and exclusions.

Most plans include a deductible, which is an amount that must be paid by the insured before benefits become payable. Some plans include a separate inhospital deductible, which must be satisfied before inpatient hospital claims are paid. Higher deductibles lead to lower claims and lower premiums.

Even after the deductible is satisfied, most plans require the insured to pay a coinsurance, which is a percentage of the remaining charges. Plans that require a higher coinsurance have lower claims and lower premiums.

Claim costs vary significantly depending on what services are covered. Some plans cover only expenses incurred while the insured is in the hospital. These plans are relatively inexpensive. Other plans are more comprehensive, covering nearly every medically related expense. Some benefits, such as immunizations, routine physicals, or prescription drugs, may be offered as an option, and an appropriate premium is added to the rate to cover them.

Cost containment features, such as medical audits and hospital stay review programs, can lower claim costs. Medical audits, particularly of hospital bills, assist in helping carriers with inappropriate billings or duplications of charges. Hospital stay review programs help to determine the appropriateness of a patient's treatment. Such reviews can lead to shorter hospital stays, thus avoiding unnecessary costs.

Limitations and exclusions keep costs down by protecting the plan from unusually large claims. Most plans have a lifetime maximum; $1 million is common. Many plans limit the amount payable for mental and nervous disorders, although state legislation may require certain minimum coverage. It also is common to exclude experimental treatments from coverage under a medical expense plan. These features limit the exposure of the plan to large claims and thus lower claim costs. (For a review of benefit limitations and exclusions, see Chapter 1: Group Major Medical Expense Insurance and Chapter 2: Individual Hospital-Surgical Insurance.)

Rate Guarantees and Renewability Provisions

Since medical expense insurance claims are highly influenced by medical inflation, the premiums must be adjusted frequently to keep pace with the rising costs. Because of the high rate of inflation in medical costs, a claim cost that is adequate this year may be inadequate next year. When medical expense insurance premiums are guaranteed to remain the same over a period of time, the premium rate must be set at the beginning of this period to reflect this guarantee. For group insurance, the premium will vary based on the length of the guarantee period (usually one to three years) and the level of medical inflation expected. At the end of the period, the group can be renewed at the renewal premium rate.

For individual insurance, historically there have been four renewability options designed to offer the insured some protection against cancellation of coverage due to deterioration of health. Each option had different implications for the degree of protection and for pricing. The options were: optionally renewable, nonrenewable for stated reasons only, guaranteed renewable, and noncancellable. HIPAA requires that all individual medical expense policies be guaranteed renewable, with specified exceptions (e.g., fraud). The HIPAA renewability provision is similar to the nonrenewable for stated reasons only provision, except that the law rather than the insurer specifies allowed reasons for nonrenewability. Contracts typically are renewed for one year with premiums adjusted for medical inflation.

Trend Analysis

Actuaries often need to make an adjustment for trend in the manual rate. Inflation in medical expense insurance historically has been much higher than general inflation. A medical rate manual typically has some specified period of time for which the rates are appropriate. If the rates are used for a policy with an effective date before or after that specified, then a trend adjustment will have to be made. Components of the trend include medical inflation, changes in utilization, cost shifting, economic inflation, and advances in medical technology. While each trend can be studied individually, it is difficult to separate them entirely. For example, new technologies influence accepted medical practices, which in turn influence utilization. Most companies analyze the overall trend in medical expense claims, as opposed to considering each item alone.

Medical inflation. Medical inflation is the increase in the costs for medical services. It may vary based on the type of service. For example, hospital costs may increase faster than physician charges. Medical inflation is measured by comparing historical data to more current cost data.

Utilization patterns. Changes in utilization can affect the trend. For example, when a group policy has been in force for some time, the average age may rise, thus increasing the frequency of claims in the group. Or if a plan is designed to discourage inpatient surgery through the use of an inhospital deductible, then the company may find that the use of outpatient services increases. Other changes in medical practice, such as the use of new drugs, affect the cost of the plan.

Cost shifting. Cost shifting occurs when one group of patients is charged more to make up for a revenue shortfall from others. For example, if a hospital provides care to a large number of persons who are unable to pay, then the hospital has to recoup those costs by charging higher prices to those patients who do pay.

Economic inflation. Inflation affects the expense portion of the premium rate. The company's expenses may rise from year to year: the cost of labor increases, the rent increases, the cost of supplies increases, and so forth. Every ongoing expense of the company is subject to inflation, and these increases are passed on to customers.

New medical technologies. As new technologies become available for medical providers, the cost of medical plans may go up or down. Some new technologies, such as laparoscopic surgery, may decrease costs since surgery that once required lengthy hospital stays can now be done on an outpatient basis or with a very short inhospital stay. In contrast, new drugs often are more expensive than older drugs, because the drug companies need to pass along the research and development costs to the consumers. However, if a drug treatment replaces a more expensive treatment, then this too represents a cost savings.

Technologies requiring the purchase of special equipment, such as ultrasound, may be the most costly of all. The equipment itself is expensive, and that cost is passed on to the patients. Furthermore, it is questionable whether the use of such equipment is always medically necessary.

Underwriting Philosophy

The underwriting practices of an insurance company have an impact on the rates that need to be charged. Practices differ based on whether the plan is sold to groups or individuals. The following section covers underwriting from the perspective of pricing. (For more information, see Chapter 6: Underwriting Medical Expense Insurance.)

For group plans. Underwriting practices vary for groups, depending on group size and participation levels. For large groups, only minimal underwriting is generally required. It is assumed that there are enough healthy people in the group to offset the high claims that might be incurred by a few sick people. Even so, there may be some nominal participation requirement, such as 50 percent, to protect the plan from antiselection.

For smaller groups (50 or fewer lives), the effects of large claims are magnified since there is not a large amount of premium to absorb them. Smaller groups typically have higher participation requirements—at least 75 percent—and more stringent underwriting. For very small groups (under 10 lives), individual underwriting may be required.

A guaranteed issue clause allows every person in a group that is eligible for the medical plan to be issued coverage regardless of medical history. For very large groups, this clause has little impact on the overall claim cost. However, for smaller groups, the impact on rating can be significant. Again, the fact that there is no large premium base to absorb especially large claims is an issue.

For individual insurance. For individual insurance, underwriting is done individually. There is greater risk for antiselection on individual medical plans since individuals with poor health can select against the company. The degree of individual underwriting has a large impact on the premiums. The stronger the underwriting, the greater the expense but the healthier the initial insured base, resulting in lower overall claim costs. Simplified underwriting can lead to more antiselection and perhaps higher claims but lower underwriting expenses. Guaranteed issue, with no medical underwriting, can be done at the least expense but can lead to substantial antiselection and extremely high claims.

A strong individual underwriting philosophy can be used to categorize insureds into the proper rating classes. Such categorization allows the company to issue coverage to substandard risks and charge the appropriate premium. People with greater risks may still be eligible for coverage but may need to pay a higher premium.

For group and individual insurance. A pre-existing condition clause, along with underwriting, can work well to keep down the cost of claims. The pre-existing condition clause simply limits the amount of benefit payable for conditions that were being treated prior to the effective date of the plan. This limitation protects the plan from antiselection.

A typical pre-existing condition clause might exclude from coverage any condition for which the insured sought treatment within a year prior to the effective date of the coverage. The exclusion can last until the coverage has been in force for only one year. Thus, with a pre-existing condition clause, insureds have no incentive to wait until they have contracted some potentially costly disease before purchasing the coverage.

Underwriting over time. While underwriting has a significant impact on the rate in the early years of a medical expense plan, over time the effects of underwriting wear off. Eventually the young people enrolled in the plan grow older and the healthy people get sick. Pre-existing limitations expire after a year of coverage. However, underwriting and pre-existing clauses continue to be important for new entrants into the plan. Thus, underwriting can help keep costs down in the early years of the plan, and it can help to limit antiselection as the plan matures.

■ Establishing Reserves

Claim reserves are set aside to specifically cover claim liabilities that have not yet been paid. Two types of claim reserves are pending reserves and incurred but not reported (IBNR) reserves.

MEDICAL EXPENSE INSURANCE

Pending Reserves

Pending reserves are established for claims that have been reported but have not yet been paid. In many cases some additional piece of information may be required before the payment can be released. Pending reserves usually are a relatively small portion of the total claim reserves for medical expense insurance.

Incurred But Not Reported (IBNR) Claim Reserves

The IBNR reserves are established for claims that have not yet been reported to the company. There is usually some lag time between the time the claim is incurred and the time it is submitted for payment. For an accurate report of a plan's expenditures, it is important that the IBNR reserves are estimated as precisely as possible.

Methods Used to Estimate Claim Reserves

There are many ways to calculate appropriate claim reserves. This discussion covers two common methods: the loss ratio method and the development method. The loss ratio method is one of the simplest methods for estimating reserves. For this method the reserve equals the earned premium times an estimated loss ratio minus paid claims. For example, consider a group with $150,000 in earned premium, an expected loss ratio of 80 percent, and paid claims of $90,000. The reserve for this group is:

$$\$150,000 \times 80\% - \$90,000 = \$30,000.$$

The development method is much more involved than the loss ratio method, and the results obtained are much more reliable. This method, also called the lag method, relies on studies and models of the runoff patterns of claims. A table is made that reports claims by the month incurred versus the month they were paid. From this table, completion factors are calculated—that is, the percentage of total claims incurred during the month that have been paid to date. Table 4.4 illustrates the development method.

■ Rating Structures

To preserve equity among policyholders, premiums often are structured into different rating classes to reflect the different rating categories. Premiums may vary by size of group, age of the insured, number of family members covered, geographic location, and other factors. There are different rating structures for group and individual medical expense insurance policies.

Table 4.4

Example of the Development Method of Estimating Claims

1. Claims are totaled by month of payment versus month incurred.

Month incurred	Jan.	Feb.	March	April	May	June	Total
Jan.	10,000	50,000	30,000	10,000	0	0	100,000
Feb.		7,000	44,000	19,000	5,000	0	75,000
March			12,000	54,000	32,000	10,000	108,000
April				10,000	49,000	33,000	101,000

2. Calculate the cumulative rate of total claims paid after one month, two months, and so on.

Month incurred	Jan.	Feb.	March	April	May	June
Jan.	0.100	0.600	0.900	1.000	1.000	1.000
Feb.		0.093	0.680	0.933	1.000	1.000
March			0.111	0.611	0.907	1.000
April				0.099	0.584	0.911

3. These factors are used to calculate expected future claims for the IBNR reserve.

Group Rating Structures

A determining factor for how many rates are developed and what those rates will be is the group's choice of family classification. Some groups have one rate for employee-only coverage and one rate for family coverage. Other groups have separate rates for employee-only, employee and spouse, employee and children (but no spouse), and employee and family.

Age-banded rates may be offered for the smallest groups. These rates are based on the age of the employee, usually in 5- or 10-year age brackets. The following is an example of typical age-banded rates:

Single Employee Rates per Month

Under age 30	$150
Ages 30–39	200
Ages 40–49	275
Ages 50–59	375
Ages 60 and over	525

MEDICAL EXPENSE INSURANCE

Example of Developing Premiums for a 200-Life Employer Group

Assumptions:

- Gender and age distributions are the same as those in the company's manual.
- No industry or occupational adjustments are made.
- The claim reserve is fully funded.
- The company uses a four-way rate structure, with the following distribution:

    100 employee-only coverages,
      30 employee and spouse coverages,
      20 employee and children coverages, and
      <u>50</u> employee and family coverages.
    200 employees total

The manual gives the following frequencies, costs, and net annual premium for an employee in a group with these characteristics.

Type of service	Annual frequency	Average annual cost	Net annual premium
Hospitalization	0.10	$7,000	$700
Surgery	0.30	1,500	450
Office visits (including tests and lab work)	0.85	500	425
Prescription drugs	0.75	200	150
Total			$1,725

The manual states that spouse costs are 20 percent higher than employee costs, and children's costs are 40 percent less than employee costs. Totaling the net annual premium listed for each service reveals that the net annual premium (or claim cost) for employees is $1,725. For spouses, add 20 percent to this cost to get $2,070. For children, subtract 40 percent from the employee cost to get $1,035.

To get the manual-expected claims for the whole group, use the information given about the number of coverages in each family category:

Manual-Expected Claims = $1,725 × (200 employees)   = $345,000
                   + $2,070 × (30 + 50 spouses) = 165,600
                   + $1,035 × (20 + 50 children) =   72,450
             Total   = $583,050

(continued on next page)

PRICING MEDICAL EXPENSE INSURANCE

(continued from previous page)

Next, add a contingency margin, expenses, and profit load. The contingency margin is 5 percent of expected claims, or $29,153. Sales and marketing expenses total 10 percent of premium, and state premium tax is 2 percent of premium. There is a home office cost of $5 per certificate per month, which equals $12,000 for this group. Finally, the company wishes to make a profit of 2 percent of premium on this case.

Based on this, the gross premium needed for this case is:

$$\frac{\text{Claim Cost} + \text{Margin} + \text{Home Office Expenses}}{1 - \text{Sales/Marketing Expenses} - \text{State Premium Tax} - \text{Profit}}$$

or

$$\frac{\$583{,}050 + \$29{,}153 + \$12{,}000}{1 - 0.10 - 0.02 - 0.02} = \$725{,}817.$$

Thus, the total expenses are:

Home Office ($5/employee/month × 200 employees × 12 months)	$12,000
Sales and Marketing (10% of $725,817)	72,582
State Premium Tax (2% of $725,817)	14,516
	$99,098

The profit is 2 percent of $725,817, or $14,516. The total of the margin ($29,153), expenses ($99,098) and profit ($14,516) is $142,767, or 19.7 percent (or 0.197) of the gross premium.

Now the gross monthly rates can be calculated. First, divide the net annual premium by $1 - 0.197$ to get the gross annual premiums, and then divide by 12 to get the monthly premiums:

	Gross Annual Premium	Gross Monthly Premium
Employee	$1,725 ÷ 1 − 0.197 = $2,148	$2,148 ÷ 12 = $179
Spouse	$2,070 ÷ 1 − 0.197 = $2,578	$2,578 ÷ 12 = $215
Children	$1,035 ÷ 1 − 0.197 = $1,289	$1,289 ÷ 12 = $107

Finally, add the appropriate premiums together to attain the desired rate structure:

		Monthly Rate
Employee	$179.02 =	$179.02
Employee & Spouse	$179.02 + $214.82 =	$393.84
Employee & Children	$179.02 + $107.41 =	$286.43
Employee & Family	$179.02 + $214.82 + $107.41 =	$501.25

MEDICAL EXPENSE INSURANCE

Individual Rating Structures

There are a number of rating classes used with individual medical expense insurance policies. The number of rating classes used and the complexity of the rate manual vary from one company to the next. This section reviews six of the more common characteristics of the individual rate structure.

Family Classes

Medical insurance often is purchased to cover family members as well as the primary insured. Premiums vary, based on the number of family members covered. Common family classes are individual, husband and wife, single parent family, and family.

Tobacco Classes

Premium structures that distinguish users of tobacco from nonusers of tobacco have been common in life insurance for years. This rating classification is becoming more common on individual medical expense insurance. The classification allows the insurance company to offer a lower and more competitive premium to nonusers of tobacco who are generally more healthy and better risks than users of tobacco.

Gender Classes

Medical claim statistics indicate a distinct difference between the level of claims for males and females. This difference often varies by age. Sex-distinct rates have been common in individual medical expense insurance for many years, but antidiscrimination laws now require companies to use unisex rates—one blended rate used for both males and females.

Underwriting Classes

In an effort to insure a greater number of people, some companies use different underwriting classes. Companies may use a standard or substandard rate class that enables them to charge the appropriate premium for the risk assumed. This way, applicants that are statistically higher risks than others may be still insurable.

Age Classes

Medical claims vary significantly by age, and most individual insurance companies charge premiums by age. Premiums may vary by each distinct age, but many companies group insureds by 5- or 10-year age bands. There are three commonly used age-rating methods:

Attained age rates. Premiums increase when the insured reaches certain attained ages. Some attained age premiums increase every year and some increase every 5 to 10 years. This rate structure typically produces the poorest persistency.

Age at entry rates. The initial premium varies based on the age at entry and remains level throughout the life of the policy. Renewal rates may change over time to reflect overall experience, but they will not change due to age. This structure typically produces better persistency than the attained age structure.

Level rates. Age classes are removed completely and a level rate is charged for all ages. This rate structure, which can be used when the age distribution is predictable, is common in the work site payroll deduction market. The simplicity of this rate structure is appealing to employer bookkeepers. It is important to accurately predict the distribution of insureds by age to reduce the risk of level rates.

Area Rating Factors

Most individual rate manuals use area rating factors to reflect the difference in the cost of medical treatment by geographical area. The base rate structure is calculated on average costs and loaded or discounted to reflect the geographical area. Geographical area may be determined by state, county, or zip code.

■ Experience Rating

Experience rating is a rating method that takes the policyholder's claims history into account in determining rates. Group medical expense insurance is a good candidate for experience rating because of the high frequency of claims and relatively low claim amounts. These characteristics make claim costs fairly predictable.

Experience Rating for Group Insurance

Experience rating is used often in group insurance because it provides greater equity among groups than manual rating. Competitive pressures also cause insurers to experience rate since groups with lower than average claims will be attracted to the lower rates that experience rating allows. If they cannot get those lower rates at one company, they might shop around for a company that will give them the lower rates.

MEDICAL EXPENSE INSURANCE

If a group is not large enough to be experience rated on its own, then its experience may be pooled with that of similar groups. This is basically the same as using a manual rate. Sometimes only claims over a certain dollar amount are pooled. An experience rate is calculated based on the smaller claims; a pooling charge is added to cover the risk of having a large claim.

For example, consider a group with 100 employees with $325,000 in claims for the previous 12-month period, including one large one of $50,000. The group is experience rated, but claims over $25,000 are pooled. The pooling charge is $15 per employee per month. The incurred claims used in rating the plan are:

$325,000 − $50,000 + ($15/employee/month × 100 employees × 12 months) = $293,000.

Note that the pooling charge is added each year even if the group had not experienced a large claim in the past year. The pooling charge has the effect of smoothing the incurred claims from year to year.

Some groups want the benefit of experience rating even though they are not large enough for their experience to be credible. In this case the company may use blending, or partial experience rating. To do this, the company assigns a credibility percentage to the group. This percentage is applied to the experience rate, while the remainder is applied to the manual rate.

Returning to the previous example, suppose that the 100-employee group was considered to be 20 percent credible. The experience rate is $244.17 ($293,000 ÷ 100 employees ÷ 12 months). Suppose the manual rate is $275.00. Using blending, the rate charged would be:

20% ($244.17) + 80% ($275.00) = $268.83.

Along with the incurred claims, the experience rated premium has another portion called retention. The retention includes charges for expenses as well as contribution to surplus. There may be a fixed retention charge that includes those expenses that are fixed costs, as well as a variable retention charge that includes premium tax and other expenses that are expressed as a percentage of premium.

At the end of a policy year if the premium charged to the experience rated group has exceeded the incurred claims plus retention, then the surplus may be placed into a rate stabilization reserve. In later years the group may experience higher than expected losses. The rate stabilization reserve would then offset all or a portion of those losses, and would help to avoid a large rate increase. Generally, a rate stabilization reserve is refundable to the policyholder if the policy terminates. This reserve also is called a claim fluctuation reserve.

Renewal Rating for Individual Insurance

For individual medical expense insurance, renewal rating procedures are just as important as the initial pricing. Medical claim costs are influenced by a number of factors and are difficult to project very far into the future with any degree of accuracy. The initial premiums may be set according to a number of actuarial assumptions, but these will change over time. Renewal premiums must account for projected changes in claim costs and be adequate to cover any rate guarantee periods. The key to managing a successful individual medical portfolio is timely rate adjustments.

Policy experience is examined periodically, often quarterly, and compared to expected results. Experience is analyzed by incurred year (or month) and by policy year. Premiums collected each month should adequately cover a certain level of claims incurred during that month. The incurred claims are the claims paid plus the outstanding claim reserve for claims incurred during that month. The incurred claim loss ratio is then compared to the expected loss ratio. Monthly experience often is not credible, and experience for several months, usually three to six months, can produce more credible results. The three- or six-month loss ratio is tracked over time to reveal any underlying trend. This experience is then projected to establish the premium rates for renewal periods.

It is important to analyze experience by policy year. Experience by policy year shows the effects of the underwriting selection. Loss ratios in the first few policy years should be lower than in subsequent years because the impact of underwriting selection lessens with time. A study of experience by policy year allows actuaries to analyze and adjust the selection factors used in the original pricing.

■ Funding Methods

When the cost of insurance benefits began to rise substantially in the 1970s, insurers and employers looked for alternative methods to finance this cost. The objectives of alternative funding methods include controlling the cash flow, decreasing or eliminating premium taxes, decreasing administrative and risk charges paid to the insurer, and reducing claim costs by avoiding state-mandated benefits.

Fully Insured Plans

The traditional funding arrangement for insurance coverage is the fully insured plan. In this plan the insurer collects the premium, pays the claims, and holds

MEDICAL EXPENSE INSURANCE

the reserves. The insurer bears the risk of higher-than-expected claims, but it also reaps the benefit of lower-than-expected claims. State premium tax is paid on all premiums collected, and the contract is subject to all insurance laws of the state of issue.

Minimum Premium Plans

One method for reducing the premium and thus increasing cash flow for the policyholder is a minimum premium contract. Under this method a separate fund is set up for claims payment. The expected claims portion of the premium is paid directly into the fund, and it does not become premium. The portion of the premium that funds expenses and reserves is paid to the insurer. The major advantage to this funding method is that premium tax is avoided on the payments made to the claims account. (This is not the case in California, where the state requires that the premium tax paid be based on the entire cost of the plan.)

The insurer is usually liable for claims that exceed the fund amount, as well as any outstanding claims upon termination. That liability is the reason a reserve is needed.

Retrospective Premium Arrangements

Under a retrospective premium arrangement, the up-front premium is reduced by some negotiated amount. Often the amount is equal to or related to the contingency margin built into the rate. At the end of the plan year, if the total plan cost is greater than the premiums paid, then the policyholder reimburses the insurer for the excess amount, possibly subject to some maximum. If, however, the plan costs are less than the premiums paid, then the insurer pays the excess premiums back to the policyholder as an experience refund. In many cases the experience refund is used to fund a rate stabilization reserve.

Self-Insured Plans

Under a self-insured plan, an employer becomes the primary risk taker and the insurer provides administrative services only (ASO), such as benefit plan design, claim processing, data recovery and analysis, and stop-loss coverage. In a self-insured plan, the employer has the responsibility to pay all claims and expenses resulting from the plan. The funds to pay these costs are deposited in a trust. An insurance company or third-party administrator usually is contracted to pay claims and handle other administrative duties for the plan. The fees for such administration often are less than retention fees in an insured contract because there is no premium tax and because there is no insurance risk to the administrator. Claim costs also may be lower because the plan is not subject to state-mandated benefits. The drawback for the employer is that it bears all the risk for excess claims. An extremely high claim could severely limit the employer's profitability.

Stop-Loss Insurance

An employer with a self-funded medical expense plan may choose to purchase protection against the risk of large claims in the form of a stop-loss policy. A smaller employer might be especially interested in stop-loss coverage, since the smaller plan is less able to absorb the costs relating to large claims.

There are two types of stop-loss insurance available. Aggregate stop-loss insurance protects against the risk of overall claims being higher than expected. An aggregate stop-loss policy may begin to pay when claims exceed 125 percent of expected claims or some other specified level. Specific stop-loss insurance protects against the risk of individual claims exceeding a predetermined dollar amount, such as $100,000.

If both aggregate and specific stop-loss insurance are purchased together, then the specific stop-loss is applied first. The reimbursement for claims exceeding the specific stop-loss limit is subtracted from the total claims; then the total is compared to the aggregate stop-loss limit to determine whether the plan is eligible for reimbursement under that coverage.

■ Regulatory Issues

Laws and regulations regarding medical expense insurance often have an impact on the rating of such coverage. When the laws relate to benefits that must be offered or to whom they must be offered, rates are affected. Some laws are quite specific regarding what may or may not be done in the rating process.

State-Mandated Benefits

Several states require that medical expense policies cover certain costs. Some popular state-mandated benefits include covering minimum hospital stays for certain surgeries or providing wellness benefits such as cancer screenings or immunizations. These required benefits can have a large impact on claim costs. In some cases the inclusion of such benefits is not required, but they must be offered as an optional coverage. In these situations it is up to the policyholder to determine whether or not to accept the additional benefits, and thus the associated costs.

Small Group Laws

In an attempt to address the problem of the uninsured by providing insurance coverage to more workers or dependents of workers whose employers had 25 or fewer employees, the National Association of Insurance Commissioners (NAIC) adopted two model laws: the Premium Rates and Renewability of Coverage for Health Insurance Sold to Small Groups Model Act and the Small Employer Health Insurance Availability Model Act. Revisions to these models were enacted in 1995.

Nearly all states have adopted some form of these laws, which affect the rating process for small employer groups. There are rules regarding how much variation may exist between a company's lowest and highest small group rates. There also are limits on premium increases, and some of the laws require guaranteed issue for small employer groups. Any company that sells medical expense insurance to small employer groups must be aware of the pricing-related requirements in these regulations.

Individual Rate Regulation

Various attempts have been made throughout the years to regulate individual health insurance rates. The current NAIC guidelines are based on criteria that measure the reasonableness of benefits in relation to premiums charged. Many states have adopted these guidelines and some states have introduced even stricter ones. To adjust premium rates on individual health policies, actuaries must demonstrate that the minimum loss ratio meets certain standards and certify that benefits are reasonable in relation to the premiums charged. These standards are:

- For a new policy, the minimum loss ratio standard must be met over the entire lifetime of the policy from inception.
- For a revised policy, the minimum loss ratio standard must be met over the entire future lifetime of the policy from the date of the rate revision.

These standards are designed to keep companies from recovering past losses on policy forms with historically high loss ratios. Some states limit the amount of rate increase that can be approved at one time and some limit the number of times a rate filing can be applied for during a certain period.

The minimum loss ratio standards vary by renewability provision and premium size. The minimum loss ratio standards can be adjusted downward for low average premium forms and upward for high average premium forms.

Health Insurance Portability and Accountability Act of 1996

The new Health Insurance Portability and Accountability Act (HIPAA) (P.L. 104-191) will affect medical expense insurance pricing in several ways. Some of the more significant requirements contained in the act that apply to group medical expense policies and relate to pricing are:

- limits on maximum length of pre-existing condition exclusion periods;
- requirements to credit prior coverage toward any new exclusion periods when an employee changes jobs;
- prohibition on discrimination based on health status in eligibility for enrollment and in establishing premium contributions;
- guaranteed renewability; and
- guaranteed issue in small group market.

In the group market, no pre-existing condition exclusion may be more than 12 months long (18 months for late enrollees). Also, the group-to-group portability provisions require companies to reduce such exclusion periods month-for-month for prior coverage when employees change group health plans. The non-discrimination provision will eliminate carving out and making special arrangements for high risk individuals in a group.

Companies that serve the small employer market (defined as 2 to 50 employees) now are required to offer such coverage to all small employers on a guaranteed issue basis. In addition, guaranteed renewal of all products offered by group carriers is required.

The Health Insurance Portability and Accountability Act will affect the pricing of individual medical policies, as well, through the following provisions:

- guaranteed issue with no pre-existing condition exclusions for individuals eligible for group-to-individual portability (unless the state has implemented a different mechanism under the act); and
- guaranteed renewability.

Because this act affects the way group and individual medical expense insurance products are designed and priced, it will likely lead to higher premiums.

MEDICAL EXPENSE INSURANCE

■ Summary

Claim costs represent the largest portion of the premium for a medical expense insurance policy. Factors that influence the claim cost include demographics, plan design, and medical expense insurance trends. Rates for group policies usually are based on an insurer's standard rate tables, and rates for individual policies usually are based on morbidity tables. Experience rating also is used often for group policies. Other items affecting the final rate are reserve calculations and the funding method for the plan. As with other types of insurance, the company's expenses and desired profit also are considered in the rating process.

■ Key Terms

Age at entry rates
Age-banded rates
Aggregate stop-loss insurance
Area rating factors
Claim costs
Claim reserve
Coinsurance
Contingency margin
Cost containment features
Deductible
Development method
Experience rating
Fixed retention
Frequency
Fully insured plan
Guaranteed issue
Guaranteed renewable

Health Insurance Portability and Accountability Act of 1996 (HIPAA)
Incurred but not reported reserves
Lapse rate
Loss ratio method
Minimum premium plan
Morbidity
Mortality
Noncancellable
Nonrenewable for stated reasons only
Optionally renewable
Partial experience rating
Pending reserves
Persistency

Pooling
Pre-existing condition
Premium rate
Rate manual
Rate stabilization reserve
Rating classes
Retention
Retrospective premium arrangement
Self-insured plan
Severity
Small group laws
Specific stop-loss insurance
State-mandated benefits
Stop-loss insurance
Trend
Variable retention

CHAPTER 5

MEDICAL EXPENSE CONTRACT PROVISIONS

79 *Introduction*

80 *Group Medical Expense Contract Provisions Relating to Policyholders*

90 *Group Medical Expense Contract Provisions Relating to Insureds*

96 *Individual Medical Expense Contract Provisions*

100 *Group and Individual Expense Contract Development*

100 *Summary*

101 *Key Terms*

■ Introduction

Medical expense insurance contracts contain a number of specific definitions and provisions that describe the terms and conditions of the insurance arrangement and the rights and obligations of the parties under the policy, including:

- requirements that a group member or individual must meet to become insured;
- types and levels of medical benefits available under the policy;
- provisions relating to claim, administrative, and legal aspects;
- circumstances under which insurance may terminate; and
- benefits available to insureds after insurance has terminated.

Some provisions are general to health insurance contracts. Others apply specifically to either the policyholder, the group members insured under a group insurance policy, or both the policyholder and the insureds or, in the case of an individual policy, the individuals covered under the policy. Other contract provisions grant specific rights to the insured, the policyholder, or the insurer. This chapter discusses group and individual medical expense insurance contract provisions and explains why these provisions are important to the parties involved.

MEDICAL EXPENSE INSURANCE

■ Group Medical Expense Contract Provisions Relating to Policyholders

The group medical expense policy is issued either as a separate policy or combined into one group policy that includes all of the coverages of the plan (e.g., comprehensive major medical benefits, dental, vision, life, accidental death and dismemberment, and short-term and long-term disability). Combining all the coverages into one group policy avoids duplication of policy provisions that are common to all coverages and reduces administrative costs. Most group insurance policies use the combined approach.

Cover Page

The policy cover page identifies and sets forth the following administrative information:

- name, address, and corporate logo of the insurer;
- policyholder's name;
- policy number;
- effective date of the policy and the anniversary date;
- issue date of the policy; and
- state of issue or situs of the policy used to determine the state laws governing the policy.

The cover page also may include the following at-a-glance information: the type of policy (group insurance), the type of coverage (life and accident and health), and an indication of whether the policy is noncontributory or contributory and participating (eligible for dividends) or nonparticipating (not eligible for dividends)

Employees to be Insured

Eligible Employees

The provision establishing the definition of eligible employees may include the following:

- a description of the relationship between the eligible employees and the employer or other entity providing the group medical benefits under the policy, including the name of the policyholder;
- a list of the eligible classes of employees (e.g., salaried and hourly employees, or employees working at a certain employer location);

MEDICAL EXPENSE CONTRACT PROVISIONS

- specific eligibility requirements, such as a probationary period, a minimum number of hours worked on a weekly basis, or membership in a union;
- a list of specific classes of employees to be excluded from coverage under the policy;
- a requirement that employees must enroll for insurance, complete an enrollment request form, and authorize payroll deductions for any contributory insurance;
- a statement about past employment with the employer being credited to a rehired employee's new period of employment, to satisfy the probationary period;
- a clear description of when an employee becomes eligible; and
- a clear description of when an employee's insurance coverage begins.

Name vs. no-name certificates. Depending on the type of certificate of insurance (name or no-name) issued by the insurer, the insurer may choose either to use the employees-to-be-insured provisions in the certificate as incorporated into the policy or to include a specific eligibility provision. Insurers using a named certificate rely on a certification label to identify the name of the insured and the actual effective date of his or her insurance as well as to indicate whether dependent coverage is provided. A no-name certificate is issued without reference to any specific insured individual.

Eligibility mandates. The Health Insurance Portability and Accountability Act of 1996 does not permit employers or insurers to establish eligibility rules for group medical expense insurance based on health status–related factors. The act also requires that:

- insurers serving the small group market (those with 2 to 50 employees) accept every small employer that applies for coverage and every eligible employee (and dependents) who applies when he or she first becomes eligible; and
- insurers give credit for prior coverage under a qualified plan to reduce preexisting condition exclusion periods, if any, as long as there was not a significant break in coverage

Eligibility Date

Usually an employee is eligible for insurance on the plan effective date if he or she is in an eligible class on that date. An employee entering service after the plan effective date is eligible the day after the date the employee completes the probationary period, if he or she is in an eligible class.

MEDICAL EXPENSE INSURANCE

Effective Date

The effective date of insurance for an employee enrolling for noncontributory insurance is the day the employee becomes eligible for insurance. For contributory insurance the effective date is:

- the day the employee becomes eligible, if the employer receives the request for insurance on or before the day the employee becomes eligible; or
- the day the employee enrolls, if the employer receives such request within the employer-specified initial enrollment period (frequently 31 days).

Exceptions

Exceptions are specific circumstances that delay the effective date of coverage, restrict coverage, or waive certain requirements. As an example of an exception, an employee not actively at work on the day coverage would otherwise begin is insured on the day he or she meets this requirement as defined by the policy. Pre-existing condition exclusions are another example of a delayed effective date for benefits under the policy associated with a pre-existing medical condition.

Special Enrollment Opportunities

Some employees decline enrollment in their employer's group health plan when they are first eligible to enroll. The Health Insurance Portability and Accountability Act of 1996 requires employers to allow employees and dependents to enroll at a later date without penalty, if they enroll within 31 days following certain specified events. Examples include when an employee loses eligibility for other group coverage, or when a child is born or adopted. A group policy may define additional special situations when employees and/or their dependents are eligible to become insured without a late enrollment penalty.

Late Enrollment

The HIPAA of 1996 does not require employers to allow employees to enroll at times other than their first enrollment opportunity or a defined special enrollment period. If an employer allows late enrollment, the group health plan must accept all late enrollees wishing to enroll. (As for other eligible employees, proof of insurability may not be required for late entrants.) In addition, HIPAA does not require insurers to accept late enrollees, as long as the insurer applies the rule uniformly and rejects all late enrollees. An insurer declining to issue coverage to late enrollees would be limiting its market, however, to employer groups that do not allow late enrollees.

MEDICAL EXPENSE CONTRACT PROVISIONS

Coverage Terminations

As part of the overall eligibility provision applicable to employees, some insurers may elect to include a list of circumstances under which coverage ends, such as for nonpayment of premium or relocation outside a network plan's service area. The placement of language and circumstances dealing with coverage termination in an eligibility provision is meant to give a complete picture of eligibility, including the loss of that eligibility.

Dependents to be Insured

Eligible Dependents

The provision pertaining to eligible dependents defines dependent(s) and children. The definition of dependent(s) usually includes a spouse, unmarried children under age 19, and full-time college students under age 23 or 25 who are primarily dependent on the employee for support.

The definition of children includes children primarily dependent upon the employee for support such as stepchildren, adopted children, children placed with the employee for adoption, foster children, and children primarily dependent upon the employee because of mental retardation or physical handicap. Children in the later category may be continued as dependents beyond the contract's limiting age.

Eligibility Date and Effective Date

The policy provides specific details about when dependents become eligible for insurance and when the insurance becomes effective.

Exceptions

The policy indicates specific circumstances that delay the effective date of coverage, restrict coverage, or waive certain requirements. Some examples are as follows:

- Dependents may not become insured before the date the employee becomes insured.
- Special rules apply for dependent child coverage pursuant to a qualified medical child support order (a court order for requiring health coverage as a part of child support).

83

Coverage Termination

The policy includes language describing the circumstances under which loss of eligibility for dependent coverage occurs.

HMO-Related Provisions in Indemnity Contracts

Employers may provide a health maintenance organization (HMO) option for employees and their dependents under the company's medical plan. Group medical expense indemnity policies written for employers recognize this option with provisions during the current plan year that:

- exclude from eligibility employees and their dependents who have elected coverage under an HMO; and
- exclude from payment of benefits any charges incurred due to services or supplies furnished under the HMO coverage.

There also are specific provisions concerning transferring from an HMO to a medical expense policy.

Transferring from HMO Coverage

The policy describes the circumstances under which an employee may transfer from HMO coverage to insurance. For example, the employee may:

- enroll for a transfer during an open enrollment period; or
- elect to transfer when he or she moves outside of the HMO service area or if the HMO ceases operations.

When Coverage Begins

This provision describes exactly when coverage begins for individuals transferring from HMO coverage to coverage under the group medical policy.

Schedule of Insurance

The schedule of insurance provision, which includes summaries of plan features, is one of the most versatile provisions in the medical policy. The following are examples of information included in this provision.

Summary of Benefit Payments under the Plan

The dollar limits and other details of payment often are outlined in the schedule of insurance. This summary includes:

- the dollar amount limits required or available under the plan, such as the deductible amount per calendar year for an individual and a family, and a list of covered expenses to which the deductible does not apply;
- a list of covered expenses and the benefit percentage at which they are paid (e.g., 100 percent, 80 percent, or 50 percent);
- an out-of-pocket maximum dollar limit after which benefits are paid at 100 percent;
- an overall dollar maximum benefit (e.g., unlimited or $1 million during an insured's lifetime); and
- any internal maximums such as calendar year or lifetime maximums.

Referencing the Schedule of Insurance

Generally, reference is made to the schedule of insurance contained in the certificate booklet issued to insureds. This process allows the certificate of insurance and the group medical policy to have one and the same schedule of insurance.

Classification of Insureds and Benefits under the Plan

A listing is included of the classification of insureds and the benefits provided to insureds by contract class. The following may appear on the list:

- class of insured employees;
- coverages included for each eligible class of insured employees and whether the coverage is provided for dependents;
- plan effective date for each class; and
- certificate booklet applicable to each class of insured employees.

Termination and Continuance of Insurance

The termination and continuance of insurance provisions describe when insurance ends and the circumstances, rights, and privileges available under the group medical expense policy to continue and extend coverage.

Termination of Insurance (When Insurance Ends)

The group medical policy provides that medical insurance terminates on the earliest of the following events:

With respect to employees, when:

Table 5.1

Table of Continuance

Reasons for cessation of active work	Maximum period of continuance
Absence due to injury or sickness that prevents the employee from performing regular work	The end of the one-year period after employment ends
Lay-off,* leave of absence, military service, or temporary transfer to part-time work	The end of the third policy month following the month full-time employment ended
	Under COBRA–18 months from date of termination*
Employer-approved leave in accordance with the Federal Family and Medical Leave Act	The end of the approved leave
Retirement	The end of the period in which the employee is no longer classified as a retired employee

*Termination of employment except for cause

- the employee leaves employment or ceases to be in an eligible class;
- the employee ceases payment required for his or her coverage;
- the employee transfers to a separate alternative employer sponsored program (e.g., an HMO plan) or
- the group medical policy or plan ends.

With respect to dependents, when:

- the employee's coverage ends;
- a dependent ceases to be an eligible dependent;
- the payment required for dependent coverage ceases;
- a dependent transfers to HMO coverage offered through the employee's employer; or
- the group medical policy or plan ends.

Continuance of Coverage

This provision allows the policyholder to deem an employee as still working for the employer for the purposes of continuing the employee's insurance and that of the employee's dependents if an employee ceases active work under certain circumstances.

Table 5.1 illustrates examples of reasons for cessation of active work and possible maximum periods of continuance allowed under a group medical policy. A dependent's insurance may continue while the employee's work status is deemed to continue after active work has ceased for a reason listed in the table of continuance.

State and Federal Continuance

State and federal continuance requirements mandate that the policy allow an employee or dependent to continue health coverage under the terms of state or federal laws. An employee or dependent may choose to continue health insurance under either the state continuance (if the state of the situs of the group policy mandates it) or the federal continuance as mandated under the Consolidated Omnibus Budget Reconciliation Act (COBRA) (if the employee's employer is subject to the federal law).

Veteran's Continuance

A continuance provision mandated by the Uniformed Services Employment and Reemployment Rights Act of 1993 requires coverage under the policy if insurance ends because the employee is recalled to active military duty.

Premium Provisions

Premium provisions give important policyholder information regarding rates and premiums, such as the premium due date and the right of the insurer to change premium rates.

An insurer may reserve the right to change premiums on any premium due date after the policy has been in effect for at least one year, subject to advance notice to the policyholder of at least 31 days. Premium rates may be changed earlier if there is:

- a change in the policy;
- an established percent increase or decrease (e.g., 10 percent) from the number of persons insured under the policy on its effective date or any subsequent policy anniversary; or
- a change in the insurer's liability by reason of state or federal requirements.

Termination of Policy and Coverages

The group medical expense policy provides the policyholder the right to terminate the policy or any medical coverage included under the policy by written notice to the insurer. Insurers are permitted to terminate the policy only in limited situations.

Termination by the Policyholder

The policyholder may terminate the group medical expense policy, or, with the insurer's consent, any medical coverage included under the policy, on any premium due date by submitting advance written notice to the insurer. If any premium is not paid before the grace period expires, the policy automatically terminates when the period ends.

Termination by the Insurer

The Health Insurance Portability and Accountability Act of 1996 limits the right to terminate group medical expense policies. An insurer can terminate only due to the policyholder's nonpayment of premium, commission of fraud, or failure to meet minimum contribution or participation levels, or the insurer's exit from the market.

General Provisions

The group medical expense policy contains a number of general provisions of an administrative nature. Some of the most commonly incorporated general provisions are described below.

- The contract provision defines the contract and how it may be changed.
- A provision on employee certificates states the insurer's obligation to prepare certificates for insured employees and deliver the certificates to the policyholder for distribution to the insured employees.
- A provision on misstatements or clerical errors indicates that adjustments will be made either in the amount of benefits payable or premiums payable due to a misstatement of the age of an insured person. A clerical error does not end insurance otherwise in force or continue it after it would otherwise have ended.
- A provision defines the grace period as a 31-day period during which insurance remains in force after the policy is in default for nonpayment of premium when the premium is due. The policy terminates at the end of the grace period, and the policyholder is obligated to pay all unpaid premiums, including the premium for the grace period.
- The retroactive rate-reduction-dividend provision outlines any right to a reduction of premium rates for a prior year based on a stock insurer's experience rating formula or the return of dividend based on a mutual insurer's dividend formula.

- The facility of payment provision describes the insurer's right to discharge its obligation of claim payment when an insured employee is deceased or legally incapable of giving valid receipt of claim.

Policy Application

A policy application is prepared by the insurer in duplicate for signature by an authorized representative of the policyholder. The application states that the policyholder applies for the insurance set forth in the policy. By signing the policy application, the policyholder's representative signifies that the policy has been approved by and accepted by the policyholder. The application is attached to and made part of the policy. The policyholder and the insurer each retain a copy of the policy and a signed copy of the policy application.

The policy application contains the following information:

- name and address of the insurer;
- name and address of the policyholder;
- policy number;
- location, city and state, where the application is signed;
- date the policy is signed; and
- signature of the person signing the application and his or her title.

Policy Riders

General Riders

A group medical expense policy may be changed by an amendment to the policy. A policy rider is used to convey the terms of the amendment, and the amendment thereby becomes a part of the policy. Policy riders are dated and numbered sequentially so that the insurer and the policyholder can easily determine the current policy provisions and level of benefits.

Examples of the types of changes that are made to a group medical expense policy by a rider are:

- change in the name of the policyholder;
- addition to or deletion of the eligible classes of employees;
- change in level of benefits (e.g., an increase in a deductible amount or the maximum lifetime major medical maximum); and
- addition of a managed care arrangement such as an HMO or PPO.

Financial Riders

Financial riders are amendments to the group medical expense policy that change the financial arrangement of the policy or method of funding for the insurance provided under the policy. The financial arrangements between the policyholder and the insurer generally do not affect the benefits available to the individual insureds under the policy. Four common financial riders are reviewed.

Combination rider. A combination rider groups the administrative costs and gains and losses under the group medical policy with the administrative costs and gains and losses under other group policies—such as group life, short-term disability, and dental policies—written to the same policyholder. The combining of experience results under all of a policyholder's policies during the year-end settlement of gains and losses under each policy provides additional financial protection and premium stability for the policyholder. The protection relies on the probability that any loss under one policy would be offset by gains under the other policies, thereby stabilizing rates under all of the policyholder's policies.

Retrospective premium rider. Under a retrospective premium rider, the insurer agrees to reduce the billed premium. This reduction is subject to the insurer's right to collect this premium at the end of the policy year should the ratio of claims to premium exceed a certain level. This financial arrangement does not change the extent of the total liability that the policyholder has with respect to premium payment. The retrospective premium arrangement is used primarily with the larger sized groups where there has been an unusual increase in recent claims that cannot be justified as a permanent shift.

Minimum premium rider. A minimum premium rider allows the policyholder to partially self-fund for a substantial portion (approximately 90 percent) of the expected medical claims. The key policyholder features of the minimum premium arrangement are:

- any cash flow savings derived from the payment of claims as they emerge as compared to premium payment;
- the avoidance of premium tax on claims paid on a self-funded basis; and
- the transfer of medical claim reserves from the insurer to the policyholder.

The minimum premium arrangement is used primarily with the larger sized groups.

Claims stabilization reserve rider. A claims stabilization or premium stabilization reserve rider permits the insurer to accumulate a portion of any dividends or retrospective premium payments into a fund that is used to offset any future premium increases.

■ Group Medical Expense Contract Provisions Relating to Insureds

Certificate of Insurance

All provisions applicable to insureds are contained in the certificate of insurance, which is issued to the individuals insured under a group medical expense policy. A certificate of insurance, which often is produced in a certificate booklet, is incorporated into and made part of the group medical expense policy.

The certificate of insurance identifies the insurer, the policyholder, the policy number, and the plan effective date. The certificate states that insurance is subject to the terms of the group medical expense policy. The certificate may broadly reference eligibility and effective dates as well as the major categories of coverage provided under the policy. It generally includes a table of contents, which makes it easier for insureds to look up key provisions applicable to the medical plan.

The insurance certification page may also state that:

- The certificate takes the place of any prior one issued to an insured covering this insurance.
- The certificate is not the insurance contract; the group medical expense policy and the policyholder's application for it are the contract.
- The certificate is evidence of insurance under the group medical expense policy.
- The insurance takes effect only for persons who become insured and stay insured according to the terms of the group medical expense policy.

Schedule of Insurance

The schedule of insurance is a part of the certificate of insurance and is filed on a separate page or form. It is a summary of key plan features and dollar limits

MEDICAL EXPENSE INSURANCE

Table 5.2

Examples of a Basic Hospital-Surgical Plan and Supplemental Major Medical Expense Plan Features and Dollar Limits

Basic medical expense insurance

Hospital services—Inpatient treatment	
Deductible amount	$250 for each confinement
Daily room and board maximum	Regular daily rate for semiprivate room
Other charges maximum	$2,000 for each confinement
Maximum number of days in hospital	31 days for each confinement
Surgical services	
Surgical benefit maximum	100% up to $1,000
Assistant surgeon benefit maximum	100% up to $750
Anesthesia benefit maximum	100% up to $750
Inhospital doctors visits	
Daily visit maximum	100% up to $50
Maximum number of days	31 days for each confinement
Supplemental accident benefits	$300

Major medical insurance

Deductible per calendar year	
Per person	$100 plus base plan benefits
Per family	$300 plus base plan benefits
Second surgical opinion	100%
Hospital preadmission testing	100%
All other covered expenses	80%
Maximum benefit	
All covered expenses except as shown below	$1 million per insured individual
Chemical dependency	$30,000 per lifetime

(see Table 5.2). The schedule of insurance may include some eligibility features such as:

- plan effective date;
- definition of eligible classes; and
- probationary period.

Eligibility and When Insurance Begins

The certificate of insurance provides specific details for prospective insured employees and dependents to determine if they are eligible for insurance, when they are eligible for it, and when it becomes effective.

Benefits Provisions

The benefits section of a certificate of insurance or group medical expense policy is the heart of any medical benefit plan. This section establishes what plan benefits an insured person is eligible to receive and what benefits the plan will not provide. It defines the benefit liability that the policyholder has agreed to provide to insured individuals and the financial risk that the insurer has agreed to accept under the group policy.

Insuring Clause

==The insuring clause is a stipulation in an insurance policy that states the type of loss the policy covers and the parties to the insurance contract==. It also defines the circumstances under which a medical charge will be considered for payment under a group medical expense policy. All claims for benefit payments presented by an insured person must meet these criteria.

The following are the key components of an insuring clause:

- type of benefits that are payable (e.g., basic hospital-surgical benefits or major medical benefits);
- type of charges for which benefits are payable (e.g., charges made by a hospital or treatment facility for hospital services; doctor charges in connection with a surgical operation for surgical services; or covered charges or covered expenses for major medical benefits);
- statement that charges must be incurred by the employee or the employee's dependent while insured under the group medical expense policy;
- statement that charges must be for services or supplies furnished or ordered by a doctor and are medically necessary for the diagnosis and treatment of an injury, sickness, or pregnancy covered by the policy.

Benefits Payable

The certificate of insurance describes the types of benefits provided under a group medical expense policy as well as the types of benefits that are limited and/or excluded. (For a review of benefits usually covered in a group plan, see Chapter 1: Group Major Medical Expense Insurance.)

The major medical maximum benefit payable in an insured person's lifetime is stated in the certificate of insurance. This maximum applies to all benefits payable while the person is insured under the major medical plan, whether such

Medical Expense Insurance

person's coverage has been continuous or interrupted, or whether the policy has been reissued.

Covered Expenses

The medical expense certificate usually states that benefits are payable for covered expenses or charges that are the reasonable and customary charges for services and supplies furnished or ordered by a doctor and are medically necessary.

Covered Expense Limits

Some covered expenses have internal limits; these limits are stated clearly in the certificate of insurance. An example of a covered expense limit would be one on expenses or charges incurred for the treatment of chemical dependency.

Expenses Not Covered

The certificate of insurance states what expenses or charges are not covered. Examples of expenses or charges for services or treatment not covered under a major medical benefits contract are found in Chapter 1.

General Limitations

This provision lists the limitations applicable to all of the separate coverages in one place within the policy or certificate of insurance. Benefits not paid for under a general limitations provision include charges for services and supplies:

- due to an occupational injury or sickness;
- for custodial care;
- furnished or paid for by any government or government agency except where otherwise prohibited by law; and
- for an injury or sickness arising out of war or an act of war.

Managed Indemnity Programs

Most group medical plans written today contain managed care provisions. The most commonly used managed care features are utilization review, preferred provider plans, and exclusive provider plans.

Utilization review. When utilization review is part of the medical expense policy, the certificate of insurance must clearly tell the insureds which medical services require utilization review, how to initiate utilization review, when to call for it, the penalties for nonnotification, and how to appeal a utilization review determination.

The utilization review process includes:

- precertification of inhospital stays and outpatient medical services;
- emergency care review;
- appeals and grievances processes; and
- a penalty if an insured person fails to initiate utilization review by calling the utilization review agency.

Preferred provider plans. When a preferred provider benefit is part of the medical expense policy, the certificate of insurance must provide an explanation of what the preferred provider benefit plan is, how the insured may access it, the benefits provided under it, the benefits available if the insured does not use the preferred provider network, and the grievance procedures available for any problems encountered using the network.

Preferred provider plans provide higher levels of benefits when the insured elects to use the services of a preferred provider and a reduced level of benefits for the services of a nonpreferred provider. As an example, the preferred provider benefits level may be at 90 percent while the nonpreferred provider benefits level may be at 70 percent. In addition, to encourage use of network doctors, all office visits may require only the payment of a nominal dollar copayment to the preferred provider.

Some preferred provider plans require that all treatment be directed and approved by a primary care physician chosen by the insured from a list of preferred provider primary care physicians.

Exclusive provider plans. When an exclusive provider benefit is part of the medical expense policy, the certificate of insurance must provide an explanation of what the exclusive provider benefit plan is, how the insured may access it, penalties applied for not using an exclusive provider, and grievance procedures available for problems encountered using the network.

Exclusive provider plans provide a high level of benefits and often are designed to be comparable to an HMO plan of benefits. Other than services for emergency care, an exclusive provider plan generally only provides plan benefits when an insured individual elects to use the services of an exclusive provider. Most exclusive provider plans require that all treatment be directed and approved by a primary physician. Some exclusive provider plans provide a limited out-of-network benefit, with the insured usually paying more in coinsurance amounts.

Coordination of Benefits

The coordination of benefits provision addresses the situation where an insured is covered for similar benefits under two or more group plans. Under this provision the benefits received by the insured do not exceed 100 percent of the allowable expenses incurred by that individual. The coordination of benefits provision is included in the certificate of insurance and generally is incorporated into and made part of the policy.

The provision includes the order of benefits determination rules, which determine which insurance plan is the primary plan—that is, the plan that pays benefits first as if there were no other coverage—and which insurance plan is the secondary plan. The benefits payable amount under the secondary plan is reduced so that the sum of the plans does not exceed 100 percent of covered charges. (For more information on coordination of benefits, including the order of benefits determination rules, see Chapter 8: Medical Expense Claim Administration.)

When Insurance Ends

The certificate of insurance provides specific details permitting an insured employee and dependent to determine when an employee's insurance ends, when a dependent's insurance ends, when insurance may be continued through a state or federal continuance mandate, when an insured is eligible for extended benefits, and when an insured is eligible for a conversion privilege.

Extended benefits are available if an insured is totally disabled on the date insurance ends. Benefits due to the condition causing the disability generally are payable until the earliest of the following times:

- the day the individual becomes eligible for benefits for that condition under another group-type plan;
- the day the disability ends; or
- three months after the individual's insurance ends.

Individual Medical Expense Contract Provisions

Individual medical expense policies are similar in many respects to group medical expense policies in the nature of the language used and the actual medical benefits provided under the terms of the policies. One important difference is that for individual insurance the individual medical expenses policyholder and the insured usually are one and the same.

MEDICAL EXPENSE CONTRACT PROVISIONS

The following are key provisions found in an individual medical expense policy, with a primary focus on major medical expense benefits.

Basic Provisions

Insuring Clause

A major medical expense insuring clause states that the insurer will pay the insured benefits for a covered loss due to the sickness and injury as described in the policy and that the benefit payment is governed by the terms of the policy.

Consideration

A consideration clause describes the relationship between the premium paid and the application completed by the applicant and the insurer's reliance on the answers to the application questions and subsequent placement of the policy in force as of the effective date. A copy of the application is attached to the policy.

Right to Examine Policy

Individual medical expense policies contain a 10-day right to examine the policy. The insurer is required to refund any premiums paid in connection with the policy if the insured is not satisfied for any reason and returns the policy to the insurer within 10 days of its receipt.

Renewal Provision

As required under the Health Insurance Portability and Accountability Act of 1996, an individual policy is guaranteed renewable at the option of the policyholder, with a few specified exceptions. (See Termination of Coverage, below.)

Table of Contents

The table of contents section lists all major policy provisions in alphabetical order and where they may be found in the policy. It provides the insured with an easy reference section to help locate the placement of key provisions within the policy.

Policy Schedule

The policy schedule is tailored to the individual policyholder. It contains an outline of important policy and benefit information, such as the following:

MEDICAL EXPENSE INSURANCE

- *Policy Data*
  Policy number
  Name of insurer
  Policy effective date
  Covered members under the contract (insured, spouse, children)
  Initial premium
  Premium payable (monthly, quarterly, semiannually, annually)
  Initial rate guarantee (12 months)
  First renewal date
  Renewal premium
- *Benefits*
  Deductible
  Insured percent
  Lifetime maximum amount
  Out-of-pocket limits for individual and family
  Cost containment provisions
  Mental illness lifetime maximum
  Routine physical examination benefit rider (per examination benefit)
  Participating provider benefit rider (PPO and non-PPO benefit levels)

Definitions

To help an insured gain a better understanding of the terms of the individual medical expense policy, the policy contains a lengthy list of definitions of key terms used in the policy.

Eligibility for Coverage

An individual medical expense policy defines eligible persons as those who meet the insurer's underwriting standards and generally include:

- the insured;
- the insured's spouse; and
- the insured's or spouse's child over 14 days and less than 19 years old, or 19 or older and under age 25 if a full-time student at an accredited educational institution or residing with the insured.

Termination of Coverage

Under an individual medical expense policy, a covered individual's coverage ends on the earliest of the following events:

- end of the grace period for an unpaid premium;
- for a spouse, the next premium due date following the date of divorce or annulment;
- for a child, the next premium due date following whichever comes first: his or her 25th birthday, his or her marriage, or the date he or she is no longer a dependent as defined in the policy;
- the insured(s) moves outside a network plan's service area; or
- when the insurer discontinues offering all coverage of this type in a state, as allowed under the Health Insurance Portability and Accountability Act of 1996.

A child with a handicapping condition that occurred before he or she reached the limiting age may have coverage continued beyond that age.

If the insured dies while the policy is in force, coverage may be continued for any surviving covered members until the last member's insurance terminates in accordance with the termination provision.

Benefits Provisions

As with the group medical expense policy, the benefits provisions in the individual medical expense policy establish what plan benefits an insured member is eligible to receive and what benefits the policy will not provide. This section defines the benefits that an insured has purchased and the financial risk that the insurer has agreed to accept under the individual policy.

In general, the benefits provided under the individual medical expense policy are similar to the benefits provided under a group medical expense policy. Many individual policies share the same structure as group policies and contain similar provisions to describe benefits payable.

Managed Indemnity Programs

Most individual medical expense policies have an element of managed care. Managed care programs such as utilization review and preferred provider plans are incorporated into the individual medical expense policy.

Extension of Benefits

Individual medical expense policies provide various levels of extended benefits. The following are reasons for extended benefits.

- The insured must be disabled or confined to a hospital or skilled nursing facility when insurance is terminated by the insurer.

MEDICAL EXPENSE INSURANCE

- Benefits are continued only for the condition causing the insured to be disabled or confined.
- Benefits are extended to the earliest of the following times: the date the individual is no longer disabled; the date the individual's maximum is paid; or the end of a specific period following the date that the insurance terminates (for example, three months).

Conversion

Conversion to an individual medical policy is available if a spouse's insurance ends due to a divorce or if a child's coverage ends due to age.

Some insurers offer conversion to a Medicare supplement policy.

Other Provisions

Individual medical expense policies contain a number of other provisions, often of an administrative nature and of critical importance to the insured and the insurer. They include premium and claim payment provisions.

Premium provisions. Premium provisions cover when premiums are due, an explanation of renewal premiums, procedures for changing the premium because of a change in residence or a change in age, the grace period provision, and a reinstatement provision that allows the insurer to accept a late premium under a grace period provision without requiring a reinstatement application. The reinstated policy may only cover a loss resulting from an injury sustained after the date of reinstatement and sickness starting more than 10 days after the reinstatement date.

Claim payment provisions. Claim payment provisions include the notice of claim and proof of claim provisions and a provision allowing the insurer to fulfill its obligation to pay a claim, in the event of the insured's death, to the estate or for benefit amounts up to a specified limit to someone related to the insured whom the insurer considers entitled to the benefits.

■ Group and Individual Expense Contract Development

Group and individual medical expense policies must stay current with changes in the marketplace and state and federal regulations. To remain current, the insurers' contract staff works closely with the legal, marketing, underwriting, medical, actuarial, and claims departments to develop new products that enhance the current offering of medical benefits. The contract development process requires that the policy forms be drafted, reviewed by all interested home office operations, and filed with and approved by the appropriate governmental jurisdictions. Insurers need to make sure that the policies and certificates of insurance issued accurately reflect the products sold.

▪ Summary

The medical expense insurance contract contains the terms and conditions of the policy. It provides the specific details concerning coverage and the rights and responsibilities of parties to the contract. The group contract is between the insurer and the group policyholder, which usually is an employer. The policyholder in an individual contract usually is the insured person.

▪ Key Terms

Benefits payable
Certificate of insurance
COBRA (Consolidated Omnibus Budget Reconciliation Act) continuance
Consideration
Continuance of coverage
Continuance of insurance
Contract
Conversion
Coordination of benefits
Cover page

Covered expenses
Effective date
Eligible dependent
Eligible employee
Eligibility date
Expenses not covered
Extension of benefits
Facility of payment
Financial rider
General rider
Grace period
HMO transfer
Insuring clause
Limitations

Managed indemnity programs
Misstatement
Policyholder
Precertification review
Premium provision
Renewal provision
Retroactive rate reduction
Right to examine
Schedule of insurance
Termination of coverage
Utilization review

Chapter 6

UNDERWRITING MEDICAL EXPENSE INSURANCE

103 *Introduction*
104 *The Underwriting Department*
106 *Risk Selection Factors*
121 *Underwriting Other Groups*
124 *Underwriting Issues for Medical Expense Insurance*
129 *Underwriting Management*
130 *Reinsurance*
131 *Summary*
131 *Key Terms*

■ Introduction

Underwriting is the process by which an insurer determines if it will accept an application for insurance and under what conditions. It involves developing risk selection practices that are designed to protect the insurer's block of business. Adverse selection is the single greatest threat to the underwriting process. Adverse selection is the actions of individuals, acting for themselves or for others, who are motivated directly or indirectly to take financial advantage of the risk classification system.

Life insurance underwriting is concerned primarily about *mortality*—the incidence of death within a given population. Health insurance underwriting is concerned primarily about *morbidity*—the incidence of accidents and sicknesses within a given population times the average cost per incident. While medical advances may reduce mortality, they often contribute to increased morbidity. For example, not many years ago twins born several months premature and weighing barely one pound had almost no chance for survival. Today, medical science can offer such premature infants a better than even chance of survival. These advances in medicine are applauded by all including the insurance industry, but they come at a tremendous cost, often running into the hundreds of thousands of dollars. Insurers can only cover these costs by increasing rates.

Underwriters use various tools and sources of information to help qualify the risk of new applications and determine under what conditions that risk will be assumed. This chapter discusses the principles involved in underwriting medical expense insurance, how those principles apply to individual situations, and the process of managing all cases collectively.

■ The Underwriting Department

The underwriting department routinely works with nearly all of an insurance company's operations, both internally and externally. The department collaborates with the claims operation and is kept up to date on any ongoing claims situations and administrative problems with the benefit design. It also works closely with the company's field sales operation and the premium/billing department and is the final authority on issues of eligibility, premium delinquency, and requests for reinstatement. The underwriting department also interacts with the company's legal department on special policyholder agreements, policyholder and insurance department complaints, and various regulatory issues.

In addition the underwriting department works with corporate compliance personnel on contract and proposal development, marketing staff on product development, actuaries on pricing, the business office on reporting, policy issuance personnel once an application is accepted, and brokers, agents, and policyholders during the proposal and renewal process. Insurance companies typically use one of two basic organizational structures in setting up an underwriting department—the functional structure or the product-line structure.

Functional Organization

The functional organizational structure is one in which the insurer establishes an individual underwriting unit assigned to individual health and life applications, with a separate group underwriting unit to handle group health and life applications. Some companies split their group underwriting department into two separate units—one to handle small groups only (e.g., 25 employees or less) and the other to handle large groups only (e.g., more than 25 employees). This structure allows underwriters to develop a high degree of expertise in the risk selection philosophy of specific market segments (individuals, small groups, and large groups).

Some companies establish separate units for Taft-Hartley type business, government business, multiple employer trusts, and other sources of business. Only the largest companies can afford to establish so many separate underwriting units. A drawback to having too many separate functional units is the possibility of separate underwriting philosophies evolving within the company and the creation of multiple identities within the same market.

Product-Line Organization

The product-line organizational structure is one in which the insurer organizes its underwriting department by product specialties. In such an organization, one underwriting unit may handle all individual health applications, while another handles all individual life applications. A separate unit may handle all group health applications, while another unit handles all group life applications or group dental and so on. Many insurers consider a product-line structure advantageous because of the highly competitive nature of the insurance industry and the need for a high level of product expertise. The insurance company may encourage separate underwriting philosophies to evolve within each product line as the level of product expertise increases.

A drawback to this organizational structure is the need to coordinate a review of multiproduct applications in order to achieve a common set of qualifications within the proposals. Without such a review, an employer applying for medical, life, dental, and long-term disability, for example, may be asked the same questions from a number of different underwriters within the same company and receive offers with differing conditions of acceptance.

Regional Organization

In addition to organizing functionally or along product line, some insurers establish regional underwriting teams that focus on specific markets (e.g., southwestern states). The regionalized team concept allows underwriters to better know their field agents and the brokerage community, the economic and risk characteristics of the region, and the region's regulatory environment. Some companies have moved to a regional headquarters type of operation so that teams can work within the same time zones and bring a local presence to remote markets.

Working with the Field Agent

Because the underwriter works in a home or regional office environment and has little to no exposure to the buyer, he or she relies heavily on the field agent. Effective communication with the field agent is vital to the underwriter, as well as to the agent.

The underwriter looks to the agent to properly and promptly communicate underwriting decisions and to reveal any risk-sensitive facts known or suspected about the applicant. And the field agent looks to the underwriter for prompt advice about the status of pending applications. In the case of an adverse decision by the underwriter, the agent needs as much background information regarding that decision as can be legally divulged by the underwriter in order to communicate sensitively and effectively with the applicant.

■ Risk Selection Factors

There are many factors that can have an impact on the desirability of a particular risk. An applicant may meet every category necessary to achieve a preferred risk status only to have one issue emerge that makes it an unacceptable underwriting risk—for example, a small group with an ongoing potentially catastrophic claim, questionable financial stability, or inadequate employer contribution level.

The underwriting department establishes risk selection criteria designed to steer the sales operations toward a more desirable risk. With each application or request for proposal, the underwriter requires detailed information about the applicant and those to be covered. Medical considerations are important in underwriting medical expense coverages. Medical history and current physical conditions are basic indicators of the probability of future problems that may result in medical expenses for hospitalization and treatment. On large groups (e.g., more than 1,000 employees), the underwriter reviews the claims history for the group as a whole and accepts that information as a reliable indicator of the claim level to expect in the future. On small groups (e.g., less than 10 employees), the experience history may have little credibility and the underwriter requires statements of health on each employee and covered dependent unit. Certain applicants may be required to provide blood samples and/or undergo a physical exam. Underwriters almost always require health statements from individual applicants and from late entrants on group policies. The underwriter examines all information presented, and sometimes requests additional information or clarification of the information submitted.

Group Medical Expense Contracts

The major risk selection factors that affect group medical expense contracts are the size of the employer group, the industry or occupations involved, the composition of the group, location, plan design, employer contribution, prior claims experience, previous group insurance plan, administration requirements, broker and agent commissions, and expected persistency.

Size

The Health Insurance Portability and Accountability Act of 1996 prohibits insurers that sell in the small group (2-50 employees) market from rejecting any small group. Underwriting is still necessary, however, for establishing small group rates.

Morbidity tends to be higher on small groups than on large groups. This is because adverse selection tends to be higher on smaller groups. For example, a small employer may want to cover an employee or family member who is ill or is facing expensive medical treatments that are expected to exceed the premiums to be paid.

The size of the employer group is an important factor in calculating administrative expense loads in a group's rates. Certain expenses as a percentage of the premium are higher on smaller groups. This is because some plan expenses are fixed regardless of the group's size (e.g., master contract issuance and premium administration). Also, broker and agent commissions tend to be higher as a percentage of premium on the smaller groups. Commission on small groups often begin at 15 percent and are graded down as the premium increases; commissions on larger groups are a flat 1 percent to 2.5 percent.

Industry

Certain industries and occupations tend to have higher morbidity than others. Examples include:

- high stress occupations such as police work or firefighting;
- occupations in which access to care is readily available, as is the case for hospital employees; and
- industries in which drug and alcohol abuse is high, such as nightclubs.

Underwriters apply industry or occupational adjustments to their rates to compensate for the higher expected morbidity. In addition, certain industries may represent unacceptable risks to an underwriter, such as groups with high employee turnover or high exposure to hazardous industrial materials.

Composition

The morbidity rate is highly sensitive to the demographics within the group. Demographic factors include classes of employees covered, age and sex distribution, and earnings.

MEDICAL EXPENSE INSURANCE

Classes of employees to be covered. Generally an underwriter seeks to cover all full-time employees who are actively at work because a large spread of risk can reduce adverse selection and spread fixed expenses over a broader base. Part-time, seasonal, and temporary employees are viewed as undesirable risks because turnover tends to be high, which increases administrative expenses. Also, the reason they are not employed full time may be because they have poor health conditions. Hourly employees may be excluded from the definition of eligibility if they are covered under separate collective bargaining agreements.

Age distribution. Insurance company manual rates usually are age sensitive, with higher rates at the older ages. Older individuals have higher morbidity than their younger co-workers and the manual rates are reflective of that higher morbidity.

Underwriters also look at a company's age distribution to see if it deviates from the norm for other reasons. For example, a group with a high average age may indicate that it is not hiring new people. If so, the average age will increase and the insurer may find its initial rates inadequate. On the other hand, a very young group may indicate high turnover, which could result in higher administrative expenses for the insurer.

Sex distribution. Female morbidity is much higher than male morbidity, especially during the childbearing years but also extending well into women's forties and fifties. Medical expense insurance premium rates are significantly higher for women during those years. An employer with a large female population typically pays much more for medical insurance than an employer with an all-male population.

Earnings. Employee earnings may affect the underwriting of the risk in several ways. Individuals with higher-than-average earnings tend to use their medical plan to a greater degree than lower paid employees. Groups with lower-than-average earnings also may present risk concerns to the underwriter. Lower wage jobs often are associated with poor work conditions, workers and family members with previously unaddressed health problems, difficulties maintaining adequate participation levels, and high turnover.

Location

Morbidity is highly sensitive to the location of a group, due to variations in health care costs and utilization. On average, hospitals in the southeastern states charge less than those in the northeast, and those in the Midwest tend to charge less than those in the southeast (see Table 6.1). However, utilization levels also differ greatly by area, and higher charges in one may be balanced out

Table 6.1

Average Charges for Inpatient Services

State	Average daily charges for room and board 1994	1995	Average total charges per day 1994	1995	Average total charges per admission 1994	1995
Alabama	$367	$451	$2,034	$2,544	$10,147	$12,108
Alaska	550	724	1,540	2,026	11,410	10,481
Arizona	612	584	2,314	2,547	12,834	12,611
Arkansas	249	318	1,174	1,559	6,482	8,793
California	908	879	3,093	3,154	15,437	16,346
Colorado	529	483	1,947	1,939	11,888	9,362
Connecticut	*	*	*	*	*	*
Delaware	*	*	*	*	*	*
District of Columbia	*	*	*	*	*	*
Florida	492	507	2,108	2,344	10,977	12,015
Georgia	431	396	1,846	1,600	9,997	8,660
Hawaii	*	*	*	*	*	*
Idaho	446	446	1,642	1,859	7,487	6,051
Illinois	576	609	2,030	2,209	11,013	10,694
Indiana	459	512	1,533	1,713	8,339	6,991
Iowa	402	389	1,514	1,442	8,231	7,251
Kansas	530	475	1,454	1,797	9,242	8,017
Kentucky	543	538	1,849	1,912	10,105	9,584
Louisiana	404	413	1,870	1,795	11,003	8,402
Maine	*	*	*	*	*	*
Maryland	511	474	1,375	1,199	5,799	4,428
Massachusetts	699	570	1,732	1,523	16,241	12,977
Michigan	717	511	2,427	1,542	11,771	9,121
Minnesota	486	515	1,448	1,844	10,017	8,461
Mississippi	235	281	1,137	1,419	6,467	6,870
Missouri	474	478	2,068	1,867	11,036	9,387
Montana	416	468	1,458	1,635	8,137	8,437
Nebraska	403	398	1,693	1,790	9,529	9,721
Nevada	474	475	2,853	3,194	14,858	14,154
New Hampshire	*	*	*	*	*	*
New Jersey	837	1,000	1,550	2,018	9,608	8,390
New Mexico	469	468	1,460	1,548	8,732	8,971
New York	701	668	1,386	1,471	7,533	7,819
North Carolina	421	470	1,677	1,713	9,021	9,087
North Dakota	277	327	914	1,451	9,252	5,701
Ohio	463	495	1,587	1,772	8,769	8,323
Oklahoma	347	361	1,666	1,527	10,075	8,283
Oregon	524	474	1,716	1,733	10,071	11,135
Pennsylvania	622	947	1,919	3,091	10,402	16,935
Rhode Island	*	*	*	*	*	*
South Carolina	394	427	1,431	2,062	8,922	10,985
South Dakota	387	363	1,532	1,495	6,114	7,117
Tennessee	365	416	1,688	1,919	8,981	10,306
Texas	493	520	2,001	2,295	9,807	11,704
Utah	517	608	1,168	1,410	11,253	11,690
Vermont	*	*	*	*	*	*
Virginia	401	498	1,430	1,991	8,642	8,794
Washington	563	647	1,699	2,149	8,743	10,949
West Virginia	373	385	1,518	1,286	8,127	6,062
Wisconsin	396	351	1,406	1,854	6,590	7,409
Wyoming	421	351	1,507	1,183	7,292	7,289
National Average	**$484**	**$496**	**$1,779**	**$1,952**	**$9,923**	**$9,959**

Source: *Current Trends in Health Care Costs and Utilization,* Mutual of Omaha Companies, 1996.

*Does not meet publication standards.

MEDICAL EXPENSE INSURANCE

by lower utilization rates (see Table 6.2). For example, although California has higher hospital rates than most states, it also has a higher degree of managed care, which tends to result in lower hospital utilization rates. Manual rates usually are automatically adjusted using the group's zip code. Groups with more than one location use a weighted average adjustment.

The underwriter also considers the group's proximity to the insurer's service facility and adjusts the administrative charge accordingly. Solicitation, installation, and ongoing service are all location-related issues considered by the underwriter. For example, it costs more to enroll 100 employees in a location 500 miles from the insurer's closest regional office than it would a group located across the street. The underwriter may be reluctant to accept a small group in an area where the insurance company has no facility. Alternatively, the group may be accepted but only if the employer pays the full cost.

In addition, certain regions of the country have higher rates of unemployment or a failing industry that threatens to destabilize the entire regional business community.

Plan Design

The two most basic elements of a plan of insurance are eligibility and benefit structure. Eligibility defines who may be insured. The benefit structure determines the scope and level of coverage to be provided.

Eligibility. Eligibility conditions must be employment related. They cannot be based on race, age, or sex since these are not conditions of employment. The Health Insurance Portability and Accountability Act of 1996 prohibits insurers and employers from establishing eligibility requirements related to the health status of an employee or dependent. Eligibility is usually defined as all full-time employees working a minimum number of hours weekly (e.g., 30 hours per week). The plan also defines dependent eligibility. Dependents usually are defined as the lawfully married spouse of the employee and all dependent children under the age of 19, or up to age 25 if they are unmarried full-time students. Some insurers also continue medical coverage beyond the limiting age for handicapped children if they are incapable of self-support. (For more information on eligibility definitions, see Chapter 5: Medical Expense Contract Provisions.)

An important eligibility provision from an underwriting perspective deals with when coverages begin. Typically coverages begin the first of the month following 30 days of full-time employment, if there is a waiting or probationary period. This reduces the cost of maintaining records for short-term employees.

Table 6.2

Inpatient Utilization Statistics

State	Admissions per 1,000 people 1994	1995	Average length of stay (days) 1994	1995	Inpatient days per 1,000 people 1994	1995
Alabama	86.5	77.5	5.0	4.8	432	369
Alaska	51.7	52.6	7.4	5.2	383	272
Arizona	57.9	63.2	5.5	5.0	321	313
Arkansas	69.6	70.4	5.5	5.6	384	397
California	52.7	52.7	5.0	5.2	263	273
Colorado	52.0	52.8	6.1	4.8	317	255
Connecticut	*	*	*	*	*	*
Delaware	*	*	*	*	*	*
District of Columbia	*	*	*	*	*	*
Florida	67.5	67.4	5.2	5.1	351	346
Georgia	73.5	68.1	5.4	5.4	398	369
Hawaii	*	*	*	*	*	*
Idaho	52.0	74.8	4.6	3.3	237	244
Illinois	69.8	66.2	5.4	4.8	379	321
Indiana	69.0	66.1	5.4	4.1	375	270
Iowa	56.7	54.4	5.4	5.0	308	273
Kansas	48.4	54.5	6.4	4.5	308	243
Kentucky	68.2	59.4	5.5	5.0	373	298
Louisiana	85.1	75.7	5.9	4.7	501	354
Maine	*	*	*	*	*	*
Maryland	39.7	50.1	4.2	3.7	167	185
Massachusetts	64.3	59.4	9.4	8.5	603	506
Michigan	43.5	56.0	4.9	5.9	211	332
Minnesota	54.9	59.8	6.9	4.6	380	274
Mississippi	112.6	76.7	5.7	4.8	641	371
Missouri	65.7	59.4	5.3	5.0	351	299
Montana	65.4	72.4	5.6	5.2	365	374
Nebraska	59.3	61.8	5.6	5.4	334	336
Nevada	56.7	62.7	5.2	4.4	296	278
New Hampshire	*	*	*	*	*	*
New Jersey	41.0	42.1	6.2	4.2	254	175
New Mexico	77.7	67.0	6.0	5.8	465	388
New York	53.2	75.0	5.4	5.3	289	398
North Carolina	49.2	59.4	5.4	5.3	266	315
North Dakota	85.0	59.6	10.1	3.9	265	234
Ohio	67.6	59.3	5.5	4.7	374	279
Oklahoma	48.8	50.6	6.0	5.4	295	275
Oregon	40.2	38.7	5.0	6.4	236	248
Pennsylvania	43.0	51.3	5.4	5.5	233	281
Rhode Island	*	*	*	*	*	*
South Carolina	85.8	85.1	6.2	5.3	535	453
South Dakota	46.0	59.6	4.0	4.8	183	284
Tennessee	77.6	78.4	5.3	5.4	413	421
Texas	75.1	71.4	4.9	5.1	368	364
Utah	79.9	87.6	9.6	8.3	770	726
Vermont	*	*	*	*	*	*
Virginia	67.3	64.8	6.0	4.4	407	286
Washington	46.0	49.0	5.1	5.1	237	250
West Virginia	55.1	72.4	5.4	4.7	295	341
Wisconsin	58.1	61.7	4.7	4.0	272	247
Wyoming	43.3	54.7	4.8	6.2	210	337
National Average	**62.3**	**63.2**	**5.6**	**5.1**	**347**	**322**

Source: *Current Trends in Health Care Costs and Utilization*, Mutual of Omaha Companies, 1996.

*Does not meet publication standards.

Benefit structure. The plan design should provide a reasonable level of benefits at a reasonable price. The underwriter is wary of a request for a plan offering a minimal level of benefits because it might suggest financial problems within that business or a high turnover rate since employees prefer working for firms offering better benefits. Rich benefits also raise a red flag for the underwriter because such benefits tend to increase utilization.

A preferred plan design is one in which the insured incurs some out-of-pocket expense. Typically the underwriter requires plan deductibles and a plan that pays 80 percent of the first $5,000 or $10,000 of charges incurred by the insured. This sharing of expenses helps control utilization as employees are more reluctant to overutilize plan benefits if they know they have to pay a $200 deductible and then 20 percent of the next $5,000 in charges out-of-pocket.

Employer Contribution

A plan may be noncontributory (the employer pays 100 percent), fully contributory (employee pays 100 percent), or something in between. Where the employees are highly compensated the underwriter may allow a lower employer contribution (e.g., 50 percent of the employee rate plus 50 percent of the dependent rate).

From an underwriting perspective, noncontributory plans are preferred because they ensure full participation. On smaller groups, the underwriter may require that the case be written on a noncontributory basis to ensure full participation. This may also be required where the employer has multiple remote locations, so as to simplify administration and enrollment.

An employer that is unwilling to contribute toward the cost of the plan (i.e., a noncontributory plan) suggests a lack of interest, which may result in poor administration and lack of cooperation with the insurer. The employer's unwillingness to contribute toward the cost of the program also may be viewed as an indicator of financial difficulties and raise questions about the company's long-term stability. Also, in such a situation minimum participation is doubtful, and, even if it is achieved initially, it is likely to be difficult to maintain.

Prior Claims Experience

For group medical expense insurance, as for virtually all insurance, the underwriter is particularly interested in what has occurred in the past. The underwriter gives less credibility to prior experience on smaller cases. For example, on groups of less than 100 employees the underwriter may combine the last two years of experience to provide greater weight to the credibility of the experience. The underwriter generally tries to normalize the claims experience by removing any large claims before projecting future liability. If a small group had several large claims on individuals who are no longer covered under the plan, the experience may be greatly discounted.

However, if those who incurred large claims in the past remain within the class to be covered and such claims are likely to continue, the underwriter may not discount those claims. On groups with 1,000 or more employees, rates often are based on the most recent 12 months of experience, with some discounting of large claims.

Previous Group Insurance Plan

To make sure the underwriter is comparing apples to apples, a copy of the in-force contract or a copy of the employee booklet or certificate of insurance is reviewed. There are several reasons for this.

First, the underwriter wants to make sure the claims experience provided was generated by the plan of benefits rated by the underwriter. This is especially important on larger sized groups where more credibility is given to the experience. If those claims were generated by a lesser plan, then the rates developed will be inadequate to support the new plan. If those claims were generated by a greater plan of benefits, the rates will not be competitive.

Second, if there are any plan disparities, it is important that the buyer be informed of these prior to plan acceptance. Unless stated otherwise, the employer may assume that the underwriter matched benefit levels.

Third, the underwriter wants to examine the extended benefits provision that defines the current carrier's liability for providing medical expense insurance to insured individuals upon contract termination. Being aware of that provision is especially important in states without some form of discontinuance and replacement (D&R) regulations. The majority of states, however, have some form of D&R laws, which define the insurer's responsibilities for individuals beyond the date of contract termination. Typically the terminated insurer is limited to covering treatment of disabled individuals that is related to the disabling condition and the succeeding carrier assumes liability for any unrelated expenses incurred by the disabled employee or dependent. From a risk management perspective, D&R laws are welcomed because when the state clearly defines the discontinuance and replacement rules, the opportunities for selection against the insurer by other insurers are eliminated.

Finally, the underwriter wants to review the previous plan's definition of eligibility, waiting periods, special leave-of-absence provisions, or other self-pay provisions when employees are not covered by insurance and they personally pay their hospital bills. Each of these provisions represents the potential for significant risk. Loose plan eligibility, the absence of a waiting period, excessive leave provisions, and indefinite self-pay terms all can increase adverse selection.

Administrative Requirements

Administrative requirements can differ by insurance company and by group policyholder. For example, billing and premium administration processes can differ (e.g., single billing versus multisite billing statements) and often the level of tolerance in premium delinquency situations differs. The underwriter considers all of these issues and addresses them during the bid process to make sure the employer has a clear understanding of the product being purchased. The sales agent usually is trained to discuss the insurer's standard way of doing things and to bring requests for nonstandard procedures to the underwriter's attention.

On large groups, a request for proposal, which is submitted by the employer's representative, outlines the employer's stated administrative requirements. The underwriter performs a thorough review of this document to make sure all such requirements are complied with or addressed in writing.

Broker and Agent Commissions

Insurance companies tend to use a standard commission schedule, which typically is graded down on smaller groups. The larger the group the more likely it is that the commission requirement is defined by the broker or agent representing the employer. Underwriters prefer level commissions rather than high first-year commissions because high first-year commissions may induce brokers and agents to move the business often.

Expected Persistency

There are substantial costs, usually referred to as acquisition expenses, incurred by an insurer when acquiring a new group. These include expenses such as those related to underwriting, proposal, sale, enrollment, contract issuance, identification cards, booklets, and billing set-up.

From a new business rating perspective, it is not possible to charge 100 percent of acquisition expenses to the first-year rates. To do so would make the first-year rates noncompetitive. Therefore, the underwriter amortizes acquisition expenses over an extended period—typically three to five years. For that reason, the underwriter wants some assurance that the new business will remain on the books until these expenses are recovered. The underwriter seeks to avoid businesses that may be short-lived, such as a special project or an employer that has a history of frequently switching carriers.

Special Situations

Stop-loss application. Under an employer-sponsored self-funded health plan, the employer assumes full risk for the obligations as defined in the plan document. The employer purchases stop-loss coverage to protect the employer's company from catastrophic loss (specific stop-loss) and/or total plan costs exceeding the employer's budget (aggregate stop-loss).

Although the employer may find many advantages to self-funding, such as cash flow and no premium tax, there is risk. An employer who purchased stop-loss coverage from an insurer may find that the renewal rate is adjusted significantly due to ongoing claims situations. The employer also may find one or more potentially catastrophic claims not covered in the renewal contract. Many insurance companies offering stop-loss coverage maintain that they do this (i.e., not cover certain claims) only on new business takeover situations.

On new business takeover situations, the underwriter is careful to make sure no undue risk is passed on to the insurance company through the transition. An employer that presently has no stop-loss coverage but now requests such coverage could be attempting to dump a catastrophic claim situation onto a new insurance company. The underwriter asks the employer to identify any ongoing potentially catastrophic claims. If such situations exist, the underwriter will want complete details.

Self-funded cases requesting an insured contract. Underwriters are wary of employers asking to insure their currently self-funded plan. Usually employers begin thinking about returning to an insured arrangement after having been exposed to abnormal risks, typically a risk that is ongoing. Underwriters try to avoid such attempts to select against their company. The employer needs to provide a sound business reason for reverting back to an insured arrangement before the underwriter will make such an offer.

Individual Medical Expense Contracts

Individual and group medical expense insurance underwriters are concerned with many of the same risk factors, such as age, sex, location, and earnings. However, the focus is very different. The group underwriter is primarily concerned with the nature and composition of the group as a whole. Employer subsidies, minimum participation requirements, and late applicant rules are relied on to prevent adverse selection within the group. But with individual insurance, each applicant must be evaluated separately. Individual underwriters cannot rely on group purchasing to bring them a reasonable spread of risks because each applicant decides individually whether or not to purchase coverage.

Underwriters of individual medical expense insurance are vitally concerned about the individual health histories and current health status of each applicant. Individual underwriters may require applicants to submit to physical exams, blood tests, and urine analyses. Underwriters of group medical expense insurance require such detailed information from all potential insureds only if the group is small (e.g., less than 10 employees), thus lessening the "average" effects of group purchasing.

Because all contracts are designed to cover a single individual or a single family, the solicitation, application, underwriting review, and contract issuance processes must be streamlined to keep the expense to premium ratios to a minimum. Typically the applicant has a limited choice of plans with little or no design flexibility. Even so, with the loss of group economies of scale, administrative expenses tend to be a higher percentage of premium for individual policies than for group policies. Commission levels are fixed and nonnegotiable. Acquisition expenses as a percentage of the premium are also higher on individual plans.

The section below discusses only those risk factors that are handled differently by individual underwriters.

Medical History

Medical underwriting is perhaps the most critical aspect of evaluating an application for an individual medical expense policy. Both the medical history and the current physical condition of the applicant are considered. The underwriter looks for a number of different things, including:

- any evidence of current medical expenses;
- any current medical condition that needs, or will shortly need, treatment; and
- any physical condition, such as a high cholesterol level, that increases the likelihood of future illness.

Sometimes one condition, such as diabetes, has current and future implications for medical expenses. Insulin-dependent diabetes requires ongoing medical care and it also can lead to serious complications. It is important to distinguish between conditions that have a tendency to recur, such as peptic ulcers, and acute disorders that do not recur once properly treated, such as bone fractures or appendectomies.

Medically evaluating an applicant requires a great deal of underwriting skill and judgment. Evaluation begins with the application and agent's statement. If evidence of impaired health is seen, then further evidence is requested and examined until the underwriter has enough evidence to confidently evaluate the risk. This evidence may include an attending physician's statement, a medical or paramedical examination (if not already required), or specific tests or studies (such as urinalyses, blood studies, or electrocardiograms.) A family history of diabetes may prompt a request for urinalysis; finding sugar in the urine may in turn prompt a request for a glucose tolerance test.

For any current or prior condition, the underwriter evaluates:

- current treatment costs;
- effect on the insured's general health;
- normal progression of the condition;
- possible future complications; and
- possible interactions with future unrelated conditions.

Since medical problems tend to increase with aging, the underwriting guidelines of most individual medical expense insurers call for more frequent use of medical examinations and attending physicians' statements on older applicants.

Occupation

The individual underwriter is concerned with the applicant's specific occupation, where a group underwriter is concerned with an entire firm's industry. To understand the distinction, think about an accountant who works for a coal mine. As a group, mine workers may represent a very high cost risk. But as an individual, the accountant may be a very good risk since he or she works in an office, not a mine.

In general, occupation is a less important factor for individual medical expense coverages than it is for disability coverages. However, it still can have a significant impact on claim costs. People in some professions may be too hazardous to insure, such as professional boxers, deep sea divers, or crop dusters. Certain other occupations have higher or lower than average costs, which is reflected in the insurer's manual rates. Even though workers' compensation is available to cover work-related injuries and illnesses, occupation is important in individual underwriting because it serves as a proxy for a number of socioeconomic

117

factors, such as education, income, and lifestyle, that do affect an individual's health and medical expenses.

Avocations

Avocations present special problems for the underwriter. Because of increased affluence, more people engage in hazardous avocations. Some insurers require completion of a special questionnaire when there is evidence that an applicant engages in a specific hazardous avocation, such as scuba diving, hang gliding, mountain climbing, or motorcycle racing. From this questionnaire, an underwriter can determine whether the exposure to danger is minimal and can be safely ignored or whether the exposure is excessive.

If most of the population participated in a particularly hazardous activity, the cost of the extra hazard would be covered by the regular premium structure. However, if only a small percentage of the population actually participates, the underwriter must determine the increased exposure to danger. Where permitted by law, the underwriter has several alternatives available, such as the use of a rider excluding the particular hazard or an extra premium.

Other Insurance

Overinsurance is insurance exceeding 100 percent of actual loss, caused by duplicate coverages. The problem is not duplicate coverage as such, but rather the problems created by overinsurance when it results in insurance payments in excess of the financial losses actually incurred by an insured.

Most group medical expense insurance contracts contain a coordination of benefits (COB) provision that avoids duplication of coverage and overinsurance. However, this provision is much less common in individual contracts. Because effective policy provisions are lacking, it becomes necessary to turn to underwriting and programming methods. A comprehensive review of other sources of coverage must be completed before the decision to accept a risk is made.

Moral Hazard

Moral hazard is an important element in individual risk selection. It is one of the elements that make the evaluation of an individual applicant most difficult. Persons who present moral hazards are those who might be dishonest in their dealings with the insurer. The underwriter must approach the subject with a fairly objective and sophisticated viewpoint, considering the type of job an individual has and his or her living environment and lifestyle. Warning signs are unethical or questionable business practices, bankruptcies, criminal records, actual or attempted overinsurance, and excessive claim experience.

Substance Abuse

The excessive use of alcohol and the incidence of drug addiction are growing problems for the underwriter. Drug addition usually results in refusal to issue coverage, but there are many degrees of excessive use of alcohol. The underwriter may take action ranging from standard issue to an extra premium rating to declining coverage.

Family Members

If coverage applied for includes medical expense insurance that extends to eligible family members as well as to the applicant, the underwriter must have information on each family member. Some insurers also may require a statement that coverage has been requested for all eligible members of the family. If any eligible family member is not included, insurers may require an explanation of this omission. The omission may be accounted for by such reasons as other insurance, known uninsurability, or military service of a son or daughter. The insurer requires this information to avoid selection against it that could result from inclusion of only those family members most likely to have claims.

Information also is requested about similar forms of insurance presently in force or applied for on any family member for whom coverage has been requested. This inquiry is important in the underwriter's attempt to avoid substantial duplication of coverage that may lead to overutilization.

Issue Options

The underwriter reviews each piece of underwriting information and determines when there is enough information to make a final underwriting decision. When issuing a decision, the underwriter does so as *standard* (exactly as applied for), *declined,* or *modified.*

Standard issue. The usual underwriting decision is to approve as applied for. Most insurers will approve 70 percent to 80 percent of their applications on this basis.

Declination of issue. The most drastic underwriting action is to decline to issue any coverage. This choice is required only for serious medical reasons or because an applicant is clearly outside a particular company's parameter of acceptable risks for occupational or financial reasons. Most companies have declination rates below 10 percent.

Modified issue. Modified underwriting approval is perhaps the most difficult aspect of individual medical expense insurance underwriting. The modification may be an exclusion rider, an extra premium, a change in benefits, or some combination of these approaches.

Health insurers have long used **exclusion riders** (also called waivers) as a means of issuing coverage to persons who would otherwise have to be declined. Such riders state that the insurer will not pay for medical expenses resulting from a particular medical problem (such as a back disorder) or an unusually hazardous activity (such as automobile racing). The rider may be worded to exclude coverage for only a specific disorder such as hernia, or it may exclude an entire system or bodily area such as disease or disorder of the stomach or intestines. The actual wording is determined by the nature and severity of the applicant's medical history or impairment, as well as by the insurer's underwriting philosophy.

Although exclusion riders generally exclude all liability for the condition named in the rider, some insurers use a limited-period waiver. For example, an insurer could exclude coverage for expenses arising from the waiver condition for two years and provide full benefits thereafter. This type of limited-period waiver is used for conditions that are not likely to recur once the patient has fully recovered.

Many insurers prefer use of the **extra premium** to the exclusion rider approach for modification of coverage for some conditions that have too many complications that would be excluded, such as obesity, hypertension, or diabetes. The payment of additional premium, which allows the insured to have full coverage, usually is more acceptable to the applicant than an exclusion. The insurer places the insured in a special rating class and charges an extra premium that is expressed as a percentage of the standard premium. The additional premium usually ranges from 25 percent to 100 percent of the standard premium, although some insurers will use even higher ratings.

Another method of modification is to **change the benefits** to something other than what the applicant requested. An example of such modification is a larger deductible on a medical expense policy. These modifications often are used when finances, business situations, or borderline medical problems indicate that standard coverage is available but some question exists regarding the overall desirability of the risk.

To offer coverage to a greater number of modified risks, some insurers have developed special policies that provide **limited coverage for specified (qualified) conditions** and full coverage for all other losses. This approach can reduce an insurer's declination rate and also permit offering coverage to applicants with serious health problems. A special policy for qualified conditions uses a separate insuring clause, worded to cover pre-existing conditions indicated on the application, as well as a special rating for the qualified condition.

■ Underwriting Other Groups

Labor Unions and Taft-Hartley Health and Welfare Trust Plans

Today it is rare for an insurer to issue a contract directly to a union, since most unions have their benefits provided through collective bargaining agreements under the provisions of the Taft-Hartley Act. Under that act, a legal trust is formed by one or more unions with an equal number of representatives from labor and business acting as trustees. Benefit levels and contribution rates per hour worked are negotiated for an extended period of time (e.g., one year to three years).

Occasionally a local union seeks benefits for members directly from an insurer. Coverage is often member-pay-all, which presents all the problems inherent in any employee-pay-all plan. In addition, membership in the union is not always compulsory, which creates a situation where those who do join the union may be doing so only to obtain the benefits available. In an extreme case, the union itself may exist solely for the purpose of obtaining insurance for its members.

Taft-Hartley Plan Underwriting Issues

There are a number of factors unique to a Taft-Hartley health and welfare trust plan that the underwriter needs to consider to determine its acceptability.

- The underwriter needs to review the trust document to make sure that the group is a Taft-Hartley health and welfare trust plan and not simply a labor union, to determine how premiums are paid, and to determine eligibility.
- The underwriter needs to review the month-by-month membership count to see if there have been any radical shifts. A steady loss in membership is a sign of a trust that may be breaking up. A sudden increase in membership may signal the addition of a large union or the merger with another trust that is shopping for better rates or benefits.

Eligibility

A prime concern to the underwriter is determining who is eligible under a Tart-Hartley health and welfare plan. There are three different methods used by unions to establish eligibility.

- One is to require that the employee work a given number of days, weeks, or months with a particular employer before becoming insured. This method is appropriate where employment is fairly stable, not cyclical or seasonal, and where there is little shifting of employees among employers.

- A second is to require that the employee accumulate a certain number of credited hours of employment during a period called an accumulation period. For example, a person who has worked 300 hours in the previous calendar quarter could be eligible for benefits during the next calendar quarter. This method is particularly applicable to industries that do not have a lot of employment stability.
- The third is to require that all hours worked by an individual be credited to a member hour bank. This is called a reserve bank arrangement. An employee who accumulates a minimum number of hours becomes eligible for benefits. For each month in which the individual is provided coverage, a specific number of hours is withdrawn from the bank. When there are no longer enough hours in the bank to provide for the next month's coverage, the insurance terminates.

The second and third methods are appropriate for industries such as the building trades where employees often work for different employers on different days. Under these unstable employment circumstances, having sufficient dollar amounts in the trust fund to cover the cyclical nature of the employment is an important underwriting consideration. (For more information on reserve funds and administrative procedures relating to the eligibility records of Taft-Hartley plans and other groups, see Chapter 7: Medical Expense Policy Administration.)

Multiple Employer Groups

In an effort to obtain the purchasing power of a large group, many small employers band together under a multiple employer trust (MET). In the past, many METs spanned state borders to form large regional and even national trusts, but recent state reform laws for small groups have made it all but impossible to provide insurance to multistate METs. Some insurers have gotten out of the MET business all together; others have set up separate underwriting units to handle METs.

Small employers may choose to participate in a MET because they cannot obtain a more competitive medical expense insurance product on their own. Those who can obtain a more competitive product tend to be the healthier groups within the business community.

Association Groups

Association groups are similar to METs with the exception that the participating employers are members of the same industry (e.g., dentists, law firms).

Many of the same concerns regarding adverse selection exist. Because participation is not compulsory, those who chose to participate might do so because they cannot find a more competitive product elsewhere. Some states do not permit the issuance of a group insurance contract to a professional association. In these cases, an insurer issues individual contracts to members of the association with some type of simplified underwriting.

Franchise Organizations

Franchise organizations are similar to association groups in that participation among franchisees usually is not compulsory, thus making adverse selection high. In cases where participation is compulsory or automatic upon achieving some level of sales or other benchmark, the underwriter may look more favorably on the risk.

Plan administration and the definition of eligibility are important underwriting factors. If participation is compulsory but plan administration lacks discipline or is decentralized, the group likely will be declined. Many underwriters would look favorably on a franchise group that agrees to cover owners and managers on a noncontributory basis. However, those same underwriters probably would decline that group if it decided to make the plan available to all other full-time employees on a self-pay basis.

Public Employers

Many medical expense insurers are reluctant to pursue business in the public sector and may categorize cities, counties, and school districts as ineligible groups. The major underwriting concerns for insurers relate to eligibility, higher average age, liability risk, and low persistency.

Eligibility

Cities, counties, and school districts tend to have loose eligibility provisions. For example, eligibility may include elected board members, part-time employees (cafeteria workers, bus drivers, auxiliary police officers), volunteer firefighters, employees on sabbatical leave, and early retirees. Cities and counties also tend to have more hazardous and/or stressful occupational classes of employees, such as police officers, sheriff's deputies, jailers, probationary workers, firefighters, and road workers.

Higher Average Age

City and county groups tend to have a higher average age than the rest of the population, which results in higher morbidity.

Liability Risk

Employee benefit plans covering employees of state and local government agencies do not enjoy the protection afforded to other group health plans under Title I of the Employee Retirement Income Security Act of 1974 (ERISA), which limits exposure to punitive damages. This means that insurers covering these employees face the risk of ruinous punitive damage awards, especially in litigious states.

Low Persistency

Changes in political party leadership and in the individuals hired to make decisions regarding group insurance often result in a change in insurers. In addition, many states have laws that require that all government insurance plans be put out to bid every few years. This situation could affect the incumbent carrier's persistency.

Social and Fraternal Organizations

Many insurers regard social and fraternal groups, in which membership is not related to occupation or employment, to be ineligible risks. There is the potential for individuals to join the group primarily for the purpose of obtaining insurance. In addition, such programs are always self-pay, which presents all the participation and adverse selection problems of any other self-pay plan.

There are, however, a few insurers that specialize in writing social and fraternal groups. Those insurers tend to treat such groups as a block of individual applicants and underwrite each application separately. The benefit of such an arrangement to the insurer is the organization's endorsement.

■ Underwriting Issues for Medical Expense Insurance

After determining that a group or an individual is a desirable risk, the underwriter then assesses the plan of medical expense benefits requested. In reviewing the plan of benefits, the underwriter has four primary concerns:

- the potential for adverse selection (e.g., paying claims related to mental and nervous conditions the same as any other condition may present an adverse selection problem for the underwriter in high stress occupations such as police work and public school teaching and administration);
- the possibility that a rich benefit plan—one with a low deductible and low coinsurance rate for the insured—will promote overutilization;
- the potential of administrative difficulties created by nonstandard benefit designs; and
- making sure all aspects of the plan requested are in compliance with state and federal mandates.

Plan Types

Comprehensive Major Medical Plans

Under most comprehensive major medical plans, the claimant is required to pay a deductible and coinsurance up to a certain out-of-pocket maximum before the insurer assumes 100 percent of the liability. Actuarial studies show that utilization falls as the claimant's share of the first dollar claims go up. The underwriter wants the deductible amount to be reasonable in relationship to the market in which the product is sold. For example, a $100 calendar-year deductible may be acceptable in the rural South, where plans with such deductibles are fairly common, but may not be acceptable in southern California, where deductibles in the $400 to $500 range are more common.

Most insurers require that their plans include cost containment features such as hospital preadmission, concurrent stay review, large-claim case management, and mental health and substance abuse review programs. In underwriting a medical expense product, both the savings and costs of these features need to be considered. It is estimated that cost containment features can reduce claims costs by 5 percent to 7 percent annually. However, they add 1.5 percent to 2.5 percent to the insurer's cost of administering the plan. Both factors need to be accounted for in the premium charged.

Supplemental Major Medical Plans

A basic hospital-surgical plan offers first dollar benefits up to certain internal limits, with the remaining charges paid under a supplemental major medical plan that is subject to a deductible and coinsurance. The first dollar feature tends to promote utilization of services, and has become cost prohibitive in most regions of the country. Where such a plan is in force, the underwriter examines claim utilization statistics regularly. As costs and utilization increase, the underwriter often moves away from such first dollar plans by implementing rate incentives or requiring separate deductibles. For example, if emergency room visits appear high, the underwriter may require an emergency room deductible.

Health Maintenance Organizations (HMOs)

Underwriters require a shift in their thinking when underwriting HMO plans. Indemnity plan underwriters use high deductibles and lower coinsurance reimbursement levels to shift costs to the patient in an effort to reduce plan utilization. HMOs use provider incentives to lower utilization, primarily by requiring the insured to use a primary care physician (PCP) as the gatekeeper to getting health care services. The PCP is prepaid a flat fee monthly and has no incentive to see that patient more often than absolutely necessary. HMOs also typically offer PCPs a bonus if they can reduce the cost of specialists' care and hospitalizations. In contrast, physicians in an indemnity environment have financial incentives to increase utilization.

Many HMOs have begun to move toward global capitation arrangements. Global capitation occurs when an HMO contracts with the local provider community to accept 100 percent of the risk for patient care. Under global capitation any risk assumed by the underwriter is automatically passed on to the provider organization. However, the contracting provider organization depends on the underwriter to use prudent risk management and selection practices in HMO underwriting. The underwriter is aware of the fact that poor risk management practices today can result in noncompetitive HMO contracts tomorrow.

Evidence of Insurability

Under certain conditions the insurer requires individual evidence of insurability for group medical expense coverage. This usually involves statements of health, medical examinations, and attending physician statements. Submission of individual evidence of insurability is limited to late entrants (those who previously waived coverage), although this information could be required for all employees and eligible dependents on small groups, such as those with less than 25 employees.

Essentially this process treats the late applicant as if he or she were applying for individual coverage. By not accepting group coverage when it was first made available, the late applicant has circumvented the protections against antiselection provided by the group insurance mechanism.

The Health Insurance Portability and Accountability Act of 1996

The key features of this act were discussed in Chapter 4: Pricing Medical Expense Insurance and Chapter 5: Medical Expense Contract Provisions. The following provisions specifically affect underwriting:

- expanding the definition of a qualified beneficiary;
- guaranteeing access to all qualified employees or dependents;
- providing guaranteed issue to groups of 2 to 50 employees;
- limiting the maximum allowable exclusion period for pre-existing conditions;
- requiring that insurers provide credit against the exclusion period for prior coverage;
- expanding the duration of COBRA eligibility;
- providing guaranteed renewability; and
- providing guaranteed availability of coverage in the individual market for certain individuals losing group coverage.

The act does not address rating issues, which leaves open the possibility of insurers' applying block rating methodology to small groups. Such rating would place employers with higher projected claims (an adverse risk) in their upper range of rating blocks, and let insurers offer discounted rates to groups projecting lower-than-average claims (a clean risk).

Reinstatement of Major Medical Plan Maximums

Most major medical plans include an automatic annual reinstatement of a portion of the plan maximum (e.g., $2,000 to $5,000 per person). Some companies consider requests to fully restore the plan maximum subject to review of a health statement, similar to that required of a late entrant. For example, employees who have used a significant portion of a limited lifetime maximum (e.g., $15,000) due to a catastrophic illness may request full reinstatement of benefits. Insurers are reluctant to do so without medical evidence suggesting that the condition is unlikely to return.

Resolicitations

When participation in the plan falls significantly below the minimum requirement, the underwriter may request a resolicitation to increase participation within the group. Under such a resolicitation, the normal late entrant requirements may be waived in whole or in part. There is the potential for adverse selection in such an open enrollment situation, and the underwriter needs to weigh the potential positive impact of the wider spread of risk against the potential negative impact of assuming unknown health risks.

Typically, resolicitation periods are short in duration (e.g., two weeks) to establish a high sense of urgency among all involved to complete the project. The underwriter needs a minimum number of additional participants to waive the evidence-of-insurability requirement. Typically that number is 75 percent of all eligible employees or 50 percent of those not presently covered, whichever is greater.

Renewal Underwriting

Group medical expense insurance policies are written with all terms guaranteed for a finite period—usually for 12 months. Prior to the end of the rate guarantee period, the underwriter indicates the conditions of contract renewal. The Health Insurance Portability and Accountability Act requires companies to renew all group contracts at the option of the policyholder. Renewal underwriting is still important, however, to the extent a group's claims experience can be reflected in its rates. It also is important to review benefit design for conformity with state and federal mandates.

The number of days of advance notice of renewal conditions is spelled out in the contract. Most contracts call for 30 days, although some states require a minimum of 60 days. Some policyholders will require more advanced notice of renewal—as many as 90 to 180 days.

Notice of renewal conditions of more than 30 days works to the underwriter's disadvantage because it gives the policyholder time to talk to other insurers. If experience improves, the underwriter is pressured to discount the renewal rates. If experience worsens, the underwriter will be held responsible for what will most likely be inadequate renewal rates. The cost of the renewal process also increases as the window of negotiations is widened.

Less frequent renewals, which is the approach preferred by most policyholders, reduces the number of times the underwriter handles the group. However, because it is difficult to predict costs and utilization beyond 12 months many insurance companies do not allow indemnity plan rate guarantees greater than a year. Because HMOs have greater control over provider charges and plan utilization, they are more willing to provide rate guarantees for up to two- and three-year periods.

The underwriter's renewal objective is to price continuing business appropriately. Each policyholder is reviewed with the same careful consideration taken during the original application, except that there is much less guesswork involved since the insurer already has claims, utilization, and other relevant data on the group. Significant changes in the plan design, employer contribution, employee and/or dependent participation, group size, economic indicators, local provider contracting, and managed care arrangements can all impact on the underwriter's analysis of appropriate rating. Detailed data analyses on the group are reviewed by the underwriter in search of any developing adverse claim situations, areas of overutilization, or adverse selection. The existence of any ongoing potentially catastrophic claims may have a significant impact on the level of reserves used for renewal pricing purposes.

Individual policies can be nonrenewed only for stated reasons. Renewal premiums are based on the experience of all similar policies, not on the health or claims experience of a particular insured. Some of the stated reasons for nonrenewal of individual policies include:

- fraud discovered on the application;
- significant medical history not revealed on the application;
- submission of dishonest or illegitimate claims;
- moving outside a network plan's service area; and
- moving outside of the United States.

Underwriting Management

The process of underwriting does not stop with the issuance of a contract or the acceptance of a renewal offer. The underwriter is responsible for the daily management of each group individually and all groups collectively.

The underwriter establishes processes to monitor and react to changes in group demographics, potentially catastrophic claim situations, changes in plan participation and employer contribution, violations of plan administration guidelines, occurrences of adverse selection developing, pockets of overutilization, and other concerns.

Benefit Changes

An employer's request for plan design modifications does not always coincide with the timing of the renewal. Off-anniversary benefit change requests occur frequently. When the underwriter receives a request for a plan design change, the group's most recent claims experience is reviewed to determine if a rate increase is needed based on the current plan of benefits. Factors that may have an impact on how much credit the underwriter will provide for the plan change requested include how the claims experience is running in relationship to the premiums received and the length of time before another rate action is permissible under the contract.

New Class Additions

Policyholders often wish to extend coverage to additional classes of employees. The additional class may be certain hourly employees previously covered elsewhere (e.g., under a Taft-Hartley trust), a division of the company previously covered under its own separate contract, or a newly acquired subsidiary.

If the number of employees to be added is insignificant in relation to the total number of employees covered, the underwriter may approve the addition without changing the existing rates. However, under certain circumstances, the underwriter may wish to underwrite the new class on its own merits. Examples of such circumstances are:

- if the number of employees to be added is significant in relation to the total number of employees already covered;
- if the new class of employees is located in an area where the cost of care is significantly different; or
- if the age or sex composition is significantly different.

The result may be an underwriting decision that requires a separate rate class for the new employees or a change in the existing rate to absorb the new class.

The underwriter may wish to impose separate restrictions or limitations on the new class. For example, if the acquisition is in a high turnover industry (e.g., a fast food establishment), the underwriter may want to establish a longer waiting period for coverage to begin in order to reduce the number of short-term employees coming into the plan.

■ Reinsurance

Most insurance companies purchase reinsurance for medical expense policies from a reinsurance specialty company to cede risks in excess of a certain amount. The insurance company transferring risk is called the ceding company. The insurance company accepting that transferred risk is called the reinsurer. The amount of risk an insurance company cedes depends on the size of its block of business and the amount of risk it feels that the block of business can absorb. The ceding company often looks to the reinsurer for guidance and expertise in risk selection, especially if the ceding company is a small insurance company. In group insurance there are two main methods in which risk is ceded: quota share and excess risk.

Quota Share

A quota share reinsurance arrangement is when the reinsurer assumes a certain percentage of all risks in exchange for an equivalent percentage of all premiums. The reinsurer makes some allowance for certain expenses incurred by the ceding company (e.g., commissions, taxes, marketing). If a portion of the risk assumed generates an experience refund to the policyholder, the reinsurer refunds the applicable percentage.

Excess Risk

An excess risk reinsurance arrangement is when the reinsurer assumes all or most of the risk in excess of the ceding company's retention limit on any single individual. For example, the reinsurer may assume the risk for all medical claims in excess of $100,000 on any one individual.

■ Summary

Underwriting medical expense insurance is an ongoing process that requires the management of individual risk situations to achieve success on an overall block basis. The major risk factors for pricing group policies include the group's demographics, plan design, prior claims experience, administration requirements, and expected persistency. For individual policy holders, the major risk selection factors are age, sex, location, earnings, and the health history and current health status of each applicant. Underwriters identify adverse risk situations and plan around them, and develop new business and renewal strategies designed to increase the insurer's market share.

■ Key Terms

Acceptable group	Coordination of benefits	Duplicate coverage
Adverse selection	(COB)	Eligibility
Census data	Credibility	Eligible group
Contributory plan	Discriminatory	Employment conditions

Enrollment
Evidence of insurability
Excess risk
Insurability
Key employees
Late entrants
Medical underwriting
Minimum participation
Multiple employer trust (MET)
Noncontributory plan
Overutilization
Participation
Persistency
Quota share
Reinsurer
Renewal underwriting
Resolicitation
Risk
Single employer group
Spread of risk
Stop-loss
Taft-Hartley health and welfare trust plans
Transferred risk
Turnover
Underwriter

Chapter 7

MEDICAL EXPENSE POLICY ADMINISTRATION

133 *Introduction*
133 *New Insurance Accounts*
139 *Continuing Administration: Customer Service*
146 *Administration of Multigroup Plans*
152 *Third-Party Administration*
153 *Administrative Services Only (ASO)*
154 *ERISA Reporting Requirements for Welfare Plans*
155 *Summary*
156 *Key Terms*

■ Introduction

Throughout the process of issue and continued administration of a group or individual medical expense insurance policy, good communication and customer service are vital. Cooperation among all the areas within the insurance company reassures group and individual customers that their insurance is in good hands. This chapter highlights some of the complex issues faced by the administrative personnel handling medical expense insurance. The various types of group plans, including nonemployer-sponsored plans, have nuances that require specialized procedures.

■ New Insurance Accounts

Once a new group or individual medical expense policy has been sold and approved, the insurer sets up policyholder service records to enable the company to perform its many and varied functions.

Group Medical Expense Accounts

Building Account Records

For insurer administered plans, information is entered and stored on two levels for group accounts: information about the group and information about the

MEDICAL EXPENSE INSURANCE

employee. For policyholder (self-) administered plans, the insurer may not store employee information since enrollment materials and eligibility information are retained by the policyholder. The policyholder certifies eligibility on the claim form at the time it is submitted to the insurer.

Group information. Group information consists of basic facts about the group plan, such as:

- the policyholder's name, address, and phone number;
- the effective date of the group policy;
- the firm's nature of business;
- the name and phone number of the person at the firm who will administer the plan;
- description of the class or classes of employees who are eligible for coverage under the plan;
- the waiting period to be applied to new employees; and
- the number of hours an employee must work each week to be eligible for coverage under the plan.

Agent or broker information, such as the name, address, and agent identification code the insurer uses, also is entered so the commission-paying process may begin.

Another component of group information entered relates to the benefits under the policy, so that claims may be paid. This information includes:

- the amount of individual and family calendar-year deductibles;
- coinsurance levels;
- out-of-pocket expense limits;
- individual copayments, if any, for services, such as physician offices visits; and
- where appropriate, managed care network information, such as the network name and the type of utilization review that will be used for the case.

Employee information. Individual employees are enrolled from information on the enrollment/application forms. This information includes demographic and employment data such as:

- name;
- date of birth;
- sex;
- Social Security number;

MEDICAL EXPENSE POLICY ADMINISTRATION

- date of hire;
- employee class;
- work location;
- names and dates of birth of dependents to be covered; and
- coverage elections.

Administration Materials

Once all the group and employee information has been recorded, various types of output can be produced. The master policy is developed based on plan provisions and benefits from the group records. Employee certificates or booklet-certificates and member identification cards are produced from the group and employee information.

The insurer provides the policyholder with an administration manual designed to provide answers to the most common questions concerning administrative and claim procedures. The manual helps eliminate the need for frequent correspondence between the policyholder and the insurer. Manuals prepared for insurer-administered plans usually are less detailed than those prepared for plans administered by the group policyholder (self-administered plans).

Usually included in the manual are:

- instructions concerning effective dates of coverage;
- verification of the accuracy of certificates;
- phone numbers and addresses for correspondence with the insurer's customer service and claims departments;
- directions for processing increases and decreases in amounts of insurance, employee terminations, continuation, conversions, and claims; and
- any insurer or policyholder-specific instructions for matters such as utilization review, flexible benefits, or medical case management.

The format of administration manuals varies among insurers. Some insurance companies include very detailed instructions; others present only general procedural steps. Instead of a manual, some insurers use a plastic card for administration and claim instructions. The card provides generic instructions and is a much abbreviated, easy-to-understand version of the manual. A significant advantage of the card is that the cost to produce it is substantially less than the cost of producing the administration manual.

For insurers producing administration manuals, word processing has made it possible to more easily tailor the manual to the provisions of a specific plan.

MEDICAL EXPENSE INSURANCE

The additional cost over the plastic card can be offset by improved administration and communication with the policyholder.

The master policy, initial billing statement, certificates of coverage or booklet-certificates, identification cards, administration manual, and managed care network provider listings are sent to the new policyholder, along with an initial supply of forms that the policyholder uses in the administration of the plan. These materials are either mailed directly to the policyholder at the place of business or sent to the agent or broker for personal delivery to the policyholder.

Frequently the materials are sent under the cover of a "welcome letter" from the insurer or, more specifically, the insurance company's customer service representative who is responsible for the administration of the group account. This letter may:

- thank the new customer for choosing the insurance company;
- explain the account numbers the policyholder and insured members should use when corresponding with the insurer or filing claims;
- list the names and addresses of service contacts; and
- for self-accounting groups, provide an explanation of how to perform some initial billing procedures.

The purpose of the welcome letter is not to give a comprehensive set of administrative instructions, which can be found in the administration manual. Rather, it is intended to outline steps to ensure a successful start to the insurer-policyholder relationship. The letter often is followed up with a phone call from the insurer's customer service representative responsible for the account, to answer any questions the policyholder's plan administrator may have.

Recordkeeping

The insurer stores all the paperwork submitted with the new case as well as the paperwork associated with the ongoing administration of the plan. New case paperwork includes the master application, the members' enrollment and medical evidence forms, the premium rate proposal used to sell the case, and any other written correspondence that has taken place during the enrollment, underwriting, and issuance phases of the new case. Insurers use a variety of methods to retain these documents for future reference.

Paper files. The method that has been around the longest is the use of paper files. This approach requires a great deal of storage space by the insurer.

Paper filing also requires more time for personnel to file and retrieve documents. Even though insurers are moving toward more advanced methods of document storage and retrieval, most still retain the paper files of their old, terminated accounts rather than move them all to a newer medium since this can be a time- and resource-consuming process that may not be justified when these files are rarely retrieved.

Microfilm and microfiche. The majority of insurers microfilm the paper documents they receive and handle. Microfilming is a quick and inexpensive method for storing large quantities of documents in a relatively small space. Although document retrieval from microfilm can be somewhat slow, some larger insurance companies are using new methods that utilize digital imaging.

An alternative to microfilm is microfiche, which also photographs the document so storage space can be greatly reduced. Although document retrieval is even slower than with microfilm, microfiche is widely used by insurers to retain large quantities of output, such as copies of billing statements or mass policyholder mailings where the retrieval rate is typically low and the photography process can be integrated with the output of the documents to improve efficiency.

Electronic on-line records. Some insurers use electronic means to document correspondence and telephone conversations with their customers. For example, a customer service representative can include in an electronic account record a summary that contains the date and time of the call, the name of the caller (if incoming) or the individual and phone number the representative called (if outgoing), and a short summary of the conversation that took place. This file is retrievable by anyone with access to the insurer's on-line system.

Electronic on-line records require no physical storage space and allow for quick and easy retrieval by the insurer's personnel. However, these records take up a lot of space in the computer's memory. Many companies have purge cycles in which older summaries are downloaded to another medium, such as microfilm or microfiche, and deleted from the computer files to free up more storage space.

Digital imaging (document scanning). The newest form of document storage is digital imaging, which scans paper items directly into the insurer's computer system. This eliminates any need for data entry and filing personnel. The information travels through the company's computer system in digital format for viewing on a computer monitor screen on an as-needed basis.

Compiling Statistical Data

During the course of each year, the group division of the insurance company compiles various kinds of statistics on policyholders that are used for a number of purposes, including the preparation of the annual statement. Other uses are:

- claim experience studies;
- expense studies;
- reports of policy lapses and reinstatements;
- determination of unearned premium reserves;
- reports on the number of insured lives, amount of insurance, and premium in force; and
- reports on first-year and renewal premiums, expense, and commissions.

Through the use of electronic data processing equipment, an insurer's administrative system can provide much of the required statistical data and analyses automatically.

Individual Medical Expense Accounts

The administration of individual medical expense insurance policies differs from that of group policies in that the insurer works directly with the insured rather than through a group policyholder. While new individual applications may come to the insurer through an agent or broker, the insurance company typically deals directly with the insured individual, sending all new policy materials directly to his or her home address.

The insured's account records are built on a single level. They contain all the demographic information about the insured, the medical benefits of the policy (calendar-year deductible, coinsurance level, out-of-pocket expense limit, and so forth), and premium billing information.

Based on the insurer's on-line account records, the insurance policy is produced. The policy describes coverages and policy provisions. Special state requirements can complicate the process, but information systems are available to help insurers produce state-specific policies.

Actual policy issue does not necessarily complete the policy issue process. Often there is additional administrative work, such as having the insured sign amendment forms with a copy returned to the insurer for the home office record. Insurers generally have an internal tracking system to make sure all the necessary administrative work is completed.

Table 7.1

A Training Model for Improving Customer Service Skills

The following are steps for insurance company personnel to take to improve customer satisfaction and problem solving:

A six-step customer satisfaction system	A four-step problem solving formula
1. Greet people	1. Understand the problem
2. Value people	2. Identify the cause
3. Ask how to help people	3. Discuss solutions
4. Listen to people	4. Solve the problem
5. Help people	
6. Invite people back	

Source: Adapted from Paula Hauser, "All about the Customer," *Comment* (September 1995), p. 11.

Because of the large number of individual policyholders serviced by the insurer's customer service department, welcome letters or phone calls are not commonly used. The insurer often relies on the agent or broker to make sure the policyholder is familiar with procedures for corresponding with and reporting changes to the insurance company.

■ Continuing Administration: Customer Service

Importance of Customer Service

Insurance companies offer products that may vary little in design and price from their competitors, so excellent customer service is often the key to attracting and retaining customers. Agents and brokers can use an insurer's customer service reputation as a selling point, but the customer service representatives in the insurer's administration department are crucial to keeping those customers on-board.

Because it is more costly for an insurer to obtain a new customer than it is to retain an existing one, customer service performance has a direct impact on the insurer's bottom line. In addition, insurers with a good customer service reputation are likely to attract and retain agents and brokers to do business with the company. Accordingly, most insurers invest a great deal in customer service training for their employees (see Table 7.1).

Corporate Commitment

Insurers with a strong customer service culture have characteristics in common, including a commitment to excellent customer service that starts at the top and an objective method for measuring their customer service performance. One insurance company chief executive officer drives his company's customer service culture with the phrase, "Quality is more a journey than a destination."[2]

Another insurer's vice president for customer satisfaction has this to say about his company's vision for excellent customer service:

> [O]ur vision is to become the ... company of choice for individuals, groups, and businesses and their employees. We believe that serving our customer is the basic reason for our existence, and doing this well will allow us to achieve our vision. To become the ... company of choice, we recognize that customers are the ones who define what is an excellent product or service, so we try to find out what they value and make it easy for them to do business with us. Finally, we believe that by taking this approach, we will attract and keep more customers, which in turn increases profitability and the value of our products and services to our customers.[3]

Without this kind of commitment from upper-level management, an initiative to improve a company's customer service culture has little chance of being successful.

Measuring Customer Service Performance

Studies show that insurance customers have the five following concerns:

- reliability (e.g., notices sent on schedule and correctly);
- responsiveness (e.g., processing all claims quickly);
- tangibles (e.g., convenient offices with modern equipment);
- assurance (e.g., that personal data will be kept confidential); and
- empathy (e.g., understandable, jargon-free correspondence and conversations).

Increasingly, health insurers are developing ways to measure their customer service performance—for example, by comparing customers' expectations to the company's performance, sending quarterly customer service surveys to customers to obtain feedback on how well the company is doing, and asking former customers why they terminated their account so the company can determine in what areas improvement is needed.

Tailoring Service to Customer Type

Customer service is tailored to the specific needs of the customer. The following section provides an overview of special customer service needs of group policyholders, group members, individual policyholders, marketers, and internal customers. At its simplest, good customer service is prompt, courteous, accurate, and confidential.

Group Policyholders

Group medical expense insurance plans are complex and often confusing to administer. Whether the plans are insurer-administered or self-administered by the policyholder, good communication between the insurer and the policyholder is essential. The policyholder relies on the insurer to be the expert in insurance and knowledgeable about all the applicable policies, procedures, and regulations affecting its group plan. The insurer, in turn, relies on the policyholder's plan administrator to provide accurate, timely reporting of information that can affect the group plan and the coverage for members. As long as both members of this team perform their respective functions well, both the insureds and the insurer benefit. Important customer service functions that insurers perform for group policyholders include providing accurate and timely information, implementing quality control measures, preparing group premium statements, and collecting due and overdue premiums. (For information about claim payments, see Chapter 8: Medical Expense Claim Administration.)

Providing accurate and up-to-date information. Customer service personnel are responsible for processing enrollments for new employees. Because the information the representative enters into the account records is taken from the enrollment form, fully completed forms with accurate information are essential. If the enrollment forms are incomplete or filled out incorrectly, the customer service representative contacts the policyholder for clarification of the details. If the plan is administered by the insurance company, the enrollment forms are maintained by the insurer. If the plan is self-administered, the forms are maintained by the policyholder.

The insurer also is responsible for the maintenance of the policy account records by recording any changes, additions, or deletions to the group's enrollment. Accurate claims handling and premium billing can occur only if the group's census and coverages are accurate in the insurer's system. Timely processing of these changes also helps ensure that billing statements reflect the most up-to-date status of the group.

The automated voice response system (AVRS) is widely used by the insurance industry for reporting and other administrative functions. AVRS provides a simple, accurate way for the group policyholder to modify its account and make requests using a telephone. A toll-free number gives the customer easy access to activities such as making account changes, ordering member booklets or identification cards, or checking on an account balance. To safeguard confidential records so that information about the group account is given only to the group policyholer and not individual employees, the policyholder is assigned a personal identification number (PIN). This number must be used to access the information. AVRS can also be used to provide account information to individual policyholders.

Using a touch-tone phone, the caller is directed through a series of menus to request information from the insurance company's computer system or make changes without talking to a customer service representative. This can be done outside of normal business hours. AVRS is another step in the insurance industry's ongoing efforts to meet the changing needs of customers.

Implementing quality control measures. As a result of the demand for accuracy and promptness in the handling of updates to the account records, insurance companies have developed stringent quality control measures. These measures may range from a formal checking process in which supervisors or a quality control department monitor the work processed by each of the service representatives to a more employee-accountable approach in which each employee is responsible for the quality and timeliness of his or her own work. Regardless of the approach, insurers realize what is at stake when errors or untimely processing occur. Not only are group policyholders and insureds affected adversely, but also the negative publicity generated by this poor customer service can be extremely difficult to overcome.

Preparing group premium statements. The accounting procedures for group premiums depend on whether the plan is self-administered or insurer administered.

With a self-administered plan, the policyholder performs most of the administrative work. The policyholder maintains detailed records of group membership, processes routine requests such as name and address changes, and in some cases prepares certificates for new group members. Each month the group policyholder prepares a premium statement that shows the computation of the premium due, which is sent with the premium to the insurance company. The home office periodically audits these computations.

If the plan is insurer administered, the insurance company performs the administrative work, which includes computing the amount of the premium due and mailing a statement to the group policyholder, usually on a monthly basis. The total amount of a group's premium may change each month because of people joining and leaving the group. If the group is comparatively small, the billing statement can list each insured group member and the premium for that member. In a large group, the statement often shows only the number of persons in each of several classifications, along with the total premium for each classification.

Issues relating to overdue premium collection. One of the most crucial and sensitive areas in the ongoing administration of a group policy is collection of due and unpaid premium.

Group health policies typically contain a 31-day grace period provision. The insurance coverage provided by the policy remains in force during the grace period. If the group policyholder does not pay the premium by the end of the grace period, the group policy will terminate. The grace period provision in a group health insurance policy specifies that if the policy terminates for nonpayment of premiums, then the group policyholder is legally obligated to pay the premium for the coverage provided during the grace period.

When a policyholder is past due in remitting its premium to the insurer, the coverage for all the members and dependents insured under the group plan is jeopardized. Insurers usually allow for an occasional late payment past the expiration of the grace period. If the policyholder routinely pays on time but due to unforeseen circumstances or an accounting error has missed a payment, it is in the insurer's best interest to work with that policyholder to try to bring the account into good standing.

When the policyholder has been late with its premium payments in excess of what the insurer is willing to allow, termination of the policy will occur. While the insurer is liable for claims incurred during the grace period, any incurred beyond that date will be denied. The insurer's customer service staff now has the responsibility of collecting the past due premium from a customer it no longer insures.

This can be a difficult task, and some insurers have specialized personnel dedicated to this one function. In addition, outside collection agencies may be retained to collect money that the insurer has been unable to collect. The insurer usually uses this avenue as a last resort since the collection agency will keep a large portion of any money it collects as its fee. Many insurers write off small balances due after internal collection attempts have failed rather than refer the account for collection by an outside agency.

Whether a group policy terminates due to nonpayment or at the policyholder's request, the insured members are entitled to conversion of their coverage to an individual plan. The notification of these rights may be done by the insurer or the policyholder, but must be done within 31 days from the date the group coverage ended. Sign-up forms and premium notifications are sent to the employees along with an explanation of how to complete and return the forms and initial premium payment.

Documenting coverage for HIPAA compliance. HIPAA requires employers (policyholders) or insurers to issue a certificate of group coverage when an insured employee or a dependent terminates coverage under the group policy. The certificate documents how long the insured had group coverage. This information is needed in order for an employee to exercise his or her "portability" rights under HIPAA. When an employee moves from one group health plan to another, HIPAA requires that qualifying previous coverage be credited to reduce any pre-existing exclusion period the employee may have under the new plan. If the employee is not eligible for group coverage and also satisfies other requirements, including having 18 months of creditable coverage, the last of which was under a group health plan, the employee is assured access to coverage in the individual market. See Appendix B for an overview of HIPAA's requirements regarding certificates of coverage.

Group Members

Group members usually get administrative information from their employer's group insurance plan administrator, but sometimes they go directly to the insurer with their questions regarding the plan. Frequently, members want to know how to go about adding a dependent, such as a spouse or newborn child, to the plan.

Because of the private nature of an individual's medical history, the insurer's customer service representatives handle all communication of this nature with confidentiality. For example, an employee may have a medical condition that he or she has revealed to the customer service representative, but the employee may not want this information known to the employer. Confidentiality and sensitivity also are called for when members or their spouses are inquiring about eligibility in the event of a divorce or legal separation.

When an employee terminates his or her job, or a dependent loses eligibility, continuation of the group insurance coverage or conversion to an individual policy is available. In the case of the terminated employee, a positive relationship may no longer exist between the employee and the former employer. Again, sensitivity and professionalism are needed when handling the requisite notifications and other communications.

Individual Policyholders

The insurer handles the ongoing maintenance of the account records for holders of individual policies much the same way as it does for members of a group plan. Communication is either with the insured policyholder directly or through the policyholder's agent or broker.

Examples of the kinds of customer service that insurers provide to individual policyholders include answering questions insureds may have regarding their policies; making administrative updates such as name, address, and dependent-eligibility-related changes; handling delinquent accounts; reinstating lapsed policies; and closing files on terminated policies. As with group insurance, HIPAA requires that insurers document how long a person was covered under an individual policy.

Agents and Brokers

While agents and brokers often are thought of as an arm of the insurer, they also are valuable customers. If they do not receive the quality service they feel they and their clients are entitled to, they are likely to find another insurer with which to do business.

The account records that the insurer's administrative personnel build and maintain are linked directly to those that calculate and pay commissions to the agents and brokers. Inaccurate and untimely handling of additions, changes, and deletions to group or individual insurance policy records can have a direct impact on the compensation the agents and brokers receive. Poor customer service in this arena is likely to send an agent or broker to another carrier quicker than any other type of service problem.

Internal Customers

Internal customers are the insurance company employees who seek information and services from the administration department. As an example, a person in the claim department needs access to information in the unit- and member-level records to pay benefits accurately and promptly. As another example, when a dispute arises over the handling of a claim, the claim examiner contacts the administration department for help in solving the problem if it involves dates of eligibility or coverage termination. For the insurer to be successful, all areas of the company must work in harmony with one another and strive for the utmost in customer service excellence.

Administration of Multigroup Plans

The predominant multigroups involved in purchasing medical expense insurance are trade and professional associations, negotiated trusteeships, and multiple employer trusts (METs). Any of these multigroup plans may be administered by the insurer, policyholder (self-administered), or third-party administrator (TPA).

Trade Associations

A trade association is made up of many single employer groups in the same industry. The ability of the administrator to conduct initial and continuous solicitation of employer members, maintain records properly, bill and collect premiums, process claims, and otherwise administer the plan in an efficient manner is essential to the success of trade association cases. To avoid termination of the group plan or the appointment of another broker, it is in the best interest of the original agent or broker to see that the administration is handled competently and that claim costs are not inflated by abuse.

To support the cost of administration when it is handled by the insurer or a TPA, the administrator normally collects an extra charge and sets aside this amount in a reserve fund for expenses, premium delinquencies, and other contingencies. Another approach is to charge the employer member a flat amount or percentage for each employee insured.

Administration Procedures

The procedures used in administering trade association groups are virtually identical with those used for small group cases. Two primary differences are the extent of involvement of the association and the allocation of premiums to a single policy issued to the association instead of each individual employer. Simplified administrative instructions and a supply of the forms necessary to enroll new employees, process changes, and file claims are sent to each participating employer.

For association plans that are not self-administered, the administrator prepares monthly list bills (statements showing all insured members and the premium for each) and sends the association copies of the bills or a listing of the premiums billed for each employer after each billing. The administrator also sends a listing of employers whose coverage has been canceled, either by request or for nonpayment of premiums, and prepares periodic summaries of premiums billed and actually collected for the association.

Special administrative problems for trade association cases include:

- working with separate (and usually small) employers that may be scattered over a wide geographic area;
- difficulty in handling billings, premium payments, recordkeeping, and processing or paying claims; and
- making sure there is at least the minimum number of enrolled employees or that a minimum percent of eligible employer units participate.

The total administrative costs on a trade association case generally are higher than those incurred for a plan of similar size that insures only a single employer. Although the continued solicitation among enrolled and new employer units (especially new employees of enrolled employer units) can be both time-consuming and expensive, it is vital to the maintenance of the proper level of participation. Unless new, younger employees enter the plan, the premium rates are likely to increase substantially as the age level of the insured employees begins to rise.

Reserve Funds

To operate a sound trade association plan, a policyholder must maintain reserve funds for unusual expenses, delinquencies in premium payments from participating employers, and rate adjustments. The monies for reserve funds normally are collected from participating employers by increasing employer premium rates sufficiently to cover these additional costs.

Audits

It is not feasible for an insurance company to audit every employer insured under a trade association plan. However, the records and books maintained by the association's administrator generally are audited periodically. A good administrator works to eliminate possible employer abuses, such as insuring only senior members of a firm when all employees are to be covered or insuring relatives who are not full-time employees of the firm.

An effective technique used by many administrators for controlling a number of potential abuses is to send annually to the employer members a form on which a certification is required. This form lists all the employees of the firms enrolled in the plan and asks specifically if all of them are working full-time, if any of them are not working the required number of hours, and if there are any eligible employees who are not insured. This certification serves the dual purpose of bringing the matter directly to the employer for review and impressing upon the employer the importance of following the enrollment procedures of the plan.

Professional Associations

Professional association cases have a number of characteristics in common with trade association cases:

- Members are engaged in the same type of occupation.
- Membership usually is scattered over a wide geographic area.
- Success of the plan is influenced by the amount of support the association gives it.
- Continued resolicitation is necessary.
- Competent, efficient administration is needed.

The major differences between the professional and trade association cases are that the administration of professional associations involves:

- dealing with individual members rather than employer-members;
- charging a premium commonly graded by age; and
- making extensive use of evidence of insurability in the underwriting of each member.

Frequent solicitation of members is necessary to maintain an adequate level of participation in the plan. In most cases, practically all solicitation is by mail. Sometimes there is active personal solicitation of individual members by direct contact from the association personnel, the administrator, or the insurer's sales force. Direct contact, if it can be accomplished at reasonable cost, achieves a higher percentage of participation than a mail-solicitation-only approach.

The constantly rising cost of medical care makes it difficult to maintain one premium rate for any extended time. Acceptance of a rate increase often is much more difficult to obtain because of the member-pay-all nature of professional association plans. If there is an increase in premium rates, both the administrator and the individuals must be sold on the new rates.

State Restrictions and Requirements

A few states exclude professional associations from among the types of groups for which group insurance can be written. Even where states permit issuance of such a group policy, other restrictions or considerations may dictate covering members through individual policies. In such cases, insurers may experience a number of varied and expensive administrative problems.

In states that require filing of individual policy forms, which are usually tailor-made, delays may result. Application forms for this kind of coverage, just as in the case with individual policies, must be filed for approval. Also, they are used by the insurer for recording information instead of enrollment cards. After two or three plan changes, insurers commonly reprint and reissue group certificates to all insured individuals; this is not possible with individual policies. Once issued, each plan change—whether a minor one or a significant benefit change—is made by attaching a rider to the initial policy. Indexing, storing, and keeping track of what policy forms have been issued, to whom, and when can be a major problem for the administrator.

Negotiated Trusteeships (Taft-Hartley Health and Welfare Trust Plans)

A negotiated trusteeship is established by a formal agreement concerning employees subject to collective bargaining, or employees of two employers who have signed the trust agreement. The administrative requirements for a trusteed health and welfare trust plan can be handled by the union, insurer, or TPA. This work is complicated by the fact that one employee may work for many employers during a one-month period. Also, one employer may hire many different employees for various periods of time during a month. Determining eligibility for an employee is made even more difficult if employers are delinquent in their contributions or fail to keep accurate records of employment. To prevent continued abuse by a few employers, some unions stop sending their members to an employer until delinquencies have been paid.

Eligibility

Eligibility for coverage under the plan normally is given in number of hours or days an employee has accumulated working for contributing employers. Many covered employees become ineligible for benefits because they do not meet the hourly requirements. They can be eligible again after they build up the necessary credits. Since almost all of these plans are noncontributory, efficient methods of enrolling new employees and recording their eligibility are necessary. (For a review of eligibility in Taft-Hartley plans, see Chapter 6: Underwriting Medical Expense Insurance.)

If administration is not efficient, certificate issue can be a serious problem since employees can become eligible for benefits on different dates. Each eligible employee is entitled to a certificate at the time of qualifying for coverage under the plan. A replacement certificate is not issued when the eligible employee changes employers.

Reserve Fund

To ensure that the administration of the plan is on a sound financial basis, a portion of the income from the fund is accumulated as a reserve. Fluctuation in premium income can be severe, and a reserve is necessary to provide for continuance of insurance and continued premium payments during a period when employer contributions are lower due to seasonal unemployment or an economic downturn. Another reason for building up a reserve is to meet the rising cost of medical care during the period of the negotiated agreement. The trustees have no power to negotiate additional income in this period, but the premium may be changed by the insurer. Contributions on behalf of employees who do not work enough hours to become eligible and contributions on behalf of employees working more than the required minimum number of hours usually are allocated to the reserve accumulation.

Code of Ethical Practices

A large percentage of trusteed health and welfare plans have a third-party administrator pay health insurance claims. Various sections of the Code of Ethical Practices adopted by the National Association of Insurance Commissioners (NAIC) for the insuring of the benefits of union or union-management welfare funds deal with this issue.

Paying benefits and conducting audits. According to the code, it is the responsibility of an insurer to pay benefits under its policies promptly, fairly, and without discrimination in accordance with policy terms. Insurers periodically audit claim payments made on their behalf by fund administrators or others. The results of such audits are available to the trustees of the fund. The insurer's actuaries, in reviewing the claim experience under the plan, are aware of the claim procedures and accounting used by the administrator, so that proper allowance can be made in the insurer's reserves for the appropriate claim lags.

Accounting statement. At the end of each policy year, the insurer of a welfare fund is required to furnish an accounting statement to the policyholder that separately includes at least the following items:

- premiums received;
- benefit payments,
- commissions, fees, and other allowances paid;
- dividends, experience-rating refunds, or contractual returns of premiums paid to the plan; and
- the resulting balance.

Summary report. Another section of the code states that insurers should encourage the trustees of each welfare fund to make a summary report of the operations of the fund at least annually to persons having a bona fide interest in the plan. To the fullest possible extent, insurers are to cooperate with the trustees in the preparation of the report. Timely reporting of premiums and claim payments by the administrator is mandatory for the insurer to comply with this stipulation.

Multiple Employer Trusts

A multiple employer trust (MET) is a legal trust established by a plan sponsor that brings together a number of small, unrelated employers for the purpose of providing group medical care coverage on an insured or a self-funded basis. The MET approach is used by many insurers for the small employer group market. Although intended primarily for the employer with fewer than 10 eligible employees, some insurers also use MET plans for larger employers.

Generally, the insurer sponsors and administers MET plans directly, but a number of successful plans have been initiated by other organizations (notably brokers) and administered by the broker, the insurer, or a third-party administrator. In all of these types of MET plans, the trustee's role usually is minimal: to receive and hold the trust funds and group policies issued by the insurer.

MET plans are similar to trade association cases that cover a large number of small employers. Administrative objectives include high efficiency and centralization, and underwriting of each employer's application for participation.

A large number of employers must participate in a MET plan if a significant amount of in-force business or premium volume is to develop. The administration is automated and simplified as much as possible to keep expenses down. Streamlined administration procedures may involve:

- providing the employer with an approved copy of the participation agreement and a policy administration guide instead of the group policy;
- the use of a preauthorized check remittance method to improve persistency;
- lock-box arrangements for premium collections to improve cash flow and increase investment earnings; and
- level first-year and renewal commission scales to simplify commission calculations.

Each MET plan may have a different anniversary for rate change purposes. Renewal action may be taken on the policy anniversary or on a postanniversary renewal rating date. The experience may be pooled for the total MET plan. If the MET plan is on a postanniversary basis, rate changes will be effective on the employer's renewal date—normally three months after the anniversary under the plan.

■ Third-Party Administration

The services provided by a TPA usually are associated with special cases, such as association plans and trusts, and sometimes with employer-employee plans that the policyholder self-administers. Regardless of the type of policyholder, the administrator performs its services in the policyholder's name. A contract or agreement with the policyholder or the insurer describes these services, which may include the following functions:

- billing premium;
- collecting premium;
- handling remittances to the insurers;
- screening employer applications for insurance coverage;
- screening individual applications for insurance;
- issuing certificates or booklet-certificates to insured persons;
- maintaining insurance records;
- processing and paying claims;
- providing information and answering policyholder questions about benefits; and
- attending meetings of trusteed plans (preparing and distributing agenda as required) and helping the trustees prepare necessary reports.

The contract or agreement contains provisions that specify other rights and duties of the parties involved and the basis for determining the administrator's fee or compensation. If engaged by the insurer, the administrator's fee may be based on a percentage of the total premium being administered. A few insurers allow TPAs to deduct the fee from the premium remitted, but most require them to remit the entire premium to the insurer and pay the administrator's fee separately. If the insurer pays claims, the administrator's fee is assumed to cover routine claim preparation and certification of eligibility for benefits. If the administrator pays claims, however, an additional fee may be paid for this function.

■ Administrative Services Only (ASO)

Many insurance companies offer their administrative and claims-paying services for self-insured plans. Under a self-insured plan, the employer assumes the risk for claims and holds funds to cover all claim costs until they are actually needed to pay claims. The hired insurance company provides administrative services and pays claims from a bank account the policyholder establishes to fund the plan. The employer pays a fee for the ASO services. The fee many be expressed as a percentage of claims paid, cost per employer, or cost per transaction.

An ASO arrangement helps the employer's cash flow because funds are made available to the plan bank account only as needed to cover paid claims. The employer also holds reserves needed to cover run-out claims and expenses if the plan is terminated. The employer can use these funds until actually needed to pay future claims and expenses. An additional advantage is that most states do not collect premium tax on fully self-insured plans.

Services Provided

An insurance company providing administrative services gives a self-insured employer only the services needed for the day-to-day operation of its group medical expense plan. These services may include:

- a prepared plan document;
- administrative manuals;
- prepared and printed materials, such as claim drafts or checks, claim forms, descriptive booklets, enrollment cards, and identification cards;
- claims payments;
- administration of cost containment programs;
- underwriting, claim, and plan management reports; and
- underwriting and actuarial services.

Risks Assumed by the Employer

Before deciding to adopt an ASO arrangement, an employer should be aware that the following risks are involved.

- The employer assumes complete financial responsibility for the cost of the plan's benefit payments and expenses. The employer must cover the entire

MEDICAL EXPENSE INSURANCE

cost of higher-than-expected claims and expenses that may occur during the life of the plan.
- Total monthly ASO plan costs vary from month to month. This makes budgeting more difficult than under an insured method, where the monthly premium represents the employer's total liability.
- The employer is the sole plan sponsor under an ASO arrangement. As a result, the liability of the plan and its operation rests entirely with the employer.
- If the covered employees contribute toward the cost of the plan, the self-insured plan is subject to trust requirements under the Employee Retirement Income Security Act (ERISA). This means the employer may be required to make special trust arrangements to protect the employees' contributions.

ERISA Reporting Requirements for Welfare Plans

ERISA has several reporting and disclosure requirements for welfare plans sponsoring medical expense insurance. The plan administrator is responsible for compliance with ERISA. In most cases the plan administrator is the group policyholder (or participating employer unit if the plan is a multiple employer trust). There may be circumstances, however, where the plan administrator is an employer association, a joint employer-employee board of trustees, or some other organization.

Summary Plan Description (SPD)

All plans subject to ERISA reporting and disclosure provisions must prepare and distribute summary plan descriptions to plan participants. The description may consist of the group insurance benefit booklet or certificate and a supplemental page that shows certain ERISA-requirement information.

When an insurer is responsible for the financing or administration (including claims payment) of the plan, the name and address of the insurer must be provided as supplemental information. The U.S. Department of Labor office where plan participants and beneficiaries can seek assistance or information regarding their rights under ERISA also must be provided.

The summary plan description must be furnished to all plan participants on or before the later of the following times:

- 90 days after the employee became a plan participant; or
- within 120 days after the plan was established or became subject to the reporting and disclosure requirements of ERISA.

When a plan is amended, a summary of the changes must be furnished to plan participants. A revised summary plan description, which includes all the changes, must be issued at least once every five years.

Plans with more than 100 participants must file a copy of the summary plan description with the Department of Labor. If different summary plan descriptions are prepared for different classes, each one must be filed. A list identifying each summary plan description must be included with the filing. The summary plan description must be refiled following an amendment to the plan. Filing deadlines for the Department of Labor have the same time limits as does the distribution of the summary plan descriptions to plan participants.

Annual Reports (Form 5500)

Plans with 100 or more participants are required to file an annual report each plan year by the last day of the seventh month following the end of the plan year. The report, Form 5500, is sent to the Internal Revenue Service and also is filed with the Department of Labor. Plans that do not file, or those that file late, are subject to financial penalties.

Plans subject to the annual report requirement also must file a Schedule A as part of Form 5500. In many cases, the insurance information needed to complete Schedule A is provided and certified by the insurance company.

Summary Annual Report (SAR)

Plans that are required to file an annual report also must prepare and distribute a summary annual report to plan participants. The report, which must follow a format prescribed by the Department of Labor, summarizes the financial information in the annual report. The plan administrator must give each plan participant a copy of the summary annual report within two months after Form 5500 is filed.

■ Summary

The administrative services needed for maintaining medical expense insurance policies involve numerous specialized procedures, ranging from gathering and storing accurate information about all group and individual accounts to collecting overdue premiums. The procedures differ for group and individual policies, and for the multigroup purchasers, such as trade and professional organizations, Taft-Hartley health and welfare plans, and multiple employer trusts. Policy administration is an ongoing process for insurers, and it requires prompt, accurate, and professional service to all customers. Welfare plans under ERISA and plans with third-party administrators and administrative services only have special administrative needs.

■ Key Terms

Accounting statement
Administration manual
Administrative services
 only (ASO)
Audit
Automated voice
 response system
 (AVRS)
Case
Code of Ethical
 Practices
Continuing
 administration
Customer service
Customer service
 representative

Digital imaging
 (document scanning)
Electronic record
Eligibility
Employee information
Employee Retirement
 Income Security Act
 (ERISA)
Group information
Insurer-administered
Microfilm/microfiche
Multiple employer trust
 (MET)
Negotiated trusteeship
New insurance
 account

Overdue premium
 collection
Paper file
Plan administrator
Policyholder
Professional association
Recordkeeping
Reserve fund
Self-administered plan
Service record
Taft-Hartley health and
 welfare trust plan
Third-party administrator
 (TPA)
Trade association
Welcome letter

Chapter 8

MEDICAL EXPENSE CLAIM ADMINISTRATION

157 *Introduction*
157 *Administrative Claim Procedures*
162 *Claim Processing and Application of Specific Policy Provisions*
180 *Authorizations Relating to Claims and Investigations*
182 *Lawsuits and Punitive Damages*
184 *Electronic Claim Processing*
187 *Summary*
188 *Key Terms*

■ Introduction

The primary function of claim administration of medical expense insurance is to provide benefits for all valid claims. To do so, the claim department is involved in numerous activities, including:

- determining eligibility;
- categorizing claims by procedure and diagnosis in order to correctly adjudicate benefits;
- applying plan provisions, such as deductibles, coinsurance, benefit maximums, schedule or plan limits, and coordination of benefits;
- obtaining authorizations to release information; and
- complying with assignments of benefits.

This chapter discusses the basic procedures by which medical expense claims are submitted and how they are processed by insurance companies.

■ Administrative Claim Procedures

Medical expense insurers have many approaches to administering the claim function. The submission of claims and administrative organization, including the use of third-party administrators (TPA) and claim services only (CSO) for group policyholders, are discussed here.

Submission of Claims

Claims usually are submitted directly by the insured. In some cases, group policyholders submit claims on behalf of their insured employees.

Direct Submission

Under the direct or certification method of submitting medical expense insurance claims, the insured is provided with claim forms and instructions on how to submit claims, and he or she sends the claim directly to the insurance company. The insurer maintains all the coverage data on insured individuals and verifies coverage at the time the claims are submitted. The insurer then makes payment of the claim directly to the insured or, if benefits are assigned, to the provider.

The direct submission of claims was developed to ease the administrative burden on the policyholder, to streamline the claim payment process, and to protect personal and medical information. It also places the insurance company in a more competitive position with service-type organizations and prepayment plans, such as health maintenance organizations (HMOs), which relieve the policyholder of the responsibility of verifying eligibility information each time a member needs health care.

For group insurance, the policyholder provides eligibility information to the insurance company on a periodic basis. Whether group or individual insurance, the data indicate a person's eligibility for coverage and the duration of that eligibility. The insurance company uses this information to determine whether a person was eligible for coverage at the time a claim was incurred. Eligibility information also is used to determine appropriate plan limits for making benefit determinations for covered individuals.

There are two ways for insureds to directly submit their claims to the insurer: the claim-kit approach and the card-only approach.

Claim-kit approach. Under the typical claim-kit approach, each insured is provided with a claim kit that includes claim forms requiring completion only by the insured and provider. The claim kit contains instructions on how to complete the form and submit the claim. For group insurance, the policyholder has no responsibility for claim form completion.

Card-only approach. Under this approach, each insured is provided with a card that identifies him or her as the insured for the benefits summarized on the card. The card, which may indicate that benefits can be paid directly to the provider by the insurer, is accepted by providers as assurance that benefits are available. No claim forms are required, and the provider of medical care submits bills directly to the insurer with sufficient identification, itemization, and other information necessary to permit payment.

Problems may arise when a patient receives services for a procedure not covered under the policy, or when some or all of his or her benefits have been depleted by earlier claims. In spite of these problems, the card-only approach is attractive to individual insureds and group policyholders because most paperwork is eliminated. The administration of card plans costs more for insurers, however, because elaborate control procedures are required to track eligibility.

Policyholder Submission

Policyholder submission is an old form of claim administration that is still in use by some groups. Under this arrangement, the policyholder provides claimants with claim forms and claimants submit claims to the policyholder. The policyholder reviews claims for completeness, certifies eligibility, and forwards the claims to the insurer.

Administrative Organization

The claim function may be conducted exclusively from the insurer's home office or regional office, as well as through field claim offices. Furthermore, it can be managed by a third-party administrator (TPA) or an insurance company providing claim services only (CSO). (For more information on TPAs and CSO, see Chapter 7: Medical Expense Policy Administration.)

Home Office Claim Administration

Home office claim administration typically refers to insurers that have a centralized claim payment operation. This type of administration may involve separate claim departments for each product line or a single claim department. The advantage of home office claim administration is the ease of communication within the claim department, such as notification of changes in administrative handling or training, and the ease of communication with other home office resources, such as attorneys and doctors.

Field Office Claim Administration

Claim administration in a field office uses essentially the same claim processing methods as home office administration. However, because of shortened lines of communication between the field office and the policyholder or insured, there

MEDICAL EXPENSE INSURANCE

is usually greater opportunity for personalized service than when all claims are handled in the home office.

Insurance companies that offer decentralized claim service maintain that it is preferable to the home office, centralized approach because:

- Policyholders or insureds receive faster claim service when it is provided by a field claim office in the same or in a nearby community.
- Many policyholders or insureds prefer local payment of claims and do not wish to deal with a remote home office.
- Field claim offices may have better opportunities than the home office to identify and control abuses in their own service areas.
- The proximity of the field claim office to providers of medical care permits prompt resolution of disputed claims.

Third-Party Administration

Another method of claim administration is claim processing by a third-party administrator (TPA). Most commonly, third parties are used by union welfare plans, multiple employer groups, association groups, and other plan sponsors that self-fund medical expense benefits. Small insurance companies may use third-party administrators to process their claims. In those cases, the third party is given a supply of drafts and the authority to pay claims with insurance company funds.

Essential Features. The essential features of third-party administration of an insured plan are as follows:

- The administrator is selected by the group policyholder and approved by the insurance company.
- The administrator normally is compensated for services by the policyholder, but occasionally arrangements are made for the expenses or charges to be paid by the insurance company.
- A signed agreement between the parties stating the functions and extent of authority of the administrator protects the policyholder and insurer against the misuse of funds.

There are a number of professional administrative firms that specialize in administering claims for insurance companies. These firms, similar to the field claim office of an insurance company, typically have a large number of employees who work full-time in a claim paying function. Some agents and brokers act as third-party administrators but on a much smaller scale.

When a self-funded group uses a third-party administrator, the essential features are similar.

- The plan sponsor selects the administrator.
- The contract between the plan sponsor and the administrator states how the claim payments will be funded and how the administrator will be compensated, and it delineates the responsibilities between the administrator and the plan sponsor.

Advantages of TPAs. There are several valid reasons for group policyholders to contract with third-party administrators.

- They often are less expensive than insurers because they have lower administrative fees.
- They often are more flexible than insurers in meeting employer needs.
- If an insurance company does not have a local claim office, a third-party administrator can make it possible to provide local claim service for the policyholder (where the volume is sufficient).

Disadvantages of TPAs. There are, however, several disadvantages of third-party administration.

- Most professional administrators use their own claim adjudication systems, which may not be directly compatible with that of the insurance company.
- Administrators may have or develop their own interpretations of policy provisions and administrative practices rather than follow those prescribed by the insurance company; for example, whether or not treatment is medically necessary might be decided differently by a TPA and an insurance company.
- The addition of a third party may add to the overall cost of the group insurance plan, which may affect persistency of the coverage since premium rates may increase.
- Third-party administrators may not have as many resources as insurers (medical consultants, legal advisers, claim consultants, and so forth).

Claim Services Only (CSO)

Most large groups are self-funded. A relatively small number of self-funded groups choose to self-administer their claims. Many self-funded groups choose to use third-party administrators. Many others contract with insurers or Blue Cross/Blue Shield plans for claim services only (CSO). These arrangements also are called administrative services only (ASO). Some organizations draw a distinction between ASO and CSO, with ASO including additional services, such as underwriting and preparing summary plan descriptions.

Claim Processing and Application of Specific Policy Provisions

Claim processing involves the application of specific or pertinent features associated with each claimant's policy. These include deductibles, coinsurance, maximum benefits, codes used in claim processing, the payment of only reasonable and customary charges, coordination of benefits, and pre-existing condition exclusions.

Deductible

The deductible is the amount of covered or eligible expense the insured must incur before the plan or policy provides benefits. The purpose of the deductible is to eliminate the claim payments and the settlement expenses associated with a great number of small losses, thus resulting in lower premiums. Individual deductibles—all cause, per cause, corridor, integrated, and variable or sliding—are addressed in Chapter 1: Group Major Medical Expense Insurance. This chapter provides detailed information on family deductibles.

A family deductible limits the total amount of deductible applied to an entire family during a calendar year. The family deductible is typically expressed as:

- the number of complete deductibles to be taken per family, usually three or two regardless of the total number of dependents; or
- the amount of deductible applied during a calendar year per family, usually not to exceed three or two times the individual deductible per person.

Number of Deductibles per Family

If the family deductible is expressed as two or three deductibles per family, the claim handling procedure generally is as follows:

- Apply submitted expenses to the per person deductible until all three (or two) individual deductibles have been satisfied, thus satisfying the family deductible. Once the family deductible has been satisfied, no additional deductibles apply to other family members for that benefit period (typically, a calendar year).
- Identify the expense that satisfied the third (or second) family member's deductible. The date that this expense was incurred is the date that the family deductible was satisfied.
- Examine or review the claims on all family members whose individual deductibles have not been satisfied. Those expenses already applied to their

individual deductible, which were incurred prior to the date the family deductible was satisfied, are still subject to the individual deductible. Expenses incurred on or after the date the family deductible was satisfied are not subject to the deductible. The insurer reconsiders these expenses and provides benefits accordingly.

Future bills are handled as follows:

- Check the incurred dates of expenses submitted to determine whether the family deductible would have been satisfied on an earlier date. If that is the case, determine the new incurred date of the family deductible and adjust other family members' claims as necessary.
- Do not apply any deductible to expenses incurred after the date the family deductible was satisfied, regardless of which family member filed the claim. Provide benefits accordingly.

Amount of Deductible per Year

- Apply the individual deductibles until the total of all deductibles in the family reaches three (or two) times the per claimant amount.

If the family deductible is expressed in this manner, it can be satisfied whether or not any single family member has satisfied his or her individual deductible. As there is no need to recalculate claims when expenses are submitted out of date order, this approach is much simpler than the three (or two) deductible approach. Most computer systems are programmed for the amount and not the number of deductibles.

Example

A policy has four covered members (i.e., insured, spouse, and two dependent children), an individual deductible of $200, and a family deductible of two individual deductibles. The husband and wife have claims that satisfy their individual deductibles on April 30 and May 31, respectively. Thus, the family deductible is satisfied on May 31. If claims for a dependent child had incurred dates in June, benefits would be provided without applying an individual deductible because the family deductible would be satisfied. If the other dependent child incurred medical services in March, and these were not submitted until later, the deductible would be applied. If these claims were sufficient to satisfy that dependent's deductible, the family deductible would have been satisfied on April 30 (husband and dependent child) instead of May 31, and the wife's claims would be recalculated, without a deductible being applied. If the family deductible was $400 instead of two deductibles, the dependent child's March claims would be considered without taking the deductible. No recalculation would be necessary.

Coinsurance

Major medical expense plans require that the insured bear a percentage (usually 20 percent) of the covered expenses in excess of the deductible. This is termed coinsurance because the insured coinsures the cost of his or her health care. Although traditional indemnity plans provide that the plan will pay a flat percentage (usually 80 percent) of covered expenses, there are numerous variations.

For example, preferred provider organizations (PPOs) and point-of-service (POS) plans reimburse covered expenses at a higher percentage if a patient uses a provider in the network rather than an out-of-network provider. Starting from a base of 80 percent, some plans provide an incentive to use network providers by paying 100 percent for network providers and 80 percent for out-of-network providers. Other plans impose a penalty for not using a network provider, paying 80 percent for network providers and 60 percent for out-of-network providers. Still other plans split the difference, paying 90 percent in-network and 70 percent out-of-network. There are many other variations.

Maximum Benefit

The aggregate all-cause maximum benefit is a feature that distinguishes major medical expense plans from basic hospital-surgical plans. Hospital-surgical plans provide fixed amounts (scheduled benefits) for a fixed number of days (during any one illness) for hospital room and board and for physician calls, and scheduled amounts for each surgical procedure. There is no overall aggregate policy limit. Major medical expense plans, on the other hand, have relatively few internal limits; rather, an aggregate limit is placed on all expenses payable by the plan.

The benefit maximum indicated in the schedule of benefits of major medical expense plans has the following features:

- The benefit maximum applies individually to *each person* covered under the plan.
- It is a lifetime limit (the maximum amount payable during the entire period that each person is covered under the plan).
- It is an aggregate, all-cause limit that applies to all covered expenses, regardless of cause, during a covered person's lifetime, unlike per cause and basic hospital-surgical plans.

In addition, many major medical expense plans include calendar year maximums for certain classes of expense, such as home health care services. In such cases, both maximums apply to each covered person. Most plans have included a lifetime and calendar year maximum for mental and nervous disorders. The Health Insurance Portability and Accountability Act of 1996 mandates that for plan years beginning in 1998, groups of more than 50 persons cannot have lifetime or calendar year limits for mental health treatment that differ from any all-cause lifetime or calendar year limits under the plan.

In plans that have per cause maximums, separate deductibles and separate maximums apply to all periods of illness due to the same cause. Some insurers provide that the total benefit payable for any one illness may not exceed the maximum benefit amount.

For example, if a plan has a $1 million lifetime major medical maximum, then once the plan has paid that amount for one individual, no more benefits would be payable. Benefits would still be payable for other family members. If, however, a plan has a per cause maximum of $50,000, then once it paid that amount for any given condition (e.g., heart disease), no more benefits would be payable for that condition. However, if the patient developed another condition (e.g., cancer), up to $50,000 would be payable for cancer (and each additional condition).

Codes Used in Claim Processing

Today's computerized claim systems are driven to a large extent by procedure and diagnosis codes. When the claim examiner enters the procedure code, the system, based on the company's use of reasonable and customary (R&C) charge data, determines the reimbursement level, taking into account the appropriate deductible and coinsurance. Diagnosis codes can be used to determine if certain limits apply, such as limits on substance abuse treatment.

Physicians' Current Procedural Terminology (CPT)

Physicians' Current Procedural Terminology is a listing of descriptive and identifying codes for reporting medical services and procedures performed by physicians (Table 8.1). It is published annually by the American Medical Association.

CPT assigns a five-digit code to each procedure or service. CPT codes generally are based on current medical practice being performed by many physicians in many locations. Using CPT codes simplifies the identification and description of services rendered to patients. CPT is also used by insurers for administrative management purposes in claims processing. Insurers accumulate charges for

Table 8.1

Current Procedural Terminology (CPT) Codes

Category	Code range
Anesthesiology	00100 to 01999, 99100 to 99140
Surgery	10040 to 69979
Radiology (including nuclear medicine and diagnostic ultrasound)	70010 to 79999
Pathology and laboratory	80002 to 89399
Medicine (except anesthesiology)	90701 to 99199
Evaluation and management	99201 to 99499

physicians' services by CPT code to build data upon which R&C allowances can be based.

Each section of the CPT contains guidelines, details about subsections, and modifiers to be used with the codes in that section. Modifiers are important because they add information to the description of the primary service and may affect the benefit amount that an insurer will allow for the service. For example, there is only one code for a specific surgery, yet a modifier may be added to indicate that multiple procedures were performed at the same operative session, or that a procedure was performed bilaterally, or certain techniques used. These indicators may signal adjustments to an insurer's reimbursement allowance for the service.

As an example, the CPT code to describe someone with abdominal pain seeing his or her primary care physician would be 99214. The doctor might also order a urinalysis, which would be billed using procedure code 81000. If the patient winds up having a routine appendectomy, the surgeon would bill using procedure code 44950, and if a hernia repair was performed at the same operative session, the surgeon would bill using 49505-51.

International Classification of Diseases (ICD)

The *International Classification of Diseases, 9th Revision, Clinical Modification: ICD-9-CM* is a standardized listing of diseases and of surgical, diagnostic, and therapeutic procedures. Published by the Health Care Financing Administration, it is designed for the classification of morbidity and mortality information for statistical purposes, and for the indexing of hospital records by disease and procedures for data storage and retrieval.

Table 8.2

International Classification of Diseases (ICD) Codes by Disease

The following are disease codes listed in Volume I.

Codes	Category
(001-139)	Infectious and parasitic diseases
(140-239)	Neoplasms
(240-279)	Endocrine, nutritional, and metabolic diseases and immunity disorders
(280-289)	Diseases of the blood and blood-forming organs
(290-319)	Mental disorders
(320-389)	Diseases of the nervous system and sense organs
(390-459)	Diseases of the circulatory system
(460-519)	Diseases of the respiratory system
(520-579)	Diseases of the digestive system
(580-629)	Diseases of the genitourinary system
(630-679)	Complications of pregnancy, childbirth, and the puerperium
(680-709)	Diseases of the skin and subcutaneous tissue
(710-739)	Diseases of the musculoskeletal system and connective tissue
(740-759)	Congenital anomalies
(760-779)	Certain conditions originating in the perinatal period
(780-799)	Symptoms, signs, and ill-defined conditions
(800-949)	Injury and poisoning

The ICD-9-CM is a three-volume publication, organized as follows:

- Volume I: Diseases: Tabular List (Table 8.2) (in three-digit codes plus one or two digits following a decimal, with the exception of V codes (Table 8.3) and E codes (Table 8.4), which are two digits plus one or two digits after the decimal).
- Volume II: Diseases: Alphabetical Index
- Volume III: Procedures: Tabular List and Alphabetical Index (surgical, diagnostic, and therapeutic procedures in two-digit codes plus one or two digits after the decimal).

Volumes I and II contain the same information, but in Volume I the diseases are listed numerically and in Volume II they are listed alphabetically. Volume III includes both the numerical and alphabetical listings of procedures.

Depending upon the requirements of the insurer, claim examiners are expected to enter at least the first three digits of at least the primary diagnosis code for each claim, with some administrators requiring all five digits for up to three

MEDICAL EXPENSE INSURANCE

Table 8.3

International Classification of Diseases (ICD) Codes by Health Status and Health Service Use

The following codes (called V codes) appear in the back of Volume I. They are a supplementary classification of factors influencing health status and contact with health services.

Code	Subject
(V01-V06)	Persons with potential health hazards related to communicable diseases
(V07-V09)	Persons with potential health hazards that require isolation and/or prophylactic measures
(V10-V19)	Persons with potential health hazards related to personal and family history
(V20-V28)	Persons encountering health services in circumstances related to reproduction and development
(V30-V39)	Live-born infants according to type of birth
(V40-V49)	Persons with a condition influencing their health status
(V50-V59)	Persons encountering health services for specific procedures and aftercare
(V60-V68)	Persons encountering health services in other circumstances
(V70-V82)	Persons without reported diagnoses encountered during examination and investigation of individuals and populations

diagnosis codes. In some cases the diagnosis code determines the level of benefits payable; in others it is recorded for statistical purposes only. Some computer systems screen all claims to make sure the patient's age and sex and the procedure code are consistent with the diagnosis code.

The ICD procedure codes are used on hospital bills. Many non-Medicare claim administrators also use these codes in their systems.

Reasonable and Customary Charges

Most definitions of covered expenses include a statement to the effect that they are subject to a reasonable and customary (R&C) charge limit. Those terms are typically defined as follows:

- *customary:* Within the range of *usual fees* (those regularly charged by an individual provider for a given service) charged by physicians of similar training and experience for the same service within a given limited geographic area.
- *reasonable:* A fee that has met the above criteria or is justifiable considering the special circumstances of the particular case involved.

Table 8.4

International Classification of Diseases (ICD) Codes by External Causes of Injury and Poisoning

The following codes (called E codes) appear at the back of Volume I. They are a supplementary classification of external causes of injury and poisoning.

Code	Subject
(E800-E807)	Railway accidents
(E810-E819)	Motor vehicle traffic accidents
(E820-E825)	Motor vehicle nontraffic accidents
(E826-E829)	Other road vehicle accidents
(E830-E838)	Water traffic accidents
(E840-E845)	Air and space transport accidents
(E846-E848)	Vehicle accidents not elsewhere classifiable
(E850-E858)	Accidental poisoning by drugs, medicinal substances, and biologicals
(E860-E869)	Accidental poisoning by other solid and liquid substances, gases, and vapors
(E878-E879)	Surgical and medical procedures as the cause of abnormal reaction of patient or later complication
(E880-E888)	Accidental falls
(E890-E899)	Accidents caused by fire and flames
(E900-E909)	Accidents due to natural and environmental factors
(E910-E915)	Accidents caused by submersion, suffocation, and foreign bodies
(E916-E928)	Other accidents
(E929)	Late effects of accidental injury
(E930-E949)	Drugs, medicinal and biological substances causing adverse effects in therapeutic use
(E950-E959)	Suicide and self-inflicted injury
(E960-E969)	Homicide and injury purposely inflicted by other persons
(E970-E978)	Legal intervention
(E980-E989)	Injury undetermined whether accidentally or purposely inflicted
(E990-E999)	Injury resulting from operations of war

Charges Subject to This Provision

Initially, reasonable and customary charge limits were applied only to surgical charges, including those for assistant surgeons and anesthesiologists. R&C charge limits are now used for many other services, including medical treatment, radiology and pathology, dental work, and medical equipment, drugs, and supplies.

The reasonable and customary charge limit may be used on plans with scheduled coverages. On such plans, the lesser of the reasonable and customary or scheduled amount is paid.

Sources of Data

On unscheduled (open-end) plans, the reasonable and customary allowances or charge limits are determined through the use of one or more sources of data

MEDICAL EXPENSE INSURANCE

either singly or in combination. As a result, the determination of reasonable and customary charge limits is not uniform among health plans. (See *Fundamentals of Health Insurance, Part B*, Chapter 3: Claim Administration.)

The sources of such data can be the sponsor or administrator of the plan, such as an employer, insurer, or other claim paying organization. These organizations in turn may have produced the data internally, if they have sufficient information, or purchased the data from external sources. Regardless of the data's source, its purpose is to *fairly represent* and be *consistent* with amounts charged by similar health care providers for identical or similar procedures, usually in a specific geographic area. From these amounts a reasonable and customary charge limit is determined by the user of the database.

In general, there are two different methods for generating a representative array of charges by procedure and by area. One is by producing a true statistical array of actual billed charges from recent claim records; the other is by modeling expected charge amounts using conversion factors and relative value units for each procedure.

For example, the HIAA operates a program known as the Prevailing Healthcare Charges System (PHCS), which relies heavily on the array approach. Billed charge data is obtained every six months from over 100 major claim paying organizations around the country, including insurance companies, third-party administrators, Blue Cross and Blue Shield plans, Delta dental plans, and self-insured groups. The data are collected, processed, and reported on the basis of four elements:

- procedure code,
- zip code area,
- date of service, and
- billed charge amount.

The charge data are compiled into mean charge, mode charge, and charges at eight different percentile levels producing a display similar to that shown in Table 8.5. The data displayed allow the users to make their own best use of the information, including the determination of reasonable and customary charge limitations.

The PHCS program also models expected charges, known as derived charges, using conversion factors and relative units where actual charge data are unavailable because the procedures are new or infrequently reported.

Relative values are intended to reflect differences—such as time, skill, severity of illness, risk to patient, and risk to physician—in procedures and services.

Table 8.5

H.I.A.A. - SURGICAL PREVAILING HEALTHCARE CHARGES SYSTEM 03/01/96 - 02/28/97

AREA - XXX

PROCEDURE	NAME	NUMBER OF CHARGES	MEAN CHARGE	MODE CHARGE	50	60	70	PERCENTILES 75	80	85	90	95
49505	REP HERNIA INGUINAL 5 YRS & UP	908	1167	1000	1199	1200	1250	1460	1500	1500	1600	1799
49507	REP HERNIA INGUIN 5 YRS & UP-INCARC	44	1426	1800*	1500	1600	1700	1800	1800	1952	1975	2000
49520	REP HERNIA INGUINAL RECURRENT	97	1321	1500	1400	1500	1500	1500	1595	1680	1800	2000
49521	REP HERNIA INGUIN RECURRENT-INCARC	11	1632	2500*	1600	1700	1960	1960	1960	2500	2500	2500
49525	REP HERNIA INGUINAL SLIDING	27	1308	1200	1200	1470	1500	1680	1800	1800	2000	2500
49550	REP HERNIA FEMORAL ANY AGE	19	1217	1540*	1200	1500	1500	1540	1540	1584	2000	2500
49560	REP HERNIA INCISIONAL INITIAL	180	1503	1500	1500	1500	1670	1800	1828	1828	2123	2200
49561	REP HERNIA INCISIONAL-INCARCERATED	37	1541	1800	1700	1788	1800	1800	1800	2000	2000	2240
49565	REP HERNIA INCISIONAL RECURRENT	32	1541	1500*	1500	1700	1800	1960	2000	2116	2116	2371
49566	REP HERNIA INCISIONAL RECUR-INCAR	12	1645	1500	1500	1850	1980	1980	2000	2000	2000	2754
49568	REP HERNIA INCISION/IMPLANT MESH	149	560	500	500	500	675	700	750	750	800	800
49570	REP HERNIA EPIGASTRIC SIMPLE	29	1063	1418*	1150	1200	1238	1418	1418	1418	1418	1500
49572	REP HERNIA EPIGASTRIC-INCARCERATED	11	1244	1766*	1320	1500	1500	1600	1600	1766	1766	1766
UN 49580	REP HERNIA UMBILICAL < AGE 5	28	1167	1216	1216	1216	1216	1250	1250	1250	1250	1250
49582	REP HERNIA UMBILICAL < AGE 5-INCARC	6	1168	1551*	615	615	1176	1500	1551	1551	1551	1766
49585	REP HERNIA UMBILICAL > AGE 5	148	1100	1000	1000	1160	1250	1470	1500	1500	1700	1800
UN 49587	REP HERNIA UMBILICAL > AGE 5-INCARC	54	1128	1100	1100	1200	1300	1320	1400	1470	1500	1600
UN 49590	REP HERNIA SPIGELIAN	8	1386	1943*	1000	1100	1100	1100	1500	1500	1943	1943
UN 49905	OMENTAL FLAP	6	1210	1540*	500	1177	1250	1250	1540	1540		
		35820	137.6		139.0	144.7	150.9	155.9	162.3	168.7	179.4	193.2
CF	40490-49999 DIGESTIVE SYSTEM											
50020	DRAIN ABSCESS RENAL/PERIRENAL	12	1098	850	850	850	900	900	992	1080	1080	3400
50080	NEPHROSTOLITHOTOMY PERCUT LESS 2 CM	9	2804	3050	2800	3050	3050	3050	3050	3050	3050	3050
50200	BIOPSY RENAL NEEDLE/TROCAR	132	475	656	480	492	523	550	552	635	656	656
50220	NEPHRECTOMY W PART URETERECTOMY	38	2545	2500	2500	2500	2900	3040	3195	3300	3300	3641
50230	NEPHRECTOMY RAD W PART URETERECT	29	3602	4000	4000	4000	4000	4494	4500	4500	4530	5280
50234	NEPHRECTOMY W URETERECT SAME INCIS	10	3530	4530	3600	3600	4530	4530	4530	4530	4530	5755
50240	NEPHRECTOMY PARTIAL	19	3435	2500	3100	3800	4150	4275	4557	4557	4537	5537
50320	NEPHRECTOMY LIVE DONOR	11	4006	5834	3570	3720	4800	5834	5834	5834	5834	5834
50360	TRANSPLANT RENAL ALLOGRAFT	28	6086	5520	5520	7187	7250	7250	7250	7250	7557	8116
50365	TRANSPLANT RENAL W NEPHRECTOMY	16	5200	5200	5200	5200	5200	5200	5200	5200	5200	5200
50390	ASPIRATE/INJECT RENAL CYST NEEDLE	43	461	571	555	566	566	571	571	571	571	740
50392	INSERT CATH RENAL PELVIS	46	593	485	551	600	600	722	722	736	736	740
50393	INSERT CATH URETER	28	657	800	618	618	800	800	853	870	876	1007
50394	INJECT FOR PYELOGRAPHY	127	144	153	150	150	153	153	153	153	153	153
50395	INTRODUCE GUIDE RENAL/URETER	41	668	509	566	700	779	809	938	965	976	986
50398	CHANGE TUBE NEPHROSTOMY/PYELOSTOMY	63	150	63	207	207	207	207	209	227	227	227
UN 50400	PYELOPLASTY (FOLEY Y) SIMPLE	8	2817	3750	1273	2015	2500	2500	3000	3750	3750	3750
50405	PYELOPLASTY COMPLICATED	15	4490	5260	5260	5260	5260	5260	5260	5260	5260	5260
50590	LITHOTRIPSY EXTRACORP SHOCK WAVE	345	2224	2100	2100	2100	2500	2646	2646	3000	3000	3025
50684	INJECT FOR URETEROGRAPHY	25	130	150	150	150	150	175	175	150	150	150
50688	CHANGE URETEROSTOMY TUBE	13	175	175	175	175	175	175	175	175	175	175
50690	INJECT FOR URETEROPYELOG/ILIAL COND	21	102	93	93	93	93	100	100	130	142	164
50715	URETEROLYSIS	11	2061	2000	2000	2000	2400	2400	2400	2435	2435	2435
UN 50740	URETEROPYELOSTOMY	5	3380	3300	3300	3300	3300	3500	3500			

COPYRIGHT HEALTH INSURANCE ASSOCIATION OF AMERICA 1975, 1997
(CPT ONLY COPYRIGHT 1983, 1996 AMERICAN MEDICAL ASSOCIATION)

AREA - XXX - XXX & AREAS (XXX,XXX)

PAGE 171

MEDICAL EXPENSE INSURANCE

Two examples of relative value listings by procedure codes are published in *Relative Values for Physicians* and the Resource Based Relative Value Scale (RBRVS), which is used by Medicare.

Conversion factors are simply the dollar amount per unit of relative value. They are calculated by dividing available, actual charge data for a procedure by the number of relative units associated with that procedure. Derived charges can then be calculated for an unavailable procedure by multiplying (1) the procedure's relative value by (2) the conversion factors of the procedure code section into which the procedure falls. Other vendors use various alternative modeling approaches to create their charge displays.

Rebuttal Actions

If a patient or physician is not satisfied with the determination of what is regular and customary, the claim office should request and evaluate any additional information that may be pertinent. Typically, an operative report would provide the appropriate information about a surgical procedure. A physician's narrative report may also be useful in supporting a specific fee for a given service. Group plans are subject to the appeal provisions of the Employee Retirement Income Security Act (ERISA). Some state insurance laws specify appeal procedures as well.

Coordination of Benefits

Coordination of benefits (COB) is a process by which two or more insurers, insuring the same person for the same or similar health insurance benefits, limit the total benefits to an amount not exceeding the actual amount of allowable health care expenses incurred.

For example, consider a person who is covered by two group health care plans for identical group medical care expense benefits and who incurs $1,000 of covered medical care expenses. Conceivably, as much as $2,000 in benefits could be collected, unless there is a COB provision in at least one of the policies. The idea behind COB is to limit the total benefits an insured can collect under both plans to not more than 100 percent of allowable expenses ($1,000 in this example). Therefore, the insured is prevented from making a profit on health insurance claims.

COB is primarily used in group insurance contracts but is also seen in some individual policies. Individual plans have comparable language to COB (e.g., variable deductible). It is necessary to review policy specifics to ensure correct claim determination. This section covers group COB.

Order of Benefit Determination (OBD)

Under COB, the first point to be determined is which plan is primary. This process may vary from state to state. Using the NAIC Model Regulation, if only one plan has a COB provision, the plan without the COB provision pays its benefits first and the plan with a COB provision coordinates its benefits with the benefits paid by the other plan.

When both plans have a COB provision, the order of benefit determination is generally as follows.

- *Nondependent/Dependent*

    The benefits of the plan that covers the person as an employee, member, or subscriber (that is, other than as a dependent) are determined before those of the plan that covers the person as a dependent.

- *Dependent Child/Parents Not Separated or Divorced*

    - The benefits of the plan of the parent whose birthday falls earlier in a year are determined before those of the plan of the parent whose birthday falls later in that year.
    - If both parents have the same birthday, the benefits of the plan that covered one parent longer are determined before those of the plan that covered the other parent for a shorter period of time.
    - However, if the other plan does not have the rule described above, but instead has a rule based upon the gender of the parent, and if, as a result, the plans do not agree on the order of benefits, the rule based on gender will determine the order of benefits.

- *Dependent Child/Parents Separated or Divorced*

    If two or more plans cover a person as a dependent child of separated or divorced parents, benefits for the child are determined in this order: first, the plan of the parent with custody of the child; then, the plan of the spouse (if any) of the parent with custody of the child; and finally, the plan of the parent not having custody of the child.

However, if the specific terms of a court decree state that one of the parents is responsible for the health care expenses of the child, and the entity obligated to pay or provide the benefits of the plan of that parent has actual knowledge of those terms, the benefits of that plan are determined first. The plan of the other parent is the secondary plan.

If the specific terms of a court decree state that the parents share joint custody, without stating that one of the parents is responsible for the health care expenses of the child, the plans covering the child follow the order of benefit determination rules for dependent child/parents not separated or divorced.

Active/inactive employee. The benefits of a plan that covers a person as an employee (or as that employee's dependent) who is neither laid off nor retired are determined before those of a plan that covers that person as a laid-off or retired employee (or as that employee's dependent). If the other plan does not have this rule, and if, as a result, the plans do not agree on the order of benefits, this rule is ignored.

Continuation coverage. The benefits of a plan that covers a person as other than a continuee are determined before those of a plan that covers that person as a Consolidated Omnibus Budget Reconciliation Act (COBRA) continuee or continuee under state law.

Longer/shorter length of coverage. If none of the above rules determines the order of benefits, the benefits of the plan that covered an employee, member, or subscriber longer are determined before those of the plan that covered that person for the shorter term.

Administration of COB

Before the provision can be used, it is necessary to determine whether other coverage exists and precisely what benefits are payable. It is almost impossible to secure this information without the cooperation of group policyholders, insureds, providers of health care, and other insurers. The importance of public support and understanding in the administration of COB provisions cannot be overemphasized

Sources of multiple coverage information. The insured is the primary source of information about other health insurance plans under which the insured or a dependent is covered. The group policyholder also can provide the insurance company with much valuable information. Questions concerning other health insurance are directed to the insured and to the policyholder on most insurers' claim forms. Physicians' (HCFA 1500) and hospitals' (UB-92) forms have specific fields in which the providers indicate other coverage of which they may be aware.

Processing multiple coverage claims. Generally claims are processed on the basis of answers to the questions on the claim forms as well as other indicators of duplicate coverage. For example, if the insured submits a medical expense claim for a spouse, and the claim form indicates that the spouse is employed, there is a fair chance that the spouse is covered under an employer-sponsored group plan. Another indication that duplicate coverage may exist is when the insured submits a copy of a bill, rather than the original. The matter will be pursued to determine if duplicate coverage exists. When the name of the insurer covering the spouse for group health insurance is obtained, contact will be made with that insurer. The advantages to insurance companies of freely exchanging information are obvious. The right to receive and release necessary information in accordance with the NAIC model provisions is instrumental in encouraging cooperation among insurers.

A telephone call to the local office of the other insurance company often is all that is needed to secure the necessary information for coordinating benefits. Some insurance companies may prefer to use a standard duplicate coverage inquiry (DCI) questionnaire. This form is designed to confirm the existence of other coverage, the allowable expenses covered by that contract, and the benefits that would have been payable in the absence of other group insurance coverage.

One problem that occurs is the attitude of some insureds toward the concept of nonduplication of benefits. Some insureds contest that if they pay premiums for their insurance (a contributory plan), they expect to receive full benefits from both insurers. Misunderstanding and dissatisfaction may develop, as well as attempts to conceal duplicate coverage.

Some delays in settling claims are a consequence of the growth of duplicate coverage. The need to establish the order of benefit payment and to determine the allowable expenses among the insurers requires communication between the insurers—a process that takes time. In many cases, the primary insurer can readily determine that it is primary and will pay its benefits without regard to the other coverage. However, the secondary insurer must find out what the primary insurer has paid before it can accurately determine its benefits. In order to avoid customer service issues arising out of claim delays, most insurers attempt to resolve COB issues within 30 days.

Examples of COB

Without COB provisions. Mrs. Jones has filed a claim for $2,400 with Company A and Company B. Company A insures Mrs. Jones as an employee under a plan covering 80 percent of eligible expenses after a $100 deductible is satisfied. Company B insures her as a dependent spouse under a plan providing 75 percent of eligible expenses after a $100 deductible is met. In the absence of COB, both companies would have to pay Mrs. Jones as follows:

MEDICAL EXPENSE INSURANCE

COMPANY A

Eligible expenses	$2,400
Less deductible	$ 100
	$2,300
× 80% coinsurance	.80
Benefit payable	$1,840

COMPANY B

Eligible expenses	$2,400
Less deductible	$ 100
	$2,300
× 75% coinsurance	.75
Benefit payable	$1,725

Without COB both insurers would pay their full benefits, which in this example would total $3,565. Thus, the insured would receive $1,165 more than the actual charge incurred.

With COB provisions. Using the same example, assume that both plans have a COB provision. Company A would pay first since it insures Mrs. Jones as an employee. Because Company A pays first, it calculates benefits in full, as though duplicate coverage did not exist.

In determining its benefits, Company B must take into consideration coverage provided by Company A. The NAIC COB provisions require that what is an allowable expense under any of the group policies must be treated as an allowable expense under each of the group policies. Therefore, in calculating its benefit Company B must include any expenses that would be allowable expenses under the Company A plan. Once Company A has determined and paid its benefits, Mrs. Jones's claim is then considered by Company B.

COB reimbursing at 100 percent of allowable expenses. In this case both companies would have to pay Mrs. Jones as follows:

COMPANY A

Eligible expenses	$2,400
Less deductible	$ 100
	$2,300
× 80% coinsurance	.80
Benefit payable	$1,840

COMPANY B

Eligible expenses	$2,400
Less Company A's benefit	$1,840
	$ 560

Under COB, Company B pays only $560 rather than $1,725 as in the previous example. Mrs. Jones receives $2,400. This method produces benefit savings for Company B of $1,165, which is credited to Mrs. Jones to be applied to any future claims she might have against Company B during the claim determination period. This credit can be used to provide benefits that would not otherwise have been paid. If, for example, the policy with Company A does not cover purchase of a hospital bed and the usual benefit for this item from Company B amounts to 80 percent, the previous benefit savings credited to Mrs. Jones may allow the Company B plan to pay the full cost of the hospital bed. The effect of COB in Mrs. Jones's case is that between the two insurers she received reimbursement of the full $2,400 of expenses and has a $1,165 credit with Company B that can be used for fully reimbursing other noncovered expenses in the claim period.

In the previous example, Mrs. Jones was reimbursed at 100 percent of incurred medical expenses, although she did not profit from the claim. Thus, in effect, COB eliminated the cost containment provisions built into the plan, namely, the deductible and coinsurance provisions. Concern about such outcomes led NAIC to recommend that states allow insurers to reduce benefits to a level below 100 percent of allowable expense. Below are examples of the two alternative methods of calculating COB.

Alternative 1: total allowable expenses with coinsurance. Under this method of calculating COB, the secondary plan is allowed to pay the difference between some percentage (typically the coinsurance level, 80 percent) of total allowable expenses actually incurred and the amount that was paid by the primary carrier. In the above example, both companies would have to pay Mrs. Jones as follows:

COMPANY A

Eligible expenses	$2,400
Less deductible	$ 100
	$2,300
× 80% coinsurance	.80
Benefit payable	$1,840

MEDICAL EXPENSE INSURANCE

COMPANY B

Eligible expenses	$2,400
× 80% coinsurance	.80
	$1,920
Less Company A's benefit	$1,840
Benefit payable	$ 80

Alternative 2: maintenance of benefits approach. Under this approach, the secondary plan (Company B) is allowed to pay the difference between what it would have paid if it had been primary and what the primary plan (Company A) has paid. This method is often called the nonduplication of benefits provision.

In the example involving Mrs. Jones, each company would pay as follows:

COMPANY B (Primary)

Eligible expenses	$2,400
Less deductible	$ 100
	$2,300
× 75% coinsurance	.75
Benefit payable	$1,725

COMPANY A

Eligible expenses	$2,400
Less dedudtible	$ 100
	$2,300
× 80% coinsurance	.80
Benefit payable	$1,840

Since $1,840 > $1,725, no benefits are due Mrs. Jones.

Since the payment from Company A exceeds Company B's payment, no benefit would be payable.

Pre-existing Condition Exclusions

Many major medical expense plans include pre-existing condition exclusion clauses. Under such provisions, a new enrollee's claims associated with a pre-existing medical condition are not covered under the contract or policy for a specified period of time (e.g., six months). Use of pre-existing condition exclusions discourages individuals from gaming the system by switching frequently between coverage and no coverage, or between more comprehensive and less comprehensive benefit plans, according to their need for medical services.

Typically, an insurer does not evaluate each individual for pre-existing medical conditions when he or she first becomes insured. Doing so would not be cost-effective. Only after a person has filed one or more claims will the claim administrator check the individual's application or other sources of medical information for the existence of pre-existing conditions. If such conditions are documented, payment may be denied for pre-existing-condition-related claims that originated during the pre-existing condition exclusion period specified in the individual's contract or policy.

Insurers must ensure that contract provisions dealing with pre-existing conditions conform with state law. Many states have placed limits on the maximum allowable exclusion period, the definition of pre-existing condition, or other aspects of pre-existing condition exclusions. The Health Insurance Portability and Accountability Act of 1996 (HIPAA) places new federal requirements on insurers' use of pre-existing condition exclusions in the group market. One HIPAA requirement, in particular, has significant implications for claim administration. Under HIPAA, insurers may not deny payment of claims under a pre-existing condition exclusion clause before an individual is notified in writing of the length of his or her exclusion period. (This requirement does not appear in the act itself, but is included in interim final regulations issued April 8, 1997 to implement the portability, access, and renewability provisions of HIPAA.)

As a result of this HIPAA requirement, insurers in the group market have significant new responsibilities when administering claims under contracts or policies that use pre-existing condition exclusions. Within a reasonable time of each new enrollee's enrollment date, the insurer must evaluate the person's documentation of prior coverage, if any (as provided for under HIPAA); reduce the exclusion period month-for-month for qualifying prior coverage; and notify the enrollee of the length of his or her exclusion period, regardless of whether the person has filed a claim. This process will add to the costs of administering group coverage that uses pre-existing condition exclusions.

The HIPAA does not place limits on the use of pre-existing condition exclusions in the individual market, with one exception. Insurers may place no pre-existing condition limitations on coverage issued to individuals eligible for group-to-individual portability under the act.

■ Authorizations Relating to Claims and Investigations

Two common authorizations relating to claims concern assignment of benefits and the release of information.

Assignment of Benefits

Assignment of benefits occurs when the insured authorizes the insurer to pay benefits directly to a health care provider (doctor, hospital, and so forth). In such a case, the insurer mails or electronically transfers funds directly to the medical provider. The standard forms (HCFA 1500 and UB-92) have specific fields to indicate the assignment of benefits. Most physician billing forms also contain fields that supply this information. The assignment of benefits may take a variety of forms but in most cases will be an actual signature of the patient or a statement of "assignment on file." When multiple insurers are involved, it is critical that the claim examiner clearly establish the insurer to which the assignment pertains.

Release of Information

The confidentiality of medical information is an important consideration in claim payment. There are federal and state laws regarding the release of medical information. The insured's signature block on most claim forms contains language authorizing the provider to release medical information necessary to process the claim. In the absence of such a release or in a state that has more restrictive requirements, the claim examiner needs to obtain a specific authorization, directly from the insured or patient, before requesting medical information from the provider.

Claim Investigation Principles

The International Claim Association (ICA), in recognition of the need to maintain public trust and confidence in the insurance industry, issued the following principles relating to life and health claim administration, which insurers can use as a guide for establishing company practices in the investigation of claims:

- ■ Any individual who has, or believes he or she has, a claim is entitled to courteous, fair, and just treatment and shall receive with reasonable promptness an acknowledgment of any communications with respect to the claim.

- Every claimant is entitled to prompt investigation of all facts, an objective evaluation, and the fair and equitable settlement of his or her claim as soon as liability has become reasonably clear.
- Claimants are to be treated equally and without considerations other than those dictated by the provisions of their contracts.
- Claimants shall not be compelled to institute unnecessary litigation in order to recover amounts due, nor shall the failure to settle a claim under one policy or one portion of a policy be used to influence settlement under another policy or portion of a policy.
- Recognizing the obligation to pay promptly all just claims, there is an equal obligation to protect the insurance-buying public from increased costs due to fraudulent or nonmeritorious claims.
- Procedures and practices shall be established to prevent misrepresentation of pertinent facts or policy provisions, to avoid unfair advantage by reason of superior knowledge, and to maintain accurate insurance claim records as privileged and confidential.
- Reasonable standards shall be implemented to provide for adequate personnel, systems, and procedures to service claims effectively. These standards shall be such as to eliminate unnecessary delays or requirements, overinsistence on technicalities, and excessive appraisals or examinations. Claim personnel shall be encouraged and assisted in further developing their knowledge, expertise, and professionalism in the field of claim administration.

Usually investigations are necessary because the claim information is insufficient or unclear or it raises doubts concerning whether the expense is eligible under the plan's provisions. It may be possible to clear up doubtful areas by a telephone call to the insured or attending physician. Claim examiners should expedite handling by placing the call, documenting the conversation, and adjudicating the expense.

Some investigations are required for losses that occur during the contestable period of the contract and written proof may be sought. Most misrepresentations concern the applicant's health history prior to the group's effective date or the date of the application for individual carriers. The objective of the claim investigation during the contestable period is to develop detailed information about the treatments of the insured that took place before these dates. Any physician who treated the insured and any hospital or clinic previously entered for treatment are contacted. Particular efforts are made to learn from the attending physician the dates of symptoms and/or treatment, the diagnosis made, and the date that the insured was told about the physician's findings. For both group and individual carriers, the information secured may lead to a pre-existing condition limitation being invoked, as described earlier in this chapter.

Other types of claim investigations include determining:

- whether treatment is medically necessary,
- the student status of a dependent, or
- whether fraud is being committed.

In all of the above investigations it is imperative that the examiner work quickly and thoroughly, document the actions he or she is taking, and communicate with the insured throughout the entire process. Many states require routine follow-up for necessary information in specific intervals. Phone inquiries may prompt providers to send the necessary information. Upon review of the information, the examiner will determine whether the claim is payable or not. If the result of the investigation is a denial of payment, a detailed, written explanation must be sent to the insured.

■ Lawsuits and Punitive Damages

Litigation on medical expense insurance claims has increased markedly in recent years. The increasing complexity of the business as well as a growing awareness on the part of claimants of the availability of litigation as a way to secure benefits to which they believe they are entitled have contributed to this trend.

Currently, there is an accepted principle of law that an insurance contract contains an implied covenant of good faith and fair dealing on the part of both parties. In addition, many state laws include provisions relating to unfair trade practices. In general, the burden of proof is on an insurer when a contested claim is the subject of litigation. This makes it imperative that insurers consider claims according to the policy, err in favor of the insured, and litigate only policy issues that are clearly defined.

An insurance claim lawsuit may be viewed as a three-tiered action: (1) breach of contract, (2) compensatory damages, and (3) punitive damages.

Breach of Contract

To decide whether a breach of contract has occurred, the court must determine whether the insurer wrongfully withheld benefits. The amount of damages involved is related to the amount of the claim withheld.

Compensatory Damages

To decide whether a claimant is entitled to compensatory damages, the court must determine whether the insurer acted in bad faith in unreasonably withholding benefits and whether such action, as a consequence, caused financial hardship to or inflicted emotional distress upon the claimant. The amounts involved here are generally somewhat higher than under a breach of contract and relate to the hardship or suffering incurred.

Punitive Damages

Extra-contractual damages meant to punish the insurer for intentional wrongdoing are called punitive damages. Historically in a legal action involving a health insurance policy, damages beyond the policy benefit limitations were not recoverable for a breach of contract, even though the breach by the insurer was found to be willful and fraudulent. This limit on damages was based either on statutory restrictions that say that only the amount due under a contract can be awarded to any party to the contract or on common law interpretation by the courts.

This historical limit changed in 1964 when a jury rendered a verdict against a liability insurer for punitive damages of $27,000. The award was eventually reduced to $1,500. In 1966, a punitive damages action under a health insurance policy resulted in a $500,000 award, which was later reduced to $200,000. Since 1966, punitive damages have been awarded in many cases for increasingly substantial amounts, some in the millions of dollars.

The general test used to determe whether punitive damages should be awarded requires the insured to show that the insurer's unreasonable conduct in denying benefits not only resulted in consequential damages but was done maliciously, fraudulently, oppressively, or unlawfully. The claim examiner, therefore, must clearly demonstrate and document the insurer's good faith in his or her claim handling.

The possiblity that employee benefit plans covered under Title I of ERISA, as amended, could be sued for punitive damages was substantially reduced, although not entirely eliminated, by the U.S. Supreme Court's decision in *Pilot Life Insurance Company vs. Dedeaux*. The Pilot Life decision held that state common law causes of action are preempted with respect to ERISA plans. As a result of this and other decisions, it appears that state laws that provide for punitive damages are preempted by ERISA. Employee benefit plans can be sued under ERISA itself for some other expenses, such as legal expenses, and the question of liability for compensatory and punitive damages under ERISA has not yet been resolved by the Supreme Court.

In any event, good claim handling practices will reduce an insurer's exposure to litigation, especially to punitive damages. The key consideration is that such practices be reasonable from the standpoint of the insured. Therefore, the claim administrator should:

- Acknowledge receipt of the claim as quickly as possible and explain to the claimant the reason for any anticipated delay.
- Investigate the claim promptly, carefully, and completely to obtain all the facts, especially those that support payment of the claim.
- Take actions that are consistent with the insurer's philosophy as well as with its established practices and procedures. Any omission may be reviewed as negligence.
- Fully document the claim file with factual information, refrain from including opinions, and detail all actions, including phone calls.
- Refrain from underlining or highlighting portions of the claim records. Underlining and highlighting can suggest that an insurer is biased regarding certain facts or opinions stated in the claim records.
- Make decisions based on hard facts, not assumptions, impressions, or prejudices.

Before denying a claim or terminating a benefit, claim administrators should ask:

- Have I acted reasonably, fairly, and promptly?
- Have I given the interest of the insured at least as much consideration as that of the insurer?
- Is there anything else I could do to find a possible cause for approval of the claim?

Claimants should be advised of their rights to appeal and encouraged to furnish additional evidence or information that might be beneficial in the claim for benefits. ERISA requires that appeal language accompany claim denials.

■ Electronic Claim Processing

Unlike the manual claim adjudication process of the past, claim adjudication today is typically handled by an automated system, whether "home grown" or purchased, that is housed on the insurer's main frame computer. The relevant data from the submitted claims are entered into the system. This data include social security number, policy number, patient name, diagnosis code(s), date of service, procedure code(s), and fee. The examiner is expected to review and evaluate the data and, depending on how advanced the adjudication system is, determine benefits and approve the claim accordingly. With a less-sophisticated system, the claim handling process involves more manual effort because the examiner has to perform more basic functions, such as the math calculations involved in determining benefits.

Some systems use programming logic that allows for certain edits to be performed prior to review by the examiner. The system flags any items of concern for the examiner to review. For example, the system may flag an out-dated procedure code, requesting the current CPT code before proceeding.

The efficiency of the claim adjudication system is enhanced by the manner in which claims are submitted, received, and presented to the system itself. There is an ever-increasing trend away from paper claim submittal toward electronic claim submittal, thereby eliminating many clerical tasks, such as opening, sorting, and distributing the mail. Such tasks are time-consuming and prone to quality control problems.

Electronic Data Interchange (EDI)

Electronic data interchange (EDI) is an automated computer systems process which transmits data between two computers. EDI has been used for over twenty years in industries such as banking, transportation, and financial services, but has not been used widely in the health care industry until the past few years. The data which is transmitted via EDI is usually in the form of a "business transaction" such as a purchase order or a payment for services or goods received. In the health care industry, business transactions which can be transmitted via EDI may include medical claim submissions, claim payments, eligibility for health care coverage and claim status requests. The ultimate goal of EDI in the health insurance industry is to electronically transmit all insurance transactions between providers and payers.

There are many tangible benefits from EDI. The benefits include improved claims quality from standard formats and transmissions, faster claim submission and payment, and significant administrative cost reductions. High administrative costs have been noted as a major reason for the high costs in today's health care industry. In the United States today there are approximately four billion medical claims submitted annually. It is estimated that $100 billion is spent annually to process the paper associated with medical claims and payment. If the health care industry coverts to EDI, the savings estimate from EDI will approximate between $8 billion and $20 billion per year.

MEDICAL EXPENSE INSURANCE

In 1990, HIAA conducted a survey of coding and claims systems used by insurance companies throughout the industry. In light of strides taken in the following five years—including Congress's review of the administrative costs of the industry; the creation and privatization of the Workgroup on Electronic Data Interchange (WEDI), which supplies information on EDI developments to the industry; and the American National Standards Institute (ANSI) development of data standards for many of the transactions used by the industry—HIAA again surveyed its members in 1995 to gather information on the status of the health insurance industry.

The results of the 1995 survey indicate that there has been a dramatic increase in the number of claims and the percent of total claims received electronically. Overall, companies reported receiving 24 percent of their claims electronically; 19 percent of physician claims, 24 percent of hospital claims and 36 percent of other claims (dental, lab, prescriptions, and so forth) were received in that way. By comparison, in 1990, respondents indicated that only 1 percent of physician and 2 percent of hospital claims were received electronically.

The push toward electronic data interchange became even more focused with the development of the rules of the Health Insurance Portability and Accountability Act of 1996 that address the problems created by the paper forms, telephone calls, and communication delays associated with insurance administration and the need to develop standards by which these transactions can be accomplished electronically. The industry estimates that full implementation of these provisions could save up to $9 billion per year from administrative overhead, which includes claim administration, without reducing the amount or quality of health care services.

The Secretary of Health and Human Services (HHS) must adopt standards for a variety of health insurance transactions by February 1998. The health insurance industry then has 24 months to implement the standards, with small plans (as defined by the Secretary) having 36 months to implement them.

Electronic Claim Adjudication

Electronically received claims can be efficiently presented to the insurer's claim adjudication system. Many systems have an interface between the EDI translator, which is responsible for mapping the format of the data received to a format usable to that given system, and the adjudication logic. The claim data can be received electronically, fed into the claim adjudication system electronically, passed through basic claim edits electronically, adjudicated according to the policy provisions electronically, and released electronically, with an explanation of benefits (EOB) forwarded to the insured and/or provider; in some instances, an electronic funds transfer (EFT) of benefits can be made to the appropriate party. Thus, electronic claim receipt coupled with electronic adjudication provides a hands-free environment within which claims are received and adjudicated in a timely and efficient manner.

These advances in claim handling, it should be noted, do not diminish the role of the examiner in the claim handling process. Electronic adjudication permits the simpler or low dollar claims to be handled by the system, freeing up the examiners to concentrate their efforts and apply their expertise to the more involved or complex claims. As claim adjudication systems evolve, the future claim environment will become more reliant on the system to perform the basic adjudication logic, using rules-based logic and case-based reasoning to correctly determine eligibility and benefits. The claim system also will use a relational database to manage eligibility and claim data, noting all actions involving a given insured, including claim handling and phone calls.

A benefit of a claim adjudication system of this nature is in its reporting and tracking capabilities. The auditing function is enhanced because reports can be generated to focus on any given segment of the claims data. Reviews of claim handling pertaining to a specific state, insured, diagnosis code, procedure code, and so forth can be performed without requiring intense clerical support.

■ Summary

The process of medical expense claim adjudication has evolved over time. In some situations, the process has been simplified, especially given the development of electronic claim receipt and sophisticated claim adjudication systems. However, in other circumstances, such as managed care, the claim handling function has become more involved. A given service may be considered in a variety of ways, depending on the policy provisions of a given insured. A hospital-surgical plan may provide one level of benefits, a major medical plan may provide a different level, while a PPO plan may provide yet another level of benefits. The ever-increasing complexities of medical practices as well as intricate coding schemes for diagnosis and procedure codes require that the examiner maintain a high level of expertise in medical terminology, computer literacy, and contract interpretation. In the future, the examiner can expect to concentrate on the more complex, high dollar claims. The examiner must be able to adapt to changes in the insurance industry and related industries while providing a high level of quality in a production-oriented environment.

■ Key Terms

Assignment
Authorization to release information
Auto-adjudicate
Breach of contract
Card-only approach
Claim-kit approach
Claim services only (CSO)
Coinsurance
Compensatory damages
Coordination of benefits (COB)
Current Procedural Terminology (CPT)
Deductible
Direct submission
Duplicate coverage inquiry (DCI)
Electronic data interchange (EDI)
Electronic funds transfer (EFT)
Explanation of benefits (EOB)
Field office claim administration
Home office claim administration
International Claims Association (ICA)
International Classification of Diseases (ICD)
Lifetime maximum
Maximum benefit
Order of benefits determination (OBD)
Policyholder submission
Prevailing Healthcare Charges System (PHCS)
Pre-existing condition
Punitive damages
Reasonable and customary (R&C) charges
Third-party administrator (TPA)

Chapter 9

MEDICAL EXPENSE INDUSTRY ISSUES

189 *Introduction*
190 *Regulatory Environment*
192 *Distribution Systems*
193 *Cost Trends*
196 *Medicare Reform*
197 *Summary*
198 *Key Terms*

■ Introduction

For the past 20 years the business of providing medical expense insurance has been in flux. Fundamental changes have taken place in who buys and sells insurance and in the products themselves. The following are some of the major changes that have affected the industry:

- Health care costs have risen dramatically for both insurers and insureds. Overall payments by private health insurers were $28.4 billion in 1975 and $166.8 billion in 1994. Individual insureds, meanwhile, paid $170 out-of-pocket in 1975 and $646 in 1994.[4]

- There has been a rapid and broad-based growth in self-insurance at the expense of fully-insured health coverage obtained from private insurers.

- Large corporate purchasers have joined forces to demand more accountability from their medical care suppliers.

- Managed care has taken root, bringing new approaches to benefit design, cost management, and almost every other aspect of the business.

- The number of uninsured Americans has steadily risen. Recent federal and state laws are helping to make medical expense insurance more accessible.

Looking ahead, the managed care movement faces major challenges from the medical community and the public. Mergers and acquisitions are transforming ownership and organizational alignments in the industry. Many of the Blue Cross-Blue Shield plans are barely recognizable as they turn for-profit, go public, and expand across state lines. And national for-profit medical systems are taking the market by storm.

MEDICAL EXPENSE INSURANCE

This chapter discusses several important trends that are shaping the future of the medical expense insurance industry: the regulatory environment, distribution systems, cost trends, and Medicare reform.

■ Regulatory Environment

Health insurance has long been regulated primarily at the state level. Over the years, however, federal legislation has been enacted to require nondiscrimination, continuation of coverage, and other benefits relating to health insurance. The passage of the Health Insurance Portability and Accountability Act of 1996 (HIPAA) is the most recent example of federal regulation of health insurance.

State Regulation

For more than 80 years, the National Association of Insurance Commissioners (NAIC), which is comprised of top state insurance regulators, has been developing model legislation. As a result of this work, insurance industry regulation follows the same broad outlines in every state. There are, however, substantial differences across states to accommodate state and regional variations in insurance markets and consumer expectations—for example, differences in the prevalence of network-based plans, the extent of large corporate purchaser activity, the involvement of private carriers in Medicaid, and county-level public programs.

While state regulation of insurance has advantages, it also has drawbacks. Multistate insurance carriers have long complained about the hassles and costs of regulatory compliance in a state-regulated industry. Covered benefits must be adjusted to satisfy each state's unique set of mandated benefits. This is especially onerous for large group employer plans that involve locations in many states. Small group reforms vary from state to state in permitted pre-existing condition restrictions, underwriting and rating practices, and other requirements. As more and more states have enacted small group and individual market reforms tailored to their industry and political environments, regulatory compliance has become increasingly burdensome for multistate insurance carriers. In response, some carriers have expressed a desire for uniform federal regulation.

ERISA Preemption and the Steady Erosion of State Authority

The Employee Retirement Income Security Act of 1974 (ERISA) was enacted to establish uniform federal regulation of retirement benefits to protect the pension rights of employees as they moved from one employer to another. While

ERISA specifically preserves the right of states to regulate insurance, its preemption of state regulation of employee benefit plans provides a legal mechanism for employment-related health plans to escape state insurance regulation by self-insuring. Meanwhile, ERISA contains only minimal federal standards for self-insured health coverage.

Self-insurance coverage has grown significantly, and by 1995 nearly half (46 percent) of employees with employer-sponsored health benefits were covered by self-insured plans.[5] Initially self-insurance was common only among very large groups (e.g., 500 or more employees). Over the years, however, smaller sized groups have been self-insuring, due in large part to a variety of creative financing options involving stop-loss coverage. Approximately 15 percent of firms with between 26 and 100 employees and 7 percent of firms with 25 or fewer employees offer self-insured coverage.[6]

Small business has begun to push for expanded opportunities to self-insure under ERISA through federally regulated (rather than state-regulated) multiple employer welfare arrangements (MEWAs). By doing this, small employers can avoid the cost and restrictions of state insurance regulations, just as the large employers do.

Most single-employer self-insured plans have provided very good coverage to employees and their dependents. Occasionally, however, abuses have occurred. Employers have been known to drop covered employees from their plans when they develop serious medical conditions, or reduce benefits under the plan to limit plan liability with respect to specific employees. Numerous attempts by states to regulate self-insured plans have been thwarted by the courts. These abuses, exceptions though they may be, provided a rationale for federal regulation of group health coverage.

HIPAA

The Health Insurance Portability and Accountability Act of 1996 created a new health insurance regulatory framework. The act automatically amends ERISA, establishing federal standards that apply uniformly to self-insured and insured group coverage, to be enforced on the federal level for self-insured plans and by state insurance regulators for insured plans.

The act makes provision for federal enforcement with respect to insurers only if states fail to "substantially enforce" the requirements of the act. Federal agencies and states are feeling their way in implementing this legislation, and it is too early to tell whether all states will do what is necessary to avoid federal regulation of insurance under this act.

The very existence of HIPAA, however, paves the way for additional federal legislation related to health insurance since it is much easier for Congress to amend existing federal law than to pass major new legislation. Indeed, two new federal health coverage mandates were enacted as amendments to HIPAA within months of its passage—one relating to mental health benefits and the other to a minimum level of coverage for hospital stays for childbirth. In light of the major federal health legislation of 1996, it appears that insurance carriers will have to juggle both state and federal regulatory requirements for the foreseeable future.

■ Distribution Systems

Another aspect of medical insurance that is facing change is the way insurers place their products with customers. While most medical expense insurance is provided under large employer-sponsored plans, a good deal is sold by agents and brokers to individuals and small employers. Medical insurance agents and brokers will face greater competition in making sales in the years ahead as alternative insurance distribution channels expand their reach.

Banks and Insurance

Banks are demonstrating increasing interest in selling insurance. In November 1996, the Comptroller of the Currency issued a statement endorsing the sale of insurance by banks. Some banking interests are interpreting the statement to mean that banks should be allowed to underwrite as well as place insurance sales.

Separately, HIPAA has created new insurance-related opportunities for banks—as medical savings account administrators. A number of banks have formed partnerships with insurance companies to market and administer medical savings accounts in conjunction with high deductible medical expense insurance. Medical savings accounts provide tax-favored treatment of out-of-pocket medical expenses.

Purchasing Groups

For several years, small business interests have advocated permitting small employers to join together in purchasing groups that could enjoy the same advantages that large self-insured firms enjoy by virtue of their market leverage and ERISA protection from state insurance laws. Large, self-insured health benefit plans avoid state-mandated benefit requirements, state insurance premium taxes and other carrier assessments, and limitations on experience rating imposed by small group reforms in a number of states. With their market clout they are able to negotiate significant discounts with providers.

To enable small employers to realize these advantages, small businesses lobbied for amendments to ERISA that would allow them to offer self-insured coverage through MEWAs governed by ERISA rather than state insurance regulations. This kind of coverage currently is not common because small group claims experience is less predictable and thus riskier than large group claims experience, and individual small employers do not have the financial resources to assume that risk. Also, self-insured MEWAs do not have a good track record and have been poorly regulated.

Congress has debated giving small employers all of the advantages cited above with the exception of, in some instances, an avoidance of state premium taxes. If this happens, it is likely to displace the currently dominant single small-employer-insured coverage.

Health insurance purchasing cooperatives (HIPCs) and association coverage continue to be popular. They, too, could receive a boost if future federal legislation exempts them from certain state insurance requirements.

Finally, it is possible that employment-based coverage will grow somewhat, at the expense of individual market coverage and uninsured status, as a result of the nondiscrimination provisions and the prohibition of small group underwriting and denial under HIPAA.

■ Cost Trends

After decades of runaway medical spending, medical inflation has slowed to a near standstill.[7] Total national health expenditures increased only 5.4 percent in 1994, down from 11.0 percent in 1990. The Milliman & Robertson Health Cost Index, based on provider survey data on hospital, physician, and prescription drug costs, showed a 3.2 percent increase in per capita spending in 1995, as compared with a 10.9 percent increase in 1990.

Evidence from employer surveys is even more dramatic. Hay-Huggins surveys of employer health costs show only a 1.2 percent increase in premiums per enrollee in 1995, in contrast to an 11.8 percent increase in 1992. KPMG Peat

MEDICAL EXPENSE INSURANCE

Marwick's surveys record 1996 premium increases lower than the overall inflation rate for a second year in a row, at an unbelievably low 0.5 percent rate of increase from spring 1995 to spring 1996. The downward trend in premiums is broad-based as well, encompassing managed care and fee-for-service plans alike.

Consumer Out-Of-Pocket Spending

While employers are enjoying some respite from health cost increases, the experience of consumers has not been so rosy. According to a Louis A. Harris and Associates survey conducted in 1996 for the Center for Studying Health System Change, 64 percent of the 5,111 respondents reported that their out-of-pocket costs increased over the past three years.[8] Twenty-six percent said their family health care costs are somewhat or completely out of control. Fully 9 out of 10 respondents expect their out-of-pocket costs to rise.

One reason consumers have not fared well is that, increasingly, employees are paying a greater share of premiums. KPMG Peat Marwick surveys show that the employee share of premiums rose from 23.6 percent in 1992 to 28.9 percent in 1995. Consequently, the 5.0 percent average annual increase in overall premiums during this period translates to a 12.3 percent average annual increase in employee premium payments.

Another reason consumer out-of-pocket spending may be increasing is associated with the steady shift of employee coverage from fee-for-service plans to network-based plans, such as health maintenance organizations, preferred provider organizations, and point-of-service plans. Employees choosing to use out-of-network providers typically experience significantly higher deductibles, copayments, and coinsurance. They also are exposed to balance-billing charges, which means they must pay 100 percent of the difference between an out-of-network provider's charges and the plan's maximum allowed rates based on usual and customary fee schedules. Providers serving patients in-network typically agree to accept the health plan's payment as payment-in-full.

Effectiveness of Managed Care

The growth of managed care has undoubtedly contributed to the lower premium increases, but just how much credit managed care deserves is unclear. Some of the lower increases might be due to the underwriting cycle in health insurance premiums, that is, when insurers experience above-average profits, premium increases often are modest two years later. Because 1993 was a very profitable year for health insurers, modest premium increases in 1995 were predictable—irrespective of managed care. Similarly, strong profits in 1994 and 1995 predict low premium increases for 1996 and 1997.[9]

Table 9.1

Pro/Con: Can Managed Care Keep Medical Spending under Control?

Much of the savings has been achieved	Managed care can deliver more savings
Long-established staff model HMOs may have achieved much of their savings potential.	Managed care plans account for nearly half of all employer-sponsored coverage; the other half and the nongroup market offer fertile ground for future savings.
To the extent that HMOs are receiving a more diverse and medically challenging population as their market share increases, it may be difficult for them to maintain their dramatic initial results in lowering medical resource use.	PPOs and POS plans are more popular than HMOs today, but over time more employers and individuals may move toward the more tightly managed plans to benefit from lower premiums or expanded benefits.
The widespread adoption of managed care tools to evaluate hospital use (e.g., retrospective and concurrent utilization review, preadmission screening) has delivered most of the likely savings in the use of hospital services.	The use of ancillary services has grown tremendously with greater discipline on inpatient hospital use. Innovative programs to assess resource use in this area are expected.
Managed pharmaceutical programs have already produced significant savings in many employer-sponsored health plans.	Creative financing arrangements are likely to continue to emerge in contracts between purchasers and payers, payers and medical providers, and purchasers and medical providers. More group purchasing by small employers may yield administrative savings.

Other possible contributors to lower premium increases include efficiencies realized from industry consolidation through mergers and acquisitions, heightened price competition in some markets, and a reaction to proposed health care reforms in the early 1990s.

The ability of managed care to continue to deliver health care cost savings is widely debated. For example, several reports in the trade press note that many HMOs are experiencing fiscal pressures and that greater premium increases may be on the way. Industry experts, however, argue that there are still savings to be made (see Table 9.1).

The Future of Medical Spending Trends

It is undeniably true that medical care financing and delivery have undergone fundamental changes in recent years. The era of unchecked spending is past. Managed care systems have brought more scrutiny and accountability to medical spending. And the conversion to for-profit status of many medical care operations imposes a new kind of financial discipline nearly unknown in the past.

MEDICAL EXPENSE INSURANCE

Still, many challenges lay ahead:

- It is unclear whether the decreases in costs due to managed care are essentially a one-time phenomenon or a continuing feature of the system.
- The responsibility for financing current public commitments to the poor and the elderly through Medicaid and Medicare will have to be dealt with.
- The nation's desire to have access to state-of-the-art medical diagnosis and treatment for all citizens has not changed, nor is it likely to change.

■ Medicare Reform

Medicare reform, like many private sector health system changes, is being driven by budget problems. The trustees of the Social Security system warned in their 1995 report to Congress that the Hospital Trust Fund, which finances Medicare Part A, is on the brink of bankruptcy. Spending growth for medical services under Medicare Part B has averaged 15 percent annual growth over the last 20 years. Without major interventions by Congress, the federal dollars needed to keep pace with Medicare spending will either deepen the federal budget deficit or crowd out already diminished discretionary spending.

Medicare's financing crisis is due in part to continued growth in medical spending. More important than per capita spending growth, however, is erosion of the Part A funding stream. As baby boomers age, the number of beneficiaries will increase far more rapidly than the number of employees paying Medicare Part A payroll taxes. The approximate ratio of workers to people aged 65 or older today is 4:1, but it is projected to decrease to 2:4 in 2035.[10]

Medicare belt-tightening in the past has been accomplished largely through reductions in provider payments. Serious debate about Medicare reform was begun in 1996 and will probably continue for a number of years. The general thrust of reform initiatives to date is to increase beneficiary enrollment in private managed care plans. Program savings are to be realized through private plans' more efficient use of medical resources and perhaps also through price competition among private plans, generated by competitive bidding for Medicare contracts. While Congress' ultimate goal might be a voucher system, which would make federal outlays predictable and controllable, it is unlikely that Congress will be willing or able to shift the risk for program spending increases to private plans or beneficiaries in the foreseeable future.

Two elements in Medicare reform proposals are of great concern to insurance carriers. One is the possibility that reform legislation will authorize the Health

Care Financing Administration, which is responsible for Medicare, to contract with unlicensed provider-sponsored network plans (PSNs) for enrollment of beneficiaries in managed care arrangements. Currently, Medicare can contract only with risk-bearing entities that are state licensed. The other is the possibility that reforms will require guaranteed issuance of Medicare supplement policies, so that beneficiaries who are dissatisfied with managed care plans can return to traditional Medicare combined with private Medigap coverage.

Insurers' objections to PSNs arise out of concerns for equity and consumer protection. At least in proposals aired to date, PSNs would enjoy a much lighter regulatory burden than that faced by licensed insurers. Federal PSN authorization would, without reasonable justification, create an uneven playing field.

Political impetus behind a Medigap guarantee issue requirement appears to be strong. Insurers are convinced, however, that this policy is ill-conceived and short-sighted. If beneficiaries are allowed to elect in and out of managed care plans at will, what is rational behavior on their part—to move into managed care plans when they are relatively healthy, and move back into traditional Medicare with Medigap when they need more medical care—will soon result in soaring prices for Medigap coverage (and quite possibly, withdrawal of the product and market exit by Medigap carriers). In addition, adverse selection against traditional Medicare will be extreme, quashing all hopes of budget control in fee-for-service Medicare.

Informed observers are not sanguine about the prospects for achieving long-term financial stability for the Medicare program. Converting Medicare to managed care and realizing savings from managed care operations will take time. Solutions must be found for major program design problems and major political barriers related to changing a federal entitlement for a politically powerful constituency.

■ Summary

Among the major issues facing medical expense insurers are the regulatory environment, distribution systems, cost trends, and Medicare reform. One of the most significant changes in recent years was the passage of federal legislation regulating health insurance. Regulation of health insurance had long been the sole domain of the states. Insurers face growing pressures to increase access to health insurance and to control the cost of health care.

■ Key Terms

Cost trends
Employee Retirement Income Security Act (ERISA)
Health Insurance Portability and Accountability Act of 1996 (HIPAA)
Health insurance purchasing cooperatives (HIPCs)
Managed care
Medical savings accounts
Medicare Part A
Medicare Part B
Medicare reform
Medigap
Multiple employer welfare arrangements (MEWAs)
National Association of Insurance Commissioners (NAIC)
Out-of-pocket spending
Provider-sponsored network plans (PSNs)
Self-insurance
Underwriting cycle

Appendix A
SUMMARY OF P.L. 104-191, THE HEALTH INSURANCE PORTABILITY AND ACCOUNTABILITY ACT OF 1996

President Clinton signed P.L. 104-191 into law on August 21, 1996. This summary, developed in August, 1996 by the Health Insurance Association of America's Policy and Information department, provides an overview of the provisions of the act of interest to the health insurance industry. (Unrelated provisions not of interest to health insurers are omitted.) The following topics are included:

A. Definitions of Health Plan, "Applicability"
B. Group Insurance Provisions
C. Individual Insurance Provisions
D. Enforcement of Insurance Provisions
E. Self-Employed Deduction for Health Insurance Premiums
F. Long-Term Care Tax Clarifications and Consumer Protections
G. Medical Savings Accounts
H. Medicare Nonduplication
I. Fraud and Abuse
J. Administrative Simplification

A. Definitions of Health Coverage, "Applicability"

The requirements of the act apply to plans providing medical care. The requirements generally do *not* apply to plans providing (only) any of a list of "excepted benefits." However, in order to be excepted, plans offering certain of these benefits must meet additional requirements.

The requirements of the act do not apply with respect to the provision of the following benefits under any circumstances:

- Coverage only for accident, or disability income insurance, or any combination thereof.
- Coverage issued as a supplement to liability insurance.
- Liability insurance, including general liability insurance and automobile liability insurance.
- Workers' compensation or similar insurance.
- Automobile medical payment insurance.
- Credit-only insurance.
- Coverage for on-site medical clinics.
- Other similar insurance coverage, specified in regulations, under which benefits for medical care are secondary and incidental to other insurance benefits.

The requirements of the act do not apply with respect to a plan's provision of the following benefits if they are provided under a separate policy, certificate, or contract of insurance, or are otherwise not an integral part of the plan:

- Limited scope dental or vision benefits.

MEDICAL EXPENSE INSURANCE

- Benefits for long-term care, nursing home care, home health care, community-based care, or any combination thereof.
- Such other similar, limited benefits as are specified in regulations.

The requirements of the act do not apply with respect to a plan's provision of the following benefits if (1) they are provided under a separate policy, certificate, or contract of insurance; (2) there is no coordination between the provision of these benefits and any exclusion of benefits under any group health (i.e., medical) plan maintained by the same sponsor; and (3) benefits are paid without regard to whether benefits are paid for the same event under any group health plan maintained by the same sponsor:

- Coverage only for a specified disease or illness.
- Hospital indemnity or other fixed indemnity insurance.

The requirements of the act do not apply with respect to a plan's provision of the following benefits if they are provided under a separate policy, certificate, or contract of insurance:

- Medicare supplemental health insurance (as defined under section 1882(g)(1) of the Social Security Act).
- Coverage supplemental to CHAMPUS (coverage provided under chapter 55 of title 10, United States Code).
- Similar supplemental coverage provided to coverage under a group health plan.

B. Group Insurance Provisions

In general, the provisions of this section do *not* apply to "one-life groups." Nor do they apply to a plan's provision of "excepted benefits" (see "A" above). Except as otherwise noted, the provisions are effective July 1, 1997.

1. *Nondiscrimination / "Whole Group" Coverage*

Neither carriers nor employer-sponsored plans (whether insured or self-insured) may "establish rules for eligibility (including continued eligibility) of any individual to enroll" in the plan based on any health status-related factor (defined below).

Rules of construction clarify that this requirement is not intended to require a plan to provide benefits not otherwise provided under the terms of the plan or to prevent a plan from "establishing limitations or restrictions on the amount, extent, or nature of the benefits" for similarly situated individuals enrolled in the plan.

Also, plans may not require an individual to pay a premium or contribution which is greater than that charged to a similarly situated individual, on the basis of any health status-related factor.

"Health status-related factors" include (with respect to an individual or a dependent): health status, medical condition (including both physical and mental illnesses), claims experience, receipt of health care, medical history, genetic information, evidence of insurability (including conditions arising out of acts of domestic violence), and disability.

2. *Limitations on Pre-Existing Condition Exclusions*

Pre-existing condition exclusions are limited to 12 months (18 months for late entrants), based on a look-back period of 6 months. No exclusions are allowed for pregnancy or for newborns or adoptees who are covered promptly (within 30 days after birth or placement for adoption). Genetic information may not be treated as a pre-existing condition "in the absence of a diagnosis of the condition related to such information."

With respect to insured coverage only, states may require shorter exclusion periods, look-back periods, or affiliation periods, and may prohibit the application of pre-existing condition exclusions entirely to additional situations or conditions.

HMOs (only) which do not impose pre-existing condition exclusions may impose a 2-month "affiliation period" instead (3 months for late entrants), or may use other alternative methods approved by the state. Affiliation periods must be applied uniformly to all applicants and must run concurrently with any employer-imposed waiting period. (Also, federally qualified HMOs are specifically authorized to use "affiliation periods" for group plans.)

3. *Crediting of Prior Coverage ("Portability")*

Carriers and employer-sponsored plans must credit qualifying prior coverage toward pre-existing condition exclusions, as long as coverage has not lapsed longer than 63 days. "Waiting periods" under group health plans are not considered lapses in coverage. With respect to insured coverage only, States may allow longer lapses before continuous coverage is broken.

"Creditable" prior coverage includes any group coverage (including FEHBP and Peace Corps), individual coverage, Medicaid, Medicare, CHAMPUS, Indian Health Service or tribal organization coverage, State high risk pool coverage, or a "public health plan" (as defined in regulations). (Generally, only coverage after July 1, 1996, will be counted as "creditable." The HHS and Labor Secretaries will develop special rules for people who need to claim credit for earlier coverage.)

Plans and carriers are required to provide documentation of coverage to individuals whose coverage is terminated, to include dates of coverage (including COBRA) and waiting periods, if any. A second copy must be provided if requested within 24 months. (Although documentation is required with respect to events occurring after June 30, 1996, the earliest date the documentation must actually be provided is June 1, 1997.)

"Receiving" plans may accept prior coverage without regard to benefits covered, or may elect to evaluate prior coverage on a "class- or category-of-benefit" basis (to be defined in regulations), but only if they do so for all participants and beneficiaries. If the latter election is made, the "receiving" plan may be charged for the reasonable cost of providing the class-of-benefit information.

It appears that the deductibles or cost-sharing applicable under prior coverage may not be considered in any way.

4. *Special enrollment periods*

The act requires special enrollment periods for employees and dependents who declined coverage initially because they had other coverage (either COBRA or employer-provided), and who have either lost eligibility for that coverage or employer contributions toward it have been terminated. Enrollment must be requested within 30 days after loss of the other coverage.

The act also requires special enrollment periods for newborns, adoptees and newly married spouses and does not permit waiting periods or delays in coverage for those who enroll within 30 days of the relevant event.

With respect to insured coverage (only), States may require additional special enrollment periods.

5. *Guaranteed Availability of (Small) Group Products*

The act requires all carriers serving the small employer market (2 to 50 employees) to accept every small employer that applies for coverage and to accept every eligible individual who applies when they first become eligible. Who is an "eligible individual" is determined by the terms of the group health plan, by the carrier's uniformly applicable rules, and in accordance with all applicable State laws.

Exactly what products must be guarantee-issued is not entirely clear. Our best guess at this point is any product that is made available to any small employer. The act does clarify that guarantee issue is

MEDICAL EXPENSE INSURANCE

not required for "health insurance coverage" that is made available to small employers only through bona fide associations.

Exceptions to the guarantee-issue requirement are allowed for inadequate network capacity, inadequate financial capacity, and applicants not in the plan's service area. Use of minimum participation or employer contribution requirements is allowed, per applicable State law.

Guarantee issue is not required in the large group market. Instead, beginning Dec. 31, 2000, States are required to report triennially to HHS, and HHS to the Congress, about health insurance access issues for large employers. Also, GAO will report to the Congress on this matter 18 months after enactment.

6. *Guaranteed Renewability of Group Coverage*

The act requires guaranteed renewal of all products by all group carriers. Nonrenewal of groups is allowed for nonpayment, fraud or misrepresentation, carrier market exit, or failure to meet minimum contribution or participation requirements.

Nonrenewal is also allowed if there is no longer any enrollee (in the group) who lives, resides or works in the plan's service area, or if the employer is no longer a member of the association sponsoring the coverage.

MEWAs and multiemployer plans must follow similar rules.

7. *Disclosure of Information*

Upon request of a small employer, carriers must provide information about the carrier's right to change premium rates (and factors affecting changes), renewability provisions, and pre-existing condition provisions, and about the benefits and premiums available "under all health insurance coverage for which the employer is qualified." Proprietary or trade secret information need not be disclosed.

The availability of this information must be disclosed in the carrier's solicitation and sales materials for small employers.

ERISA plans are required to notify participants about material reductions in covered services or benefits.

C. Individual Insurance Provisions

The individual market provisions apply to carriers serving the individual market. The act specifies that carriers offering coverage only in connection with group health plans or through one or more bona fide associations are not required to offer coverage in the individual market.

These provisions take effect July 1, 1997 with respect to new and existing business.

1. *Guarantee Issue Requirements*

A carrier offering coverage in the individual market may not decline to offer coverage to, or deny enrollment of an eligible individual and may not impose any pre-existing condition exclusions with respect to such coverage. There are standard exceptions to this requirement for insufficient network or financial capacity.

This requirement does not apply in States with acceptable "alternative mechanisms." (See below.) In States without an acceptable alternative mechanism, a carrier may limit the coverage offered as described in section 3. below.

2. *Eligibility for Guarantee Issue of Individual Coverage*

The act defines eligible individuals as individuals: with 18 or more months of aggregate creditable coverage; with most recent prior coverage from a group health plan, governmental plan, or church plan (or health insurance coverage offered in connection with any such plan); ineligible for group health coverage, Medicare Parts A or B, Medicaid (or any successor program), and without any other health insurance coverage; not terminated from their most recent prior coverage for nonpayment of premiums or fraud; and who, if eligible for continuation coverage under COBRA or a similar state program, elected and exhausted this coverage.

3. *"Guarantee Issue" Products*

The act requires individual carriers to offer coverage to eligible individuals under all policy forms—with exceptions. In a state where the federal (fallback) requirements are in effect, a carrier may elect to limit the policy forms offered to eligible individuals as long as it offers at least two different policy forms, both of which are designed for, made generally available and actively marketed to, and enroll both eligible and other individuals by the carrier.

In addition, the 2 policy forms must meet one of the following: (1) the 2 policy forms have the largest and next to the largest premium volume; or (2) the 2 policy forms are representative of individual health insurance coverage offered by the carrier in the state. A carrier must apply the election uniformly to all eligible individuals in the state for that carrier, and the election will be effective for policies offered for not less than 2 years.

The 2 representative policy forms must include a lower- and higher-level of coverage, each of which has benefits substantially similar to other individual health insurance coverage offered by the carrier in the state. The lower-level policy form must have benefits with an actuarial value at least 85 percent, but not greater than 100 percent of a weighted average benefit. The higher-level policy form must have benefits with an actuarial value: (1) at least 15 percent greater than the actuarial value of the lower-level policy form; and (2) between 100 and 120 percent of the weighted average benefit. Both products must include benefits substantially similar to the carrier's other individual products.

The weighted average may be either: (1) the average actuarial value of the benefits from individual coverage provided by the carrier; or (2) the average actuarial value of the benefits from individual coverage provided by all carriers in the state. The weighted average must be based on coverage provided during the previous year and exclude coverage of eligible individuals. Actuarial values must be calculated based on a standardized population and a set of standardized utilization and cost factors.

If a carrier elects to offer 2 representative policy forms, they each must be subject to a risk-spreading mechanism (among carriers or among policies of a carrier), or to a mechanism that otherwise provides for some financial subsidization for eligible individuals, including through assistance to participating carriers. The conference report clarifies that it is the intent of Congress that "the risk spreading mechanism and financial subsidization standards provide meaningful financial protection and assistance for eligible individuals."

4. *Alternative State Mechanisms*

A state may notify the HHS Secretary that it intends to implement (or already has implemented) an alternative mechanism to achieve the act's goals. A state alternative program is presumed to be acceptable unless the Secretary finds otherwise. In states implementing an acceptable alternative mechanism, the federal (fallback) requirements do not apply.

To be an acceptable alternative, a state program must provide all eligible individuals with a choice of coverage where pre-existing condition exclusions are not imposed; and at least one of the choices must provide comprehensive or standard coverage.

General types of state programs which the Secretary may find acceptable include health insurance coverage pool or programs, mandatory group conversion policies, guarantee issue of 1 or more individual policies, open enrollment by 1 or more individual carriers, or a combination of such programs. Specifically, a state program may be found acceptable if it is consistent with the NAIC Individual Health Insurance Portability Model Act, the individual coverage requirements in the NAIC Small Group and Individual Health Insurance Availability Model Act, or the covered benefits and rating requirements of the NAIC Model Health Plan for Uninsurable Individuals Act.

MEDICAL EXPENSE INSURANCE

5. *Guaranteed Renewability of Individual Coverage*

The act requires guaranteed renewal, or continuation in force, of all products by all individual carriers. Nonrenewal is allowed for nonpayment, fraud or misrepresentation, carrier market exit, cases where the individual no longer lives in the network plan's service area or in an area in which the carrier is authorized to do business, or, for coverage made available to bona fide associations, if membership in the association ceases.

Association carriers must comply with these provisions.

D. Enforcement of Insurance Provisions

With respect to carriers, the act leaves enforcement to the States, with the possibility of a federal takeover if the state does not perform. "[E]ach State may require that health insurance issuers that issue, renew, or offer health insurance coverage in the State" meet this act's requirements. If a State "fails substantially" to enforce a provision or provisions of the act, the HHS Secretary will enforce them. The Secretary's enforcement tool is a civil money penalty of up to $100 "for each day for each individual with respect to which" a failure occurs. Detailed procedural rules and safeguards are established. Penalties will not apply under certain circumstances or if promptly corrected.

Enforcement with respect to group health plans (i.e., employer-sponsored plans) is by the Secretary of Labor, with similar penalties enforced through the tax code.

E. Self-Employed Deduction for Health Insurance Premiums

The act increases the percentage of health insurance premium expenses that self-employed individuals can deduct from their income for federal income tax purposes to 40% in 1997, 45% in 1998 - 2002, and ultimately 80% in 2006 and thereafter.

F. Long-Term Care Tax Clarifications and Consumer Protections

The act includes very favorable long-term care tax clarification and standards provisions. Effective January 1, 1997 (except as otherwise noted), it:

- Matches the tax treatment of reserves under IRC §807 with the NAIC minimum reserving requirements, but delays the effective date until 1998.
- For tax purposes, treats LTC insurance like accident and health insurance.
- Treats LTC services and premiums as medical expenses (except if paid to a relative), with additional limits on the premium deduction based on age. Allows self-employed individuals a partial deduction for LTC premiums.
- Allows employees to exclude from income the value of employer contributions under IRC sec. 106, but does not allow inclusion of LTC insurance in a cafeteria plan.
- Appears to allow employer deduction of LTC contributions, but does not address whether such contributions have the effect of delaying compensation.
- Specifies that per diem policies qualify but are subject to a $175 (indexed) daily benefit cap, integrated with other LTC policies (see next bullet). The benefit cap does not apply to reimbursement-type products. Aggregates per diem contracts and per diem LTC riders; any excess of aggregate per diem payments is taxed unless actual costs for LTC services in excess of the limit are incurred.
- Adds an integration rule for per diem policies only. The $175 daily limit for per diem policies is reduced by the amount of any reimbursement from non-per diem LTC contracts. Adds a special rule that per diem policies issued on or before 7/31/96 are not required to meet the integration rules.
- Adds a requirement that the policy must include at least 5 of the 6 activities of daily living (ADLs) listed. The benefit trigger is being unable to perform at least 2 ADLs (out of either 5 or 6 ADLs).

APPENDIX A

Severe cognitive impairment without dependency on ADLs (for example, Alzheimer's patients) is a separate trigger.
- Requires coordination with Medicare. (The Medicare duplication language was included in Title II.)
- Allows LTC riders for chronically ill; includes LTC riders in the accelerated death benefit provisions.
- Allows tax-favored treatment for existing policies which complied with state standards at the time of issuance for policies issued before 1-1-97. Allows tax-free exchange of existing LTC contracts for new qualified LTC contracts until 1998.
- Includes selected consumer protection provisions of the January 1993 NAIC Model Act and Regulations; includes mandatory offer of nonforfeiture.
- Allows states to adopt more stringent consumer protection standards.
- Provides that the Secretary of the Treasury determines if the requirements of the NAIC Model Act and Regulation have been met.
- Establishes a new excise tax for failure to meet certain consumer protections, but applies it to the issuance of qualified LTC contracts rather than to all LTC contracts.
- Creates reporting requirements for all LTC benefits, including total payments, taxpayer identification and type of contract.
- Includes accelerated death benefit provisions for amounts received under life insurance contracts by individuals who are terminally ill or chronically ill.
- Does not allow withdrawal from retirement accounts for the purchase of LTC insurance or tax-free exchanges of life insurance for LTC insurance.
- Adds tax qualified treatment for certain state-maintained plans.
- Adds a request for a study of the impact, including marketing and other effects, of the per diem limits.

G. Medical Savings Accounts

A medical savings account (MSA) is a trust or custodial account created to pay the qualified medical expenses of the account holder. Banks, insurance companies and certain other approved entities may serve as an MSA trustee.

The act establishes a four-year pilot project for federally tax-favored treatment of contributions to medical savings accounts. For the pilot project, there is a cap on the number of taxpayers allowed to benefit annually from a tax-favored MSA - generally 750,000 taxpayers. In determining the number of taxpayers opening MSAs, individuals who were uninsured during the previous 6 months will not be counted.

The MSA provisions are effective for taxable years beginning after December 31, 1996.

1. *Eligible Individuals*

MSAs are available to employees covered under an employer-sponsored high deductible plan of a small employer (fewer than 50 employees) and to self-employed individuals covered under a high deductible plan. To be eligible, such individuals must not be covered under any other health plan (other than a plan that provides certain permitted coverage).

Permitted insurance is: (1) Medicare supplemental insurance; (2) insurance if substantially all of the coverage provided under such insurance relates to (a) liabilities incurred under workers' compensation law, (b) tort liabilities, (c) liabilities relating to ownership or use of property (e.g., auto insurance), or (d) other similar liabilities, (3) insurance for a specified disease or illness, and (4) insurance that provides a fixed payment for hospitalization.

205

2. Tax Treatment of and Limits on Contributions

Individual contributions to an MSA are deductible (within limits) in determining adjusted gross income (AGI). In addition, employer contributions are excludable (within the same limits), except that this exclusion does not apply to contributions made through a cafeteria plan. Contributions may be made either by an employee or by an employer on behalf of the employee, but not by both in any given year.

For self-employed individuals, the deduction cannot exceed an individual's earned income from the trade or business. For employees, the deduction cannot exceed the individual's compensation from the employer sponsoring the plan. The maximum annual contribution that can be made to an MSA for a year is 65 percent of the deductible under the high deductible plan in the case of individual coverage and 75 percent of the deductible in the case of family coverage. No other dollar limits on the maximum contribution apply.

3. Definition of High Deductible Plan

A high deductible plan is a health plan with an annual deductible of at least $1,500 and no more than $2,250 in the case of individual coverage and at least $3,000 and no more than $4,500 in the case of family coverage. In addition, the maximum out-of-pocket expenses with respect to allowed costs (including the deductible) must be no more than $3,000 in the case of individual coverage and no more than $5,500 in the case of family coverage. Beginning after 1998, these dollar amounts are indexed for inflation. A plan does not fail to qualify as a high deductible plan merely because it does not have a deductible for preventive care as required by State law.

As under present law, State insurance commissioners would have oversight over the issuance of high deductible plans issued in conjunction with MSAs and could impose additional consumer protections. It is intended that the NAIC will develop model standards for high deductible plans that individual States could adopt.

4. Taxation of MSA Distributions

Distributions from an MSA for the medical expenses of the individual and his or her spouse or dependents generally are excludable from income. However, this holds only if the individual for whom the expenses were incurred was eligible to make an MSA contribution at the time the expenses were incurred. This rule is designed to ensure that MSAs are in fact used in conjunction with a high deductible plan, and that they are not primarily used by other individuals who have health plans that are not high deductible plans.

Medical expenses are defined as under the itemized deduction for medical expenses, except that medical expenses do not include expenses for insurance other than long-term care insurance, premiums for health care continuation coverage, and premiums for health care coverage while an individual is receiving unemployment compensation under federal or state law.

Distributions that are not for medical expenses are includable in income. Such distributions are also subject to an additional 15 percent tax unless made after age 65, death, or disability.

5. End of Pilot Project

After December 31, 2000, no new contributions may be made to MSAs except by or on behalf of individuals who previously had MSA contributions and employees who are employed by a participating employer. An employer is a participating employer if (1) the employer made any MSA contributions for any year to an MSA on behalf of employees or (2) at least 20 percent of the employees covered under a high deductible plan made MSA contributions of at least $100 in the year 2000.

Self-employed individuals who made contributions to an MSA during the period 1997-2000 also may continue to make contributions after 2000.

6. Measuring the Effects of MSAs

The General Accounting Office is directed to contract with an organization to conduct a study regarding the effects of MSAs in the small group market on (1) selection including adverse selection, (2) health costs, including the impact on premiums of individuals with comprehensive coverage, (3) use of preventive care, (4) consumer choice, (5) the scope of coverage of high deductible plans purchased in conjunction with an MSA and (6) other relevant issues, to be submitted to the Congress by January 1, 1999.

The intent of Congress is that the study be broad in scope, gather sufficient data to fully evaluate the relevant issues, and be adequately funded. It should measure the impact of MSAs on the broader health care market, including in-depth analysis of local markets with high penetration. It should evaluate the impact of MSAs on individuals and families experiencing high health care costs, especially low- and middle-income families.

H. Medicare Nonduplication

The conference agreement basically reflects the House provisions for Medicare Duplication with one important modification—the inclusion of new federal disclosure notices.

As expected the conference report:

- contains two important "safe harbors" for supplemental insurance and long-term care insurance policies;
- clarifies that supplemental insurance policies that pay benefits regardless of what Medicare pays will not be in violation of the Medicare "anti-duplication" laws;
- ensures that long-term care insurance policies, including home health care, respite care, community-based services and other types of long-term care insurance policies may coordinate with Medicare and will not be in violation of the Medicare "anti-duplication" laws.

In addition, the agreement provides relief from pending or future lawsuits based on the premise that either long-term care insurance policies or supplemental insurance policies sold between 1990 and the date of enactment violated the Medicare "anti-duplication" laws. This retroactive legal protection was crafted very narrowly to address only the problems created by the Omnibus Budget Reconciliation Act (OBRA) 1990 amendments.

As expected, the one change from the House-passed provisions on Medicare Duplication was the inclusion of new disclosure statements for all supplemental and long-term care insurance policies. These new disclosure language is less onerous, and more accurate than the old disclosure notices.

Although the HIAA language protecting direct response companies from having to submit disclosure notices after an application for coverage had been received was ultimately rejected, the final language on direct response companies did not require a disclosure notice be provided upon the initial solicitation, which is what the Administration had pushed for. Instead, direct response companies must furnish the appropriate disclosure notice to individuals when providing an application for coverage.

I. Fraud and Abuse

Subtitle A—Fraud and Abuse Control Program: Establishes a program to coordinate Federal, State, and local law enforcement programs to control fraud in health plans. Empowers the Secretary and Attorney General to share data with health plans. Establishes (in the federal hospital insurance trust fund) a health care fraud and abuse account into which criminal fines and civil penalties will be deposited. A Medicare Integrity Program is established.

Subtitle B—Revisions to Current Sanctions for Fraud and Abuse: Persons convicted of a felony relating to health care fraud will be mandatorily excluded from participating in Medicare and state health care programs. There are intermediate sanctions for Medicare health maintenance organizations (section 1876, 42 U.S.C. is amended). The Secretary of HHS may terminate a contract with an eligible section 1876 organization or may impose intermediate sanctions such as civil money penalties or suspension of enrollment of individuals. There is an additional exception to anti-kickback penalties for risk-sharing arrangements.

Subtitle C—Data Collection: Establishes a national health care fraud and abuse data collection program for reporting final adverse actions against health care providers, suppliers or practitioners. Each Government agency and health plan is required to report any final adverse action (not including settlements in which no findings of liability have been made) taken against a health care provider, supplier, or practitioner.

Subtitle D—Civil Monetary Penalties: Recoveries related to federal health care programs will be deposited into the Federal Hospital Insurance Trust Fund.

Subtitle E—Revisions/Amendments to Criminal Law: Amends the United States Code by adding the federal offense of health care fraud in any health care benefit program, which includes public and private plans. An authorized investigative demand procedure including subpoena authority is allowed in any case relating to a federal health care offense.

Key Provisions in the Act:

- The Secretary of HHS will provide guidance regarding application of health care fraud and abuse sanctions. The guidance includes modifications to existing safe harbors pertaining to the Medicare program, additional safe harbors specifying payment practices that will not be treated as criminal actions, advisory opinions, and special fraud alerts.

- The Secretary of HHS will consult with providers and health plans in establishing standards related to the exception for risk-sharing arrangements to the anti-kickback penalties. A negotiated rule making process is included in the provision for an additional exception to anti-kickback penalties for eligible organizations under section 1876 or for risk-sharing arrangements.

- Of particular interest to Medicare carriers, the Medicare Integrity Program includes language stating that entities need to comply with conflict of interest standards generally applicable to Federal acquisition and procurement. (Note that this language is from the Senate version of the bill. The House version had a higher standard and required an entity to demonstrate to the Secretary of HHS that the entity's financial holdings would not interfere with its ability to perform the functions required by the contract.)

- Although the act empowers the Secretary of HHS and the Attorney General to share fraud data with health plans, it is unclear whether the sharing is a "two-way" street between the government and health plans or is a one-way flow of information from the private sector to the government.

J. Administrative Simplification

The act seeks to improve the efficiency and effectiveness of the health care system, including federal and private programs, by encouraging the development of a health information system through the establishment of standards and requirements for electronic transmission of certain health information.

The HHS Secretary will adopt standards for transactions and data elements to enable health information to be exchanged electronically. There are also standards for security of health information. The use of standards will apply to health plans, clearinghouses and only those health care providers who transmit health information in electronic form.

The term "health plan" means an individual or group plan that provides, or pays the cost of medical care. Such term includes the following: group health plans, health insurance issuers, health maintenance organizations, part A or B of the Medicare program, the Medicaid program, Medicare supplemental policies, long-term care policies, employee welfare benefit plans, other federal public plans, and the Federal Employees Health Benefit Plan.

The standards must be adopted by the Secretary within 18 months of enactment; then health plans have 24 to 36 months to implement the standards.

These requirements supersede state laws, except where the Secretary determines the state law is necessary to prevent fraud and abuse, ensure appropriate State regulation of insurance and health plans, or involves state reporting on health care delivery or costs. Another exception is if the State law relates to the privacy of health information. There are penalties for failure to comply with standards. The language includes a provision for protecting trade secrets.

There are provisions requiring consultation with specified organizations prior to the adoption of standards. The specified groups are: the Workgroup for Electronic Data Interchange (WEDI); the National Uniform Billing Committee; and the National Uniform Claim Committee. (NOTE that HIAA is a voting representative in each of these organizations.) Also, the Secretary will have assistance from and rely upon the recommendations of the National Committee on Vital and Health Statistics.

Key Provisions in the Act:

- The act excludes the definition for coordination of benefits and instead says the Secretary will adopt standards for transferring among health plans appropriate standard data elements needed for coordination of benefits.
- The standards adopted are prohibited from requiring disclosure of trade secrets or confidential commercial financial information by participants in the health information network.
- The standards will provide for standard unique health identifiers for each individual, employer, health plan and health care provider for use in the health care system. When adopting identifier standards, the Secretary of HHS can consider multiple uses for identifiers (presumably this means that existing identifiers such as the social security number may be used.)
- The exceptions to State law pertaining to privacy of health information can potentially cause health plans to comply with multiple operational standards for privacy of health information.

Appendix B
COMPLYING WITH THE HEALTH INSURANCE PORTABILITY AND ACCOUNTABILITY ACT OF 1996

This material below, *Complying with the Health Insurance Portability and Accountability Act of 1996: A Guide for Employers and Health Insurers,* was prepared prior to the publication of any guidance or regulations from the federal agencies responsible for implementing the act. Interim final rules for Title I (access, portability, and renewability provisions) developed by the Departments of Labor, Health and Human Services, and Treasury were published in the *Federal Register,* on April 8, 1997. Treasury guidance on medical savings accounts was published December 16, 1996 in Internal Revenue Bulletin 1996-51 (Revenue Service Notice 96-53). Additional Treasury guidance was published May 12, 1997 in Internal Revenue Bulletin 1997-20 (Revenue Ruling 1997-19). The Department of Justice, on January 22, 1997, released guidelines on the Fraud and Abuse Control Program, as mandated by the Health Insurance Portability and Accountability Act of 1996.

A Guide for Employers and Health Insurers

By Dean A. Rosen, Esq.* and Richard Meltzer, Esq.**

I. Overview of the Health Insurance Portability and Accountability Act

A. Political Background

The Health Insurance Portability and Accountability Act of 1996, P.L. 104-191, ("HIPAA" or "the Act")[1] represents the most sweeping federal reform of the health care system since the enactment of Medicare and Medicaid three decades ago and includes several of the most significant changes to employee benefit law since passage of the Employee Retirement Income Security Act (ERISA) in 1974.

---

*Mr. Rosen is Majority Counsel to the Ways and Means Health Subcommittee of the United States House of Representatives. During the development and enactment of the Health Insurance Portability and Accountability Act, he served as Majority Health Policy Counsel to the U.S. Senate Committee on Labor and Human Resources, chaired by Senator Nancy Landon Kassebaum.

**Mr. Meltzer is a principal in the law firm of Washington, Counsel, P.C., specializing in the areas of tax law, health care and benefits law, and environment and energy matters.

[1] The legislation also is commonly referred to as the "Kassebaum-Kennedy Act," after its chief sponsors Senators Nancy Landon Kassebaum (R-Kan.) and Edward M. Kennedy (D-Mass.).

The bipartisan legislation originally was introduced in the Senate as "The Health Insurance Reform Act," S. 1028, by Republican Senator Nancy Landon Kassebaum of Kansas and Democratic Senator Edward M. Kennedy of Massachusetts on July 13, 1995. Senate bill 1028 focused primarily on guaranteeing the availability and portability of health coverage to certain individuals and expanding the purchasing clout of small employers through health insurance purchasing cooperatives. The Senate Committee on Labor and Human Resources voted to report the legislation favorably by a unanimous 18-0 vote on August 2, 1995.

In April 1996, both the Senate and the House of Representatives passed legislation containing the core elements of the original Senate bill. However, the House bill, H.R. 3103, substantially expanded upon these core elements to include numerous changes to the tax code, medical liability reforms, and new rules designed to streamline medical claims processing and combat health care fraud and abuse. The final Senate bill also contained a controversial provision requiring certain health plans to provide coverage for mental illnesses commensurate with physical illnesses. Despite months of partisan wrangling over whether or not to include some of the controversial provisions of the House-passed bill and the Senate mental health parity provision, the conference report representing agreement between the House and Senate was passed 421-2 in the House on August 1, and 98-0 in the Senate on August 2.[2] On August 21, 1996, President Clinton signed HIPAA into law.

B. Overview

HIPAA creates a federal framework for reforms of the group and individual health insurance markets. The Act's federal standards apply to insurers, health maintenance organizations (HMOs), and employer plans, including those that self-insure. Within this framework, the Act generally provides the states with significant latitude to go beyond the federal standards in regulating the insurance market. Thus, the Act retains the traditional state role as primary regulator of health insurance while at the same time setting forth a new role for the federal government in regulating the private health insurance and employee health benefit market.

C. Basic Provisions of the Act

The provisions of the Act found in Titles I and IV guarantee the availability of health insurance coverage for certain employees and individuals, sharply limit the use of so-called "preexisting condition" exclusions, prohibit employers and insurers from discriminating against workers based on health status, and make it easier for people to obtain health coverage when they change jobs or lose their job, regardless of their health status. While many states have had similar laws on the books for several years for small employers who purchase traditional insurance coverage, HIPAA for the first time extends these important consumer protections to people who work for large firms and those covered by self-insured group health plans.

Title II of the Act institutes new federal penalties for health care fraud and abuse and a new federal program to streamline and simplify the electronic transmission of billing records and other medical data.

Titles III and V of the Act contains several changes to the tax code designed primarily to make health coverage more affordable for small employers and individuals. First, HIPAA gradually increases the tax deduction for health insurance for the self-employed from the current 30 percent to 80 percent. Second, it establishes a pilot project that allows small businesses and the self-employed to contribute to tax-preferred medical savings accounts (MSAs). When combined with a high-deductible insurance plan that covers catastrophic illnesses, MSA funds can be used to pay for routine medical costs. Third,

---

[2] Ultimately, the mental health parity provision was dropped from the final version of the legislation and a compromise provision was included to make medical savings accounts available on a limited basis to certain small employers and self-employed individuals.

the Act liberalizes the tax treatment of long-term care expenses and accelerated death benefits. Fourth, it allows penalty-free withdrawals from Individual Retirement Accounts for certain medical expenses.

D. Applicability

The reforms contained in HIPAA relate both to the group and individual health insurance markets and apply to health insurers, HMOs, and group health plans sponsored by employers, unions, churches, governments, and associations, including self-insured plans. The provisions of the Act (other than those relating to individual coverage) apply to group health plans with two or more participants who are active employees on the first day of the plan year. A group health plan is defined as an employee welfare benefit plan to the extent that the plan provides medical care to employees or their dependents directly or through insurance, reimbursement or otherwise.

State and local government plans are covered, unless they elect to be excluded under specific procedures specified in the Act. State and local government plans electing not to be covered under the Act must make this election at the beginning of each plan year (or for the duration of a collective bargaining agreement for those plans covered by such arrangements). These plans also must notify enrollees of their decision to opt-out of the requirements of HIPAA and the consequences of such decision. Regardless of whether they opt-out, state and local governmental plans must provide certifications of creditable coverage to enrollees who leave the plan.

It is important to note that HIPAA does not apply to certain types of benefit arrangements. First, the Act does not apply to certain benefits deemed to be outside of the scope of the Act entirely, including (1) coverage only for accident, or disability insurance, or any combination thereof; (2) coverage issued as a supplement to liability insurance; (3) liability insurance; (4) workers' compensation insurance; (5) automobile medical payment insurance; (6) credit-only insurance; (7) coverage for on-site medical clinics; and (8) other similar coverage, as may be specified by the Secretary of HHS in regulations, where benefits for medical care are secondary or incidental to other insurance benefits.

Second, the Act does not apply to (1) limited scope dental or vision benefits; (2) benefits for long-term care, nursing home care, home health care, community-based care, or any combination thereof; or (3) similar limited benefits as may be specified in regulations where those benefits (a) are provided under a separate policy, certificate, or contract of insurance, or (b) otherwise are not an integral part of the plan.

Third, the Act does not apply to (1) coverage only for a specified disease or illness; or (2) hospital indemnity or other fixed indemnity insurance if (a) these benefits are provided under a separate policy, certificate, or contract of insurance; (b) there is no coordination between the provision of these benefits under any group health plan maintained by the same plan sponsor; and (c) such benefits are paid with respect to an illness or event without regard to whether benefits are provided for that event under any group health plan maintained by the same plan sponsor.

Finally, the Act's requirements do not apply to benefits provided under a separate policy, certificate, or contract of insurance if the benefits are supplemental to Medicare or supplemental to military health care.

E. The Act's Structure and Enforcement Scheme

HIPAA provides for enforcement of the new federal group health plan availability and portability requirements through the Internal Revenue Code (IRC), Employee Retirement Income Security Act (ERISA), and through civil monetary penalties that may be imposed by the Secretary of Health and Human Services (HHS) under the Public Health Service Act (PHSA). The states generally are responsible for implementing and enforcing the Act's group and individual market reforms as they relate to insurers, health maintenance organizations (HMOs) and other "health insurance issuers."

The Act amends ERISA, the PHSA, and the IRC. In general, requirements relating to group health plans are found in the ERISA and IRC amendments; requirements on health insurance issuers, such as insurance carriers and HMOs, are found in the PHSA and ERISA amendments. Tax changes, such as the increase in the self-employed deduction, establishment of tax-favored MSAs, and long-term care provisions, are amendments to the IRC.

1. Internal Revenue Code Enforcement Relating to and Group Health Plans

HIPAA's group health plan requirements incorporated into the IRC generally impose a tax for any failure of a group health plan to comply with the Act's requirements. The tax may be imposed on the employer sponsoring the group health plan or on the plan itself in the case of a multiemployer plan or a multiple employer welfare arrangement (MEWA). HIPAA's group health plan requirements contained in the IRC do not apply to governmental plans or to plans which on the first day of the plan year cover fewer than two current employees. In addition, no tax may be imposed on a small employer (defined as a company that employed an average of 50 or fewer employees on business days during the preceding calendar year) that provides health care benefits through a contract with an insurer, health maintenance organization, or other "health insurance issuer" where the violation is solely because of the coverage offered by the issuer.

The amount of the tax that may be imposed is generally equal to $100 per day for each day during which a failure occurs until the failure is corrected. The tax applies separately with respect to each individual affected by the failure. Thus, plans covering large numbers of individuals may be subject to significant monetary penalties for violations of the Act. Generally, no penalty may be assessed if the violation is unintentional or if the failure was corrected within 30 days. The maximum tax for unintentional violations that can be imposed is the lesser of $500,000 or 10 percent of the employer's payments under group health plans during the taxable year in which the failure occurred (or 10 percent of the amount paid by the multiemployer plan or MEWA for medical care during the plan year in which the failure occurred). Finally, the Secretary of Treasury is given discretion to waive or all or part of the tax if it is determined that payment would be excessive relative to the failure involved.

2. ERISA Enforcement Relating to Group Health Plans and Health Insurance Issuers

HIPAA's requirements with respect to group health plans with two or more employees on the first day of the plan year are enforced under Title I of ERISA as under current law. Sections 502, 504, and 510 of ERISA are most relevant for purposes of HIPAA enforcement. Under section 502 of ERISA, employee benefit plans that fail to comply with applicable requirements can be sued for relief and subject to civil monetary penalties. Such plans also may be sued to recover any benefits due under the plan. Section 504 of ERISA provides the Secretary of Labor with investigative authority to determine whether any person is out of compliance with the law's requirements. Section 510 prohibits a health plan from discriminating against a participant or beneficiary for exercising any right under the plan.

The Secretary of Labor does not enforce the Act's requirements with respect to health insurance carriers, HMOs or other "health insurance issuers." However, the private right of action under part V of ERISA would apply to health insurance issuers. The Act also provides that states may enter into an agreement with the Secretary of Labor for delegation to the state of some or all of the Secretary's authority under sections 502 and 504 of ERISA to enforce the requirements of HIPAA in connection with MEWAs providing medical care which are not group health plans.

3. State/PHSA Enforcement Relating to Health Insurance Issuers

HIPAA provides that each state may require that health insurers that issue, sell, renew, or offer health insurance coverage in the state meet the Act's requirements and each state may impose penalties (as determined under state law) for non-compliance. In the case of a determination by the Secretary of HHS that a state has failed to "substantially enforce" a provision or provisions of the Act, the Secretary is required to enforce such provision or provisions insofar as they relate to the issuance, sale, renewal, and offering of health insurance coverage in connection with group health plans in the state. In this case, secretarial enforcement would apply only in the absence of state enforcement and with respect to group health plans that are non-federal government plans.[3]

If a state fails to substantially enforce a provision or provisions of the Act, the Secretary of HHS may impose penalties for noncompliance in an amount not to exceed $100 per day per individual. In determining the penalty, the Secretary must take into account the previous record of compliance and the gravity of the violation. No penalty may be assessed if the violation is unintentional or if the failure is corrected within 30 days. HIPAA provides for administrative and judicial review of penalty assessments. Penalties are to be paid to the Secretary of HHS and are available for the enforcement of those provisions with respect to which the penalty was imposed.

There are special enforcement rules governing the individual market, which will be discussed in more detail in section IV. below.

4. Coordination of Enforcement

It is unclear to what extent penalties authorized under the IRC, ERISA, and the PHSA may apply simultaneously to a group health plan or health insurance issuer. However, the Act expressly requires the Secretaries of Treasury, Labor and HHS to ensure, through the execution of an interagency memorandum of understanding, that regulations, rulings and interpretations of the Act are administered so as to have the "same effect at all times." HIPAA also requires the Secretaries to coordinate enforcement of the Act, to assign priorities to each agency for enforcement of the Act, and to avoid duplication of enforcement efforts. Interim final regulations are expected to be issued in April 1997, three months prior to the general effective date of the Act.

II. New Responsibilities for Employers and Group Health Plans Under the Act

The requirements discussed in sections II.A. through II.F. below apply both to group health plans and health insurance issuers.[4] The requirements described in sections II.G. and II.H. apply only to group health plans.

A. Limitations on Preexisting Condition Exclusions

1. Previous Law

No provision.

2. HIPAA Requirements

The Act for the first time restricts the ability of group health plans (those covering 2 or more participants who are active employees on the first day of the plan year) to exclude coverage of preexisting conditions. If a condition is otherwise covered under a group health plan, the plan cannot deny coverage for the condition merely because an individual suffered from it before enrolling in the plan. These preexisting condition requirements apply both to the group health plan itself and to health insurance issuers providing coverage in connection with group health plans. Generally, the requirements are effective for plan years beginning after June 30, 1997. For collectively bargained arrangements,

---

[3] This structure was necessitated largely by the recently-enacted unfunded mandates legislation which generally prohibits the federal government from requiring states to take actions, including those relating to enforcement of federal laws, which would impose costs on the states exceeding certain thresholds.

[4] A "health insurance issuer" is defined by the Act as "an insurance company, insurance service, or insurance organization (including a health maintenance organization . . .) which is licensed to engage in the business of insurance in a state and which is subject to state law which regulates insurance (within the meaning of 514(b)(2) of ERISA).

the requirements are effective on the later of (a) the date on which the last collective bargaining agreement relating to the plan terminates; or (b) July 1, 1997.

The Act contains a limited exception allowing group health plans to exclude from coverage for up to 12 months following enrollment preexisting conditions for which "medical advice, diagnosis, care, or treatment was recommended or received" during the six-month period immediately before the individual enrolled in the plan. This 12-month exclusion is reduced by the individual's period of "creditable coverage," which generally is the period during which the individual had other health coverage immediately before enrolling in the plan without a break in coverage of 63 days or more. The concept of creditable coverage is discussed in more detail in section II.B. below. For individuals enrolling in a group health plan at a time other than the first available opportunity to do so or outside of a special enrollment period, the maximum allowable preexisting condition period is extended from 12 months to 18 months.

It is the combination of the HIPAA's preexisting condition limitations and required crediting for previous coverage that provide portability under the Act for individuals to move from one health benefit arrangement to another without interruptions in coverage. Once an individual obtains health insurance coverage, he or she will be able to use evidence of that coverage to reduce or eliminate any preexisting condition exclusion that otherwise would apply under the terms of a group health plan. Thus, the portability made possible by HIPAA works much like transferring course credits from one school to another. While an individual has changed schools and courses, the successful completion of courses in the previous school is applicable towards satisfaction of the requirements for graduation from the new school.

HMOs that do not use preexisting condition periods may substitute "affiliation periods" of up to 60 days (and up to 90 days for late enrollees).[5] However, those periods must be applied uniformly to all "similarly situated" individuals without regard to health status. Also, to avoid abuse of the affiliation period exception, the Act provides that affiliation periods must run concurrently with waiting periods. HMOs may use alternative methods to address adverse selection if such alternative methods are approved by the state in which coverage is being provided.

HIPAA contains several important exceptions to the general rules regarding preexisting condition exclusions. "Genetic information," which is not defined by the Act, cannot be considered a preexisting condition in the absence of a diagnosis of a condition related to that genetic information. Thus, the detection of a gene which causes breast cancer or a family history of breast cancer cannot be used to exclude an individual from coverage under the group health plan if the individual herself is not diagnosed with breast cancer during the six-month period prior to her enrollment under the group health plan. In addition, a group health plan may not impose preexisting condition exclusions relating to pregnancy, or to newborns or adopted children who are enrolled for coverage within 30 days of birth or placement for adoption.

The Act contains no limitations on waiting periods, so long as such waiting periods are applied uniformly without regard to the health status of the potential plan participants or beneficiaries. For example, group health plans may require that all employees, or all part-time employees, work for 6 months before they become eligible to enroll for coverage under the plan. It is important to note, however, that (a) waiting periods do not count as gaps in an individual's creditable coverage period, even if a waiting period means that an individual in fact is without coverage for 63 days or more; and (b) the preexisting condition period otherwise applicable to an individual is reduced by the duration of any waiting period.

3. Action Necessary for Compliance

By the commencement of the plan year beginning after June 30, 1997 (a) review plan documents and insurance policies to identify provisions that may conflict with the Act's preexisting condition

---

[5] Note that it is only HMOs, rather than other types of network plans, that may utilize affiliation periods.

APPENDIX B

requirements; (b) determine the financial impact of the restrictions on preexisting condition exclusions imposed under the Act; and (c) consider appropriate plan design changes and any adjustments in contributions or premiums necessary to adapt to the new requirements.

B. Tracking and Reporting Creditable Coverage

1. Previous Law

No provision.

2. HIPAA Requirements

The Act's reporting and crediting requirements apply to group health plans and health insurance issuers offering coverage in connection with group health plans.

Beginning June 1, 1997, group health plans and health insurance issuers providing coverage in connection with group health plans must begin providing certifications of coverage to all individuals whose coverage is terminated under the plan for any reason. For events occurring after June 30, 1996 and before October 1, 1996, plans are required to provide certifications only by written request. Individuals seeking to establish creditable coverage for periods prior to July 1, 1996 may present other evidence of creditable coverage and group health plans and health insurance issuers must make a good faith effort to credit such coverage.

Group health plans must begin crediting individuals' prior "creditable coverage" at the beginning of the first plan year on or after July 1, 1997.[6] Generally, group health plans must credit coverage that individuals had as of June 30, 1996. Individuals can earn creditable coverage for most types of health benefit arrangements, including group health plans, COBRA continuation coverage, individual health insurance, Medicare, Medicaid, and most other government-sponsored health plans. Individuals lose all creditable coverage if they experience a gap in creditable coverage of 63 or more continuous days immediately prior to enrollment in a new plan.

Generally, the type and level of coverage an individual has during a period of creditable coverage is not relevant. However, a group health plan may elect to require new enrollees to demonstrate prior creditable coverage for a specific class or category of benefits before crediting that coverage toward the plan's preexisting condition exclusion period for that particular class or category of benefits. Group health plans and health insurance issuers providing coverage in connection with group health plans must apply this alternative method of crediting coverage uniformly to all participants and beneficiaries and must provide prominent notice to participants and beneficiaries of the election of this method and of its significance. Moreover, the conference report makes clear that the term "classes or categories" is meant to be interpreted broadly. Thus, for example, a group health plan could require individuals to have prior prescription drug coverage before reducing the exclusion period for preexisting conditions under the plan's own prescription drug benefit. The plan could not, however, deny coverage to a specific brand name pharmaceutical because that brand was not covered under the prior plan. Nor could the plan single out participants or beneficiaries with high claims experience or potential high claims costs and apply this alternative method only to them.

Group health plans must provide certifications of coverage for former participants' and beneficiaries' automatically whenever regular or COBRA continuation coverage ceases, and upon request within 24 months thereafter. Group health plans also must provide certifications by separate classes or categories of benefits to a new plan in which a former participant or beneficiary enrolls, if the new plan requests this information and pays the previous plan the reasonable costs of gathering and providing the information.

---

[6] Collectively bargained arrangements are required to begin crediting coverage on the later of (1) the date on which the last collective bargaining agreement relating to the plan terminates; or (2) July 1, 1997.

3. Action Necessary for Compliance

As soon as possible, establish procedures for recording periods of creditable coverage for participants and beneficiaries and determine the levels of coverage that was offered to employees and dependents to the earliest date possible, including coverage that was provided as of June 30, 1996.

By June 1, 1997 (a) establish procedures to provide certifications of creditable coverage to participants and beneficiaries ceasing coverage under the group health plan; and (b) establish reasonable costs to be charged to plans that request certification of classes and categories of benefits.

By the commencement of the plan year beginning after June 30, 1997 (a) review plan documents and insurance policies to identify provisions that may conflict with the Act's crediting requirements; (b) consider appropriate plan design changes and any adjustments in contributions or premiums necessary to adapt to the new requirements; and (c) decide whether to require new enrollees to demonstrate creditable coverage for specific classes or categories of benefits.

C. Special Enrollment Periods

1. Previous Law

No provision.

2. HIPAA Requirements

The Act requires group health plans to offer special enrollment periods to two classes of individuals. These special enrollment rules generally apply to all group health plans beginning in plan years after June 30, 1997. For collectively bargained arrangements, these requirements are effective on the later of (a) the date on which the last collective bargaining agreement relating to the plan terminates; or (b) July 1, 1997. The requirements apply both to group health plans and to health insurance issuers offering coverage in connection with group health plans.

The first class of individuals consists of employees and dependents who otherwise are eligible to enroll in the plan but did not do so initially because they had other coverage. If an employee or dependent in this circumstance subsequently loses the other coverage and requests enrollment in the plan within 30 days after losing the coverage, the plan must allow enrollment in the plan without waiting for the plan's next open enrollment period.

To qualify for special enrollment, the employee or dependent must meet three conditions at the time he or she declines coverage (a) he was covered by other coverage at the time of initial eligibility for enrollment in the plan; (b) he stated in writing at that time that enrollment was being declined because of the other coverage (but only if the employer or health insurance issuer required the statement and explained its significance); and (c) the other coverage was either COBRA continuation coverage that was exhausted or coverage other than COBRA continuation coverage that was terminated due to termination of employer contributions toward the coverage or loss of eligibility for the coverage (e.g., as a result of legal separation, divorce, death, termination of employment or reduction in the number of hours of employment).

The second class of individuals to whom group health plans must offer special enrollment is new dependents. If dependents are eligible for coverage under the plan, individuals who become dependents as a result of marriage, birth, or placement for adoption generally must be allowed to enroll in the plan and have 30 days after they first become dependents to enroll. The same special enrollment period applies (a) to the person (generally the employee) through whom the dependent claims dependent status if that person is not already enrolled in the plan; and (b) in the cases of birth or placement for adoption, to the spouse of the person through whom the dependent claims dependent status if the spouse is not already enrolled in the group health plan and is otherwise eligible for coverage under the plan. This rule is designed primarily to make it easier for families to be enrolled for coverage under the same plan. It could, however, lead to adverse selection in some plans.

Individuals enrolling in a group health plan during a special enrollment period are not considered "late enrollees" and therefore may be subjected to no more than a 12-month exclusion period for preexisting conditions (rather than the 18-month exclusion that otherwise applies), subject to further reduction by the individual's period of prior creditable coverage. Moreover, no preexisting condition limitations may be applied to newborns and adopted children who become eligible during special enrollment periods and no preexisting condition limitation may apply to pregnancy regardless of whether the individual had prior creditable coverage.

3. Action Necessary for Compliance

By the commencement of the plan year beginning after June 30, 1997 (a) review plan documents and insurance policies to identify provisions that may conflict with the Act's special enrollment requirements; (b) consider appropriate plan design changes and any adjustments in contributions or premiums necessary to adapt to the new requirements; and (c) modify plan administrative procedures to conform to the Act's special enrollment requirements.

D. Discrimination Based on Health Status Prohibited

1. Previous Law

Section 510 of ERISA prohibits employee benefit plans from discriminating against a particular participant or beneficiary for exercising any right to which he or she is entitled under the provisions of the employee benefit plan. Section 105(h) of the IRC prohibits discrimination in favor of highly compensated individuals by self-insured employer-sponsored health plans.

2. HIPAA Requirements

The Act prohibits group health plans from discriminating against employees and dependents based on several "health status-related factors." Plans cannot (a) deny eligibility or continued eligibility for enrollment nor (b) charge an employee or dependent a higher premium or contribution than premiums or contributions charged to "similarly situated" individuals under the plan based on (i) health status, (ii) physical or mental conditions, (iii) claims experience, (iv) receipt of health care, (v) medical history, (vi) genetic information, (vii) evidence of insurability (including conditions arising out of acts of domestic violence or participation in recreational activities such as motorcycling or horseback riding), or (viii) disability. HIPAA's prohibitions against discrimination based on health status-related factors generally are effective for plan years beginning after June 30, 1997 and apply both to group health plans and health insurance issuers offering coverage in connection with group health plans.[7] They are applicable to all employees and their dependents, regardless of whether such individuals have prior creditable coverage.

HIPAA does not require group health plans to offer specific types of benefits nor does it prohibit plans from placing limitations on the benefits they do offer, even though the limitation may adversely affect certain participants or beneficiaries.[8] However, if a plan offers benefits or imposes limits on benefits, it must do so for all "similarly situated" individuals enrolled in the plan without regard to the health status-related factors." This generally means that plans can draw eligibility and coverage distinctions based on factors legitimately unrelated to health, such as union membership, part-time status, and employment site.

---

[7] For collectively bargained arrangements, these requirements are effective on the later of (1) the date on which the last collective bargaining agreement relating to the plan terminates; or (2) July 1, 1997.

[8] But see sections II.E. and II.F. describing requirements added to HIPAA by the FY97 Departments of Veterans Affairs and Housing and Urban Affairs appropriations bill requiring plans to provide certain coverage for maternity stays and mental health (P.L. 104-204).

The Act does not restrict the amount that health insurance issuers offering coverage in connection with group health plans can charge employers or similarly situated individuals overall. However, issuers and plans are prohibited from singling out individuals for higher premiums, deductibles, or copayments or dropping them from coverage based on their health status, including a preexisting condition. The Act does permit issuers and group health plans to provide premium discounts or rebates, or to modify copayments or deductibles in return for adherence to programs of "health promotion and disease prevention."

3. Action Necessary for Compliance

By the commencement of the plan year beginning after June 30, 1997 (a) review plan documents and insurance policies to identify provisions that may conflict with the Act's nondiscrimination requirements; and (b) consider appropriate plan design changes and any adjustments in contributions or premiums necessary to adapt to the new requirements.

E. Newborns and Mothers Health Protection Act

1. Previous Law

State insurance laws often require health insurance issuers to provide coverage for a variety of medical procedures and expenses. Group health plans that purchase commercial insurance generally must comply with these state mandated benefit laws. However, ERISA preempts state mandated benefit laws to the extent that such laws apply to self-insured plans and ERISA generally does not require private health plans to provide specific types or levels of coverage. Beginning in 1995, several states enacted legislation requiring health insurers offering coverage in the state to provide coverage for a minimum length of stay following the birth of a child.

2. Newborns' and Mothers' Health Protection Act Requirements

Shortly after Congress passed HIPAA, it added provisions to Title VI of the appropriations bill for the Departments of Housing and Urban Development and Veterans Affairs (P.L. 104-204) that amended HIPAA to require group health plans (and individual health plans) to provide coverage for a minimimum hospital stay of 48 hours following vaginal delivery and 96 hours following caesarean delivery. The attending physician, in consultation with the mother, may authorize an earlier discharge. But health plans may not take steps to encourage earlier discharges, such as penalizing providers or patients, or providing financial incentives to patients. Moreover, plans may not increase otherwise applicable copayments and deductibles to discourage stays up to the applicable 48 or 96 hour periods. Generally, state laws relating to health insurance issuers that provide greater protections to consumers are not preempted.Thus, a state law could require coverage for 72 hours, instead of 48 hours.

There are several differences between this hospital stay requirement and the general provisions of HIPAA relating to group health plans. First, these provisions are effective for plan years beginning after January 1, 1998 (rather than June 30, 1997). Second, the requirements are enforced through ERISA and PHSA, but not through IRC penalties. Finally, group health plans are required to provide a separate notice of these requirements to covered employees and dependents no later than 60 daysafter they become effective.

The Secretary of HHS is directed to appoint an advisory panel to study perinatal and maternity care, and to report to Congress on recommended improvements in such care. An initial report is due 18 months after enactment.

3. Action Necessary for Compliance

By the first plan year beginning after January 1, 1998, modify plan documentsand administrative procedures to reflect the new federal maternity stay requirements. Notify participants and beneficiaries of the new requirements no later than 60 days after the beginning of the plan year. HMOs and other network plans should review and modify agreements with providers, as necessary, to ensure that they

APPENDIX B

do not include financial incentives or penalties that may be inconsistent with the maternity stay requirement. For insured plans, determine whether applicable state law imposes additional requirements or requirements that would be deemed more beneficial to consumers.

F. Mental Health Coverage Requirements

1. Previous Law

State insurance laws often require health insurance issuers to provide coverage for a variety of medical procedures and expenses. Group health plans that purchase commercial insurance generally must comply with these state mandated benefit laws. However, ERISA preemptsstate mandated benefit laws to the extent that such laws apply to self-insured plans and federal law does not require private health plans to provide specific types or levels of coverage. Several states have enacted mental health parity requirements applicable to insurance coverage sold in the state.

2. New Mental Health Coverage Requirements

The Mental Health Parity Act of 1996 (Title VII of the FY97 appropriations bill for the Departments of Housing and Urban Development and Veterans Affairs) amends HIPAA to require group health plans with 50 or more employees to apply the same annual and lifetime dollar limits to both mental health benefits and physical health benefits for plan years beginning after January 1, 1998.

Group health plans may apply a single dollar limit to all physical and mental health coverage in the aggregate, or may apply separate but equal dollar limits to physical and mental health coverage. For plans that apply different annual or lifetime limits to different types of medical/surgical benefits, the Secretary of Labor is directed to issue regulations addressing ways in which these plans can apply an average of the different dollar limits for mental health benefit coverage.

There are several exceptions to these mental health requirements. First, as noted above, the requirements apply only to companies that employed an average of 50 or more employees during the previous year.[9] Second, the provisions currently are scheduled to sunset on September 30, 2001. Third, plans are not required to provide mental health coverage. Fourth, the provisions do not apply to coverage for substance abuse or chemical dependency. Fifth, plans are not prohibited from utilizing restrictions other than lifetime or annual dollar limits. Therefore, for example, a plan could increase co-payments or deductibles for mental health coverage, or limit the number of treatments or visits covered. Finally, the mental health requirements will not apply to those plans that experience cost increases as a result of the provisions of one percent or more. Because the language of the Mental Health Parity Act is ambiguous, it is unclear whether group health plans utilizing this final exception must be prepared to show proof of actual cost increases in a previous plan year, or whether estimates of projected increases will be sufficient.[10]

3. Action Necessary for Compliance

By the first plan year beginning after January 1, 1998, modify plan documents, policies, and administrative procedures to reflect the new federal mental health parity requirements. If necessary, consider alternative cost-sharing requirements or plan designs to discourage unnecessary mental health treatments. For insured plans, determine whether applicable state law imposes different or more strict requirements.

---

[9] Note, however, that state laws requiring mental health parity will apply to firms with fewer employees that purchase insurance coverage.

[10] Note also that the requirements are enforced through ERISA and PHSA, but not through IRC penalties.

G. Expanded ERISA Reporting and Disclosure Requirements

1. Previous Law

Plan administrators of employee benefit plans subject to Title I of ERISA, including group health plans, are required to file reports periodically with the Secretary of Labor and to disclose plan information to participants and beneficiaries. Among the documents required to be filed and provided to participants and beneficiaries is a summary plan description (SPD) that describes the terms of the plan and informs participants and beneficiaries of their rights and obligations under the plan.

The SPD generally must be updated every five years. If a change in the terms of the plan or in other information disclosed in the SPD occurs in the interim, a summary of material modifications (SMM) must be filed with the Secretary and provided to participants within 210 days after the close of the plan year in which the change is adopted or occurs.

2. HIPAA Modifications

HIPAA modifies the SPD and SMM requirements applicable to group health plans. The SPD now must disclose whether an employer or a health insurance issuer is responsible for financing or administering plan benefits. If an issuer is responsible for financing or administering plan benefits, the name and address of such issuer must be included in the SPD. The SPD also must inform participants and beneficiaries how to contact the office at the Department of Labor responsible for advising them of their rights under HIPAA.

In addition, the Act considerably reduces the period within which an SMM must be provided to participants and beneficiaries and filed with the Secretary of Labor. If a plan modification involves a "material reduction in covered services or benefits under a group health plan," participants and beneficiaries must be notified and the SMM must be filed with the Secretary within 60 days after such material reduction is adopted. Alternatively, SMMs may be furnished at regular intervals of not more than 90 days. This option may prove less burdensome for group health plans that intend to make frequent changes during any plan year involving "material reductions in covered services or benefits."[11] For changes which do not involve a "material reduction," the notification period remains 210 days following the close of the plan year.

These changes generally are effective for plan years beginning after June 30, 1997. For collectively bargained arrangements, these requirements are effective on the later of (a) the date on which the last collective bargaining agreement relating to the plan terminates; or (b) July 1, 1997.

3. Action Necessary for Compliance

By the commencement of the plan year beginning after June 30, 1997 (a) modify administrative procedures necessary to furnish SMMs within the shortened period required by the Act; and (b) prepare an SMM describing changes adopted in response to HIPAA. Provide the SMM to participants and beneficiaries within 60 days after the changes are adopted if such changes involve a "material reduction in covered services or benefits," or within 210 days after the close of the plan year if such changes do not amount to "material reductions."

H. COBRA Requirements Expanded and Clarified

1. Previous Law

The Consolidated Omnibus Budget Reconciliation Act of 1985 (COBRA) requires most group health plans to offer certain employees and their dependents the option to purchase continued health coverage

---

[11] In addition, the Act directs the Secretary to promulgate regulations by February 21, 1997 providing alternative methods to notification by mail.

in the case of certain qualifying events, such as termination or reduction in hours of employment, that otherwise would cause them to lose coverage. Qualified beneficiaries must be given the same options with respect to changes in coverage as similarly-situated active employees.

Generally, the maximum period of COBRA coverage is 18 months. Employers may charge qualified beneficiaries 102 percent of the applicable premium for COBRA coverage. However, individuals determined under the Social Security Act to be disabled at the time of the qualifying event (generally, the loss of employment) may extend their eligibility for COBRA to 29 months. During this extended period, which is designed to fill the gap between their loss of employer-sponsored coverage and eligibility for Medicare disability coverage, employers may charge qualified beneficiaries 150 percent of the applicable premium for COBRA coverage. However, it was not clear whether this extended COBRA coverage applied to any qualified beneficiary or only to the covered employee.

COBRA coverage can be terminated before the end of the applicable coverage period in certain circumstances, including where (a) an employer ceases to maintain any group health plan; (b) the qualified beneficiary fails to pay the required premium; or (c) the qualified beneficiary becomes covered under another group health plan that does not contain any "exclusion or limitation with respect to any preexisting condition of such beneficiary." The scope of the preexisting condition coverage rule was unclear. For example, it was unclear whether qualified beneficiaries were required to actually have the preexisting condition that was limited or excluded by the other plan in order to maintain their COBRA coverage.

2. HIPAA Modifications

The Act clarifies that the extended period of COBRA coverage in the case of disability applies both to covered employees and to qualified beneficiaries of the covered employee. The Act also makes the extended period of COBRA disability coverage available to all qualified beneficiaries who become disabled, as determined by the Social Security Administration, within 60 days after the qualifying event.

Reflecting requirements added elsewhere by HIPAA relating to preexisting condition limitations and creditable coverage, the Act provides that COBRA coverage may be terminated by an employer before the end of the applicable coverage period if a qualified beneficiary becomes covered under another group health plan, even if the other plan contains a preexisting condition limitation, as long as the preexisting condition limitation or exclusion does not apply to the qualified beneficiary, or is satisfied by the qualified beneficiary.

The Act also modifies the definition of qualified beneficiary to include a child born or placed for adoption with the covered employee during a period of COBRA coverage. Under previous law, newborns or adopted children could be denied COBRA coverage because generally they were not eligible for enrollment until the group health plan's next open enrollment period. This modification means that newborns and adopted children may be immediately eligible for COBRA coverage. Also, because the Act requires group health plans to allow participants to change their coverage status upon the birth or placement for adoption of a child, COBRA beneficiaries will now be able to change their coverage status upon the birth or adoption of a child.

These COBRA modifications are effective January 1, 1997, regardless of when the plan year begins or whether the relevant qualifying event occurred before, on, or after such date. Group health plans are required to notify each qualified beneficiary who has elected COBRA coverage of the changes to the COBRA rules contained in HIPAA no later than November 1, 1996.

3. Action Necessary for Compliance

If they have not yet done so, group health plans should immediately notify qualified beneficiaries of the changes made by the Act to COBRA. Group health plans also should modify their COBRA election forms and administrative procedures to conform to the Act's modifications.

III. New Responsibilities For Health Insurance Issuers In the Group Insurance Market

The requirements described in sections II.A. through II.F. above apply to both group health plans and health insurance issuers offering coverage in connection with group health plans under the Act. The requirements described in sections II.G. and II.H. apply only to group health plans. This section will describe those responsibilities and requirements added by HIPAA to the PHSA that apply solely to health insurance carriers, HMOs and other "health insurance issuers" in the group insurance market.

A. Guaranteed Issue Requirements In the Small Employer Market

1. Current Law

The McCarran Ferguson Act of 1945 (P.L. 79-15) exempts the business of insurance from antitrust regulation to the extent that it is regulated by the states and indicates that no federal law should be interpreted to override state insurance regulation unless it does so explicitly. Section 514(b)(2)(A) of ERISA leaves to the states the regulation of insurance, while employee benefit plans are not insurance and are regulated by the federal government. Many states have adopted rules requiring health insurance carriers to issue coverage to small employers. State rules differ markedly, however. For example, states have adopted varying definitions of "small employers." Moreover, some states require the issuance of all health insurance policies, while some require the issuance only of specified benefit packages. And states have adopted different requirements regarding the amount that may be charged to employers for coverage.

2. HIPAA Requirements

The Act requires health insurance issuers offering coverage in the small group market in a state (a) to accept all small employers (those that employed an average of 2-50 employees during the previous calendar year and who employ at least two employees on the first day of the plan year) applying for coverage; and (b) to accept every eligible individual who applies for coverage during the period in which such individual first becomes eligible under the terms of the group health plan. While there is some ambiguity in the Act, it is likely that this requirement will be interpreted to require issuers to provide guarantee issue for small employers to all policies that issuers offer in the small group market.

The Act leaves to state law determinations, if any, regarding how much issuers may charge small employers for such coverage.

An issuer may deny coverage to small employers if it demonstrates to the state, if required, that it does not have the financial reserves necessary to underwrite additional coverage. The issuer also must apply the financial capacity limit to all employers in the small group market in the state, consistent with state law, and without regard to claims experience or health status-related factors. An issuer denying coverage on the basis of financial capacity may not offer coverage in the small group market in the state for 180 days or until the issuer has demonstrated to the state that it has sufficient reserves, whichever is later. The Act allows states to make determinations of adequate capacity on a service-area-specific basis.

In addition, issuers offering coverage in the small group market under network plans with limited coverage areas may (a) limit coverage to those small employers with eligible employees or dependents who live, work, or reside in the plan's service area; or (b) within the service area, deny coverage to small employers if the issuer demonstrates to the state, if required, that it will not have the capacity to deliver services adequately to additional groups of small employers. Issuers offering coverage through network plans that deny coverage on the basis of capacity limits must deny coverage to small employers uniformly without regard to claims experience or any health status-related factor. An issuer denying coverage on the basis of capacity is prohibited from offering coverage in the small employer market in the applicable service area for 180 days.

HIPAA allows health insurance issuers to establish employer contribution rules or group participation rules, as allowed under applicable state law. Employer contribution rules generally require employers to make a minimum contribution toward the premium payment of employees or dependents. Group participation rules generally require employers to enroll a minimum number of employees or minimum percentage of employees in order to obtain coverage from the issuer.

While the Act requires issuers to renew coverage and continue coverage to bona fide associations, the guaranteed issue requirements do not apply to health insurance issuers that make coverage available in the small group market only through one or more "bona fide associations." Bona fide associations are defined in the Act as associations that (a) have been actively in existence for at least five years; (b) have been formed and maintained in good faith for purposes other than obtaining insurance; (c) do not condition membership on any health status-related factor; (d) make health insurance coverage offered through the association available to any member, or individuals eligible for coverage through a member (such as a dependent), regardless of any health status-related factor; (e) do not make health insurance coverage offered through the association available other than to, or through, members of the association; and (f) meet additional requirements that may be imposed by state law.

While HIPAA does not require issuers to issue coverage to large employers (those with more than 50 employees), the Governor of each state must submit, by December 31, 2000 and every three years thereafter, a report to the Secretary of HHS on the access of large employers to health insurance coverage in the state. The Secretary must submit triennial reports to Congress based on these reports. In addition, the General Accounting Office (GAO) is directed to prepare a report by February 21, 1998 on the access of large employers to health insurance coverage.

3. Action Necessary for Compliance

By July 1, 1997, health insurance issuers offering coverage in the small group market, as defined by the Act, should (a) review current practices relating to access and coverage in the small employer market; (b) adopt procedures necessary to comply with the Act's guaranteed access provisions; (c) assess the financial impact of the Act's guaranteed issue provisions and make any necessary adjustments, consistent with state law, to account for the new requirements; and (d) determine whether applicable state law imposes more rigorous guaranteed issue requirements.

B. Guaranteed Renewal Requirements In All Markets

1. Previous Law

The McCarran Ferguson Act of 1945 (P.L. 79-15) exempts the business of insurance from federal antitrust regulation to the extent that it is regulated by the states and indicates that no federal law should be interpreted to override state insurance regulation unless it does so explicitly. Section 514(b)(2)(A) of ERISA leaves to the states the regulation of insurance, while employee benefit plans are not insurance and are regulated by the federal government. Many states have enacted laws requiring insurers to renew group health insurance coverage in the small group market.

2. HIPAA Requirements

The Act requires health insurance issuers offering group health insurance coverage in either the small or large group market (or both) to renew or continue in force coverage at the option of the plan sponsor of the plan. The Act leaves to state law determinations, if any, regarding how much issuers may charge small employers for renewing coverage. Group health plans may determine which participants and beneficiaries are eligible for continued enrollment consistent with the nondiscrimination rules described in section II.D.

The Act provides certain exceptions to the guaranteed renewability requirement for one or more of the following (a) nonpayment of premiums; (b) fraud; (c) violation of participation or contribution rules; (d) termination of coverage in the market in accordance with applicable state law (as discussed below); (e) for network plans, no enrollees connected to the plan live, reside, or work in the service area of the issuer, or the area for which the issuer is authorized to do business and, in the case of the small group market only if the issuer would deny enrollment to the plan under regulations governing guaranteed availability of coverage; and (f) for coverage made available to bona fide associations, if membership in the association ceases, but only if coverage is terminated uniformly without regard to any health status-related factor of a covered individual.

The Act also allows exceptions to guaranteed renewability if the issuer or plan no longer offers a particular type of group coverage in the small or large group market so long as the issuer, in accordance with applicable state law (a) provides prior notice to each plan sponsor, and to participants and beneficiaries; (b) provides the plan sponsor the chance to purchase all (or, in the case of large employers, any) other health insurance plan offered by the issue in the applicable market; and (c) applies the termination uniformly without regard to the claims experience of the sponsors or any health status-related factors of any participants or beneficiaries or any participants or beneficiaries who may become eligible for coverage.

Health insurance issuers offering coverage in the group market may discontinue all coverage in a state if they cancel all current policies in the applicable small or large group market and provide at least 180 days prior notice to all covered individuals and to applicable state authorities. In this instance, the issuer is prohibited from offering any coverage in the applicable market in the state involved for five years.

Issuers are permitted to modify the health insurance coverage offered to large employers, and to small employers if modifications are made effective on a uniform basis among group health plans offering that particular type of coverage.

3. Action Necessary for Compliance

By July 1, 1997, health insurance issuers offering coverage to both large and small employers should (a) review current practices and policies relating to renewal to determine whether they comply with the Act's requirements; (b) adopt policies and administrative procedures necessary to comply with the Act's guaranteed renewal provisions; (c) assess the financial impact of the Act's guaranteed renewal provisions and make any necessary adjustments, consistent with state law, to account for the new requirements; and (d) determine whether applicable state law imposes more rigorous renewability requirements.

C. Disclosure Requirements for Small Employers

1. Previous Law

The McCarran Ferguson Act of 1945 (P.L. 79-15) exempts the business of insurance from federal antitrust regulation to the extent that it is regulated by the states and indicates that no federal law should be interpreted to override state insurance regulation unless it does so explicitly. Section 514(b)(2)(A) of ERISA leaves to the states the regulation of insurance, while employee benefit plans are not insurance and are regulated by the federal government. Several states have adopted rules requiring health insurance carriers to disclose the terms of the policies offered to small employers.

2. HIPAA Requirements

In an effort to provide small employers with more complete and accurate information when they are deciding whether to provide health insurance coverage to their employees, HIPAA contains disclosure requirements that are more detailed than those currently in place in most states.

The Act requires health insurance issuers offering coverage in the small group market to make a "reasonable" disclosure to small employers, as part of their solicitation and sales materials, of the availability of information regarding the terms and conditions of coverage available to each small employer. At the request of a small employer, issuers must disclose those provisions of policies available to small employers (a) regarding the issuers' right to change premium rates and the factors that could affect such changes; (b) relating to renewability and coverage for preexisting conditions; and (c) relating to the benefits and premiums under all health insurance coverage for which the employer is qualified. The information must be presented in a manner designed to be understandable by the average small employer and sufficiently detailed to reasonably inform small employers of their rights and obligations under the health insurance coverage.

Issuers need not disclose information that would be considered proprietary or trade secret information under applicable law.

3. Action Necessary for Compliance

By July 1, 1997, health insurance issuers offering coverage in the small employer market should (a) review current practices and policies relating to disclosure of information to determine whether they comply with the Act's requirements; (b) modify sales and solicitation materials to provide reasonable disclosure to small employers of the availability of more detailed information regarding the terms and conditions of available coverage; (c) develop non-proprietary information to provide to small employers consistent with the Act's disclosure requirements relating to premiums, preexisting conditions, renewability, and benefits; (d) adopt policies and administrative procedures necessary to comply with the Act's disclosure requirements; and (e) determine whether applicable state law imposes more rigorous disclosure requirements.

D. State Flexibility and Preemption

1. Previous Law

The McCarran Ferguson Act of 1945 (P.L. 79-15) exempts the business of insurance from federal antitrust regulation to the extent that it is regulated by the states and indicates that no federal law should be interpreted to override state insurance regulation unless it does so explicitly. Section 514(b)(2)(A) of ERISA leaves to the states the regulation of insurance, while employee benefit plans are not insurance and are regulated by the federal government.

2. HIPAA Structure

While the Act contains new federal insurance standards, it attempts to preserve to the extent possible the current division of responsibility for enforcement and preemption between the states and the federal government. HIPAA provides a narrow preemption of state law relating to health insurance issuers offering health insurance coverage in the group market. At the same time, HIPAA effectively imposes uniform standards for self-insured ERISA plans by expressly providing that nothing in the Act should be interpreted to affect or modify the preemption provisions of ERISA contained in section 514(b)(2)(A).

For health insurance reform requirements under the PHSA relating to health insurance issuers, the Act contains two different rules of preemption. First, it provides a very narrow preemption for most state laws, including those relating to guaranteed issue and renewal and those outside of the scope of the Act, such as community rating. The Act provides that any provision of state law which establishes, implements, or continues in effect any standard or requirement solely relating to health insurance issuers in connection with health insurance coverage is not superseded unless the standard or requirement "prevents the application" of a federal requirement contained in HIPAA.

Second, the Act contains different preemption rules for state laws relating to portability. The Act provides that state laws applicable to a preexisting condition exclusion which differ from the standards in the Act are superseded, unless they (a) shorten the look back period for determining a preexisting condition limitation (from six months to any shorter period of time); (b) shorten the length of a preexisting condition exclusion (from 12 months, or 18 months for late enrollees, to any shorter period); (c) lengthen the break in coverage time allowed from 63 days to any greater period; (d) lengthen the time for enrollment of newborns or adopted children from 30 days to any longer period; (e) prohibit the imposition of any preexisting condition exclusions in cases not described in the Act; (f) require additional special enrollment periods or events which trigger special enrollment periods; or (g) reduce the maximum period permitted for an affiliation period.

Congress apparently believed that it was necessary to adopt this special preemption construct relating to portability to ensure that the processes necessary to establish and certify creditable coverage established by the Act would not be frustrated by overly burdensome or conflicting state laws.

IV. New Responsibilities for Health Insurance Issuers in the Individual Insurance Market

Currently, the individual health insurance market is regulated solely by the states. As of December 1995, 11 states required that individual insurers write policies on a guaranteed issue basis; 16 states required guaranteed renewal of insurance in the individual market; and 22 states limited the use of preexisting condition limitations. In addition, approximately 25 states had adopted high-risk pools for certain uninsurable individuals.

HIPAA contains federal requirements guaranteeing the availability of individual health insurance coverage to certain qualified individuals with prior group coverage, without limitation or exclusion of benefits, and guaranteeing the renewability of individual health insurance coverage in most cases. The Act does not require that individuals without any prior coverage be insured. Nor does it provide portability for individuals moving from one individual health insurance policy to another. Furthermore, it leaves to the states decisions regarding limitations, if any, to be imposed on premiums charged for individual health insurance coverage guaranteed by the Act.[12]

Health insurance issuers need not comply with the Act's individual market guaranteed issue or renewal provisions if they (a) offer insurance coverage only in connection with group health plans (as defined by the Act); (b) make insurance coverage available to individuals only through one or more associations; or (c) provide individual coverage only through conversion policies. Note, however, that all issuers in the individual market must provide certifications of prior creditable coverage in the same manner as health insurance issuers offering coverage in connection with group health plans.

Because current individual market requirements differ so markedly from state to state and because each state is likely to adopt distinct rules in response to HIPAA, this portion of the outline does not contain a section describing the status of "previous law" nor a section describing "actions necessary for compliance."

A. Guaranteed Access for Eligible Individuals

The Act requires each health insurance issuer that offers health insurance coverage in the individual market in a state to offer coverage to each "eligible individual" (as defined by the Act). Further, it prohibits such issuers from imposing any preexisting condition exclusions on such eligible individuals. These requirements do not apply to issuers in states that have acceptable alternative mechanisms, as described in section IV.C. below. In addition, health insurance issuers in states that have not adopted acceptable alternative mechanisms may limit coverage as described in section IV.B. below.

To qualify as an "eligible individual" under the Act, an individual must (1) have 18 or more months of aggregate creditable coverage (without a break of 63 days or more); (2) with his or her most recent coverage from a group health plan, governmental plan, or church plan; (3) be ineligible for group health coverage, Medicare Parts A or B, and Medicaid; (4) not have been terminated from his or her most recent coverage for nonpayment of premiums or fraud; (5) if eligible for COBRA continuation coverage (or a similar state program such as "mini-COBRA"), have elected and exhausted this coverage.

While the language of the Act is vague, it is likely that the duration of an individual's COBRA coverage alone will be sufficient to qualify for individual coverage under the Act. For example, an individual who elects and continues COBRA coverage for a full 18 months need not have been covered for an additional 18 months or more while he or she was an active employee.

---

[12] As in the group market, the Act does allow issuers to offer premium discounts, or modify otherwise applicable copayments or deductibles in return for adherence to health promotion or disease prevention programs.

The Act contains exceptions to guaranteed issue in the individual market for both network and non-network plans similar to the exceptions discussed for health insurance issuers offering coverage to small employers in section III.A.2 above.

B. Plan Options for Issuers

The Act requires individual health insurance issuers to offer coverage to eligible individuals under all policy forms offered by the issuer, with certain exceptions. First, issuers may decline to offer coverage under all policy forms if the state is implementing an acceptable alternative mechanism (as described in Section VI.C. below).

Second, if a state is not implementing an acceptable alternative mechanism, issuers may elect to limit policy forms offered to eligible individuals so long as they offer eligible individuals at least two different policy forms, both of which are designed for, made generally available and actively marketed to, and have enrollment which consists of both eligible and other individuals. In addition, the two policy forms must meet one of the following requirements (1) they must be the two policy forms which have the largest and next to largest premium volume; or (2) they must offer coverage to eligible individuals (a) with both a "higher-level" and "lower-level" policy form (as determined consistent with actuarial standards specified under the Act); (b) coverage that provides benefits "substantially similar" to other individual health insurance coverage offered in the state by the issuer; and (c) that is subsidized, risk-adjusted, or covered by a public or private risk-adjustment mechanism. Issuers must apply this election uniformly to all eligible individuals in a state, and the election will be effective for at least two years.

C. State Alternative Mechanisms

HIPAA provides significant latitude for states to implement "acceptable alternative mechanisms" (AAMs) designed to provide access to eligible individuals. State AAMs must (1) provide a choice of health insurance coverage to all eligible individuals in the state, including at least one policy form providing comprehensive coverage; and (2) not impose any preexisting condition exclusions on eligible individuals.

A state is presumed to be implementing an AAM if the Governor notifies the Secretary of HHS by April 1, 1997, that the state has adopted or intends to adoptan AAM by January 1, 1998 (or by July 1, 1998 for those states in which the legislature does not meet until after August 21, 1997). States that do not have AAMs in place by either the January 1, 1998 or July 1, 1998 deadlines may adoptAAMs at any time in the future. In this case, the AAM will be deemed acceptable unless the Secretary determines that it is not acceptable within 90 days after the submission by the state of certain required information.

AAMs may take the form of either (1) a qualified high-risk pool (consistent with principles specified in the Act); (2) individual market reforms modeled after the Small Employer and Individual Health Insurance Availability Model Act (adopted by the National Association of Insurance Commissioners on June 3, 1996); (3) any other mechanism that provides for "risk adjustment, risk spreading or a risk spreading mechanism (among issuers or policies of an issuer)"; or (4) any other mechanism that allows individuals to choose all health individual health insurance policies available in the state.

States electing to adopt AAMs must provide information to the Secretary every three years to ensure that the AAM is continuing to be implemented. If the Secretary finds that the state is not implementing an AAM, it must allow the state a "reasonable" opportunity to modify the mechanism to comply with HIPAA's requirements. If, after a reasonable opportunity, the state still is not implementing an AAM, the requirements described in sections IV.A. and IV.B. above will apply in the state.

D. Guaranteed Renewal in the Individual Market

The Act requires health insurance issuers offering individual health insurance coverage to renew such coverage at the option of the individual. There are exceptions to these guaranteed renewal requirements for one or more of the following (1) nonpayment of premiums or untimely payment; (2) fraud; (3)

termination of coverage in the market (as outlined below) in accordance with applicable state law; (4) for network plans, the individual no longer lives, resides or works in the service area the issuer is serving, but only if coverage is terminated uniformly without regard to any health status-related factor; (5) for coverage made available to bona fide associations, if membership in the association ceases, but only if the coverage is terminated uniformly without regard to any health status-related factor.

HIPAA allows issuers to discontinue a particular type of coverage in the individual market only if they (1) provide prior notice to each covered individual; (2) offer each individual the option of purchasing any other individual health insurance coverage policy offered by the issuer; and (3) act uniformly without regard to any health status-related factor of enrolled individuals or individuals who may become eligible for such coverage. Issuers also may discontinue offering all health insurance coverage in the individual market in a state if they cancel all current policies and provide at least 180 days prior notice to all covered individuals and to applicable state authorities. In this case, an issuer may not issue individual coverage in the state for five years. Finally, issuers may modify policy forms offered in the individual market if such modifications are consistent with state law and are effective on a uniform basis among all individuals holding that policy form.

It is important to note that the Act's guaranteed renewal provisions apply to all individuals enrolled in individual coverage, regardless of whether they were originally offered coverage as "eligible individuals" under the Act.

E. State Flexibility

In addition to providing great latitude for states to adopt alternative mechanisms to the Act's guaranteed availability requirements as described in section IV.C. above, HIPAA contains a very narrow preemption of state individual market rules. It provides that nothing in the Act shall be interpreted to prevent a state from establishing, implementing or continuing in effect standards and requirements relating to health insurance issuers offering coverage in the individual market, unless such standards or requirements prevent the application of a requirement in the Act.

F. Enforcement

Each state may require health insurance issuers that issue, sell, renew, or offer health insurance coverage in the individual market to meet the individual reform provisions of the Act. If a state fails to "substantially enforce" the federal requirements, the Secretary of HHS will provide enforcement through the PHSA in the same manner as for a substantial failure of enforcement by a state in the small group market.[13]

G. Additional State Reforms

Because there are several gaps in HIPAA's individual portability provisions which might inhibit the ability of individuals who do not have group health insurance to gain access to coverage or move from one benefit arrangement to another, it is possible that states may enact laws expanding on the Act's individual market reforms. It is likely that states will impose some rate limitations in the individual market. In addition, some states may adopt reforms allowing individuals to move from one individual health insurance plan to another and making it easier for eligible individuals and other individuals to obtain access to individual health insurance plans.

V. Medical Savings Account Demonstration Project

A. Previous Law

Prior to the Act, MSAs without tax-advantages could be offered by employers to employees. In general, the pre-1997 MSAs functioned as personal savings accounts for the payment of unreimbursed medical

---

[13] Again, this structure was necessitated largely by the recently-enacted unfunded mandates legislation which generally prohibits the federal government from requiring states to take actions, including those relating to enforcement of federal laws, which would impose costs on the states exceeding certain thresholds.

APPENDIX B

expenses. Proponents of MSAs argued that contributions to, earnings of, and disbursements from medical savings accounts needed to receive tax treatment similar to that afforded Individual Retirement Accounts ("IRAs") to provide effective health care coverage to significant numbers of people. Concern about the impact of MSAs caused the Congress to establish an MSA demonstration project that generally provides tax-advantaged MSAs to a limited number of participants during a prescribed period of time.

The other alternative to MSAs prior to enactment of the Act was the Flexible Spending Account for health care ("health FSA" or "health FSAs"). In general, a health FSA is offered under an employer-sponsored cafeteria plan on a salary reduction basis and the benefits also are not subject to tax. Although the covered benefits are similar to those covered by MSAs, any amounts left in a health FSA at the end of the year are forfeited. The Act does not preclude the establishment of either an MSA without tax advantages or the health FSA.

B. HIPAA Requirements

1. General

Title III of the Act authorizes the establishment of a limited number of tax-advantaged medical savings accounts ("MSA" or "MSAs") during the years 1997 through 2000. During the four years of the demonstration project, up to 750,000 taxpayers (exclusive of previously uninsured taxpayers) will be permitted to set up MSAs for themselves and their dependents. An MSA is a trust or custodial account exclusively for the benefit of the account holder and is subject to rules similar to the rules of IRAs. An MSA trustee can be a bank, insurance company or other person who satisfies the requirements of the Secretary. During the period of the demonstration project, studies of the effects of MSAs[14] on federal revenues, participants, and health care costs and services generally will be conducted so that the Congress can make an informed judgment about whether or not to maintain or expand the program.

2. Employment Status

Subject to certain aggregate limits, individuals whose sole health care coverage is a high deductible insurance plan may participate in an MSA if they are either self-employed or employees covered by a small employer plan. A self-employed individual includes two percent or more shareholders in an S-corporation as well as general partners of a partnership. A self-employed individual is not precluded from establishing an MSA merely because he or she is eligible to participate in an employer-sponsored plan (or his or her spouse is eligible to participate in an employer-sponsored plan). A small employer must have an average of fifty or fewer employees during either of the two calendar years preceding the year in which the MSA is established or, in the case of a new employer, a reasonable expectation that fifty or fewer employees will be hired during the first year of business. For purposes of determining the number of employees, controlled groups of corporations (IRC Sec. 414(b)), unincorporated trades or businesses under common control (IRC Sec. 414(c)), affiliated service groups (IRC Sec. 414(m)) and certain other businesses (IRC Sec. 414(o)) are treated as a single employer. Having satisfied the initial test of eligibility and made MSA contributions, a small employer may retain eligibility for one year following the year in which the average number of employees exceeds two hundred. Should an employer no longer be a small employer for purposes of the Act, employees for whom MSAs were established can continue to make contributions to their accounts.

3. Aggregate Limits

The authority granted to a self-employed individual or a small employer to establish an MSA will be terminated after the earlier of (a) December 31, 2000, or (b) a determination by the Department of the Treasury that the number of taxpayers who have made or received contributions to MSA accounts

---

[14] Unless otherwise indicated, all references to MSAs are to tax-advantaged MSAs.

231

exceeds 750,000. The Act also imposes interim annual limits on the authority to establish an MSA in 1997 and 1998.

4. High Deductible Plan Requirements

Individuals are eligible to participate in an MSA only if they are covered by a high deductible health plan during the years in which contributions to the MSA are made by them or on their behalf. In the case of an individual MSA, a high deductible health plan is defined as a plan with an annual deductible of at least $1,500, but no more than $2,250. In the case of an MSA for an individual and one or more dependents, a high deductible health plan is defined as a plan with an annual deductible of $3,000, but no more than $4,500. In addition, annual out-of-pocket expense maximums with respect to covered benefits cannot exceed $3,000 for one person or $5,500 for more than one person. After 1998, each of the limits will be adjusted for inflation. In the case of an employee of a small employer, the high deductible plan must be established and maintained by the small employer. In the case of a self-employed individual, the high deductible plan cannot be established or maintained by an employer. Despite the general requirement that an MSA participant cannot be covered by any health plan other than a high deductible plan, the Act provides exceptions for coverage for accidents, disability, dental care, vision care, long-term care, Medicare supplemental insurance, specific disease or illness insurance, fixed hospitalization insurance and workers' compensation. Individuals covered under Medicare are not eligible for an MSA.

5. MSA Contribution Limits

MSA contributions made by or on behalf of individuals are limited to sixty-five percent of the annual deductible amount for the high deductible insurance and to seventy-five percent of the annual deductible amount for contributions made by or on behalf of individuals and dependents. The annual contribution limit is the sum of each monthly limit. In addition, deductions from income tax for contributions made on behalf of employees by a small employer cannot exceed the amount of compensation paid to the employee by the employer sponsoring the high deductible plan and, in the case of the self-employed, deductions cannot exceed the net earnings from the trade or business with respect to which the high deductible health plan is established.

An individual cannot contribute to an MSA plan to which his or her employer contributes or the employer of his or her spouse contributes. An individual who can be claimed as a dependent by another taxpayer may not make contributions. Employer contributions cannot be made through a cafeteria plan (of course, an employer could make health FSA contributions through a cafeteria plan). After tax contributions are prohibited, and excess contributions are subject to an excise tax. An employer must make comparable contributions on behalf of all employees with comparable coverage during a calendar year. Comparability is achieved by making contributions of equal dollar amounts or equal percentages of the high deductible insurance deductible amount. Employees with less than a full year of employment must receive a pro rata contribution.

6. Tax Treatment

Contributions for a calendar year may be made until the due date of the taxpayer's return without regard to extensions. Subject to the annual limits, individual contributions to an MSA are deductible for purposes of determining adjusted gross income (*i.e.*, regardless of whether the taxpayer itemized deductions). Small employer contributions to MSAs are excluded from gross income and from the employment taxes of employers and employees. MSA interest earnings are excluded from gross income. Distributions from MSAs are exempt from federal income tax to the extent that the distributions are used to pay for certain unreimbursed medical expenses, qualified long-term care insurance (see Title X below), COBRA and other continuation coverage required by federal law, and for health plan insurance received in connection with unemployment compensation. Permitted unreimbursed medical expenses are defined in Section 213(d) of the Internal Revenue Code, subject to exceptions for long-term care insurance expenses, health care continuation premiums, and premiums for health care coverage in connection with unemployment compensation.

Distributions not used for medical expenses are taxable and (unless made after age sixty-five, death or disability) subject to a fifteen percent tax penalty. MSA balances remaining at the death of the participant may pass to a surviving spouse who is the named beneficiary of the MSA without federal income tax liability. In addition, the balance may be deducted from the decedent's estate pursuant to the estate tax marital deduction. The balance in the decedent's MSA also is treated as an MSA in the name of the surviving spouse if the latter is a named beneficiary. However, designation of a beneficiary other than the surviving spouse causes the account balance to be included in income of the beneficiary in the year of the decedent's death (reduced by any amounts used to pay qualified medical expenses of the decedent within one year of death). If there is no named beneficiary, the MSA balance is included in the income of the decedent in the year of death.

C. Action Necessary for Compliance

Self-employed individuals and small business within the meaning of the Act should determine whether participation in an MSA with a high deductible health plan makes health care and financial sense for themselves and their employees. If participation in an MSA does make sense, each participant should consider seriously naming his or her spouse as the beneficiary.

VI. New Federal Fraud and Abuse Provisions

A. Fraud and Abuse Control Program

1. Previous Law

The Secretary of Health and Human Services and the Attorney General are responsible for the investigation and prosecution of fraud in federal health care programs. The Secretary has the authority to impose civil monetary penalties and to exclude fraudulent health care providers from federal health care programs. The Attorney General is authorized to initiate criminal prosecutions. States are authorized to investigate and prosecute Medicaid fraud.

2. HIPAA Requirements

The Secretary and the Attorney General are directed to establish a national health care fraud and abuse control program to coordinate federal, state and local law enforcement efforts. The scope of the joint and coordinated program includes investigations, audits, evaluations and inspections related to the delivery of and payment for health care. Data captured in these efforts will be shared among public representatives and private third party payers. As a part of the joint effort, guidelines will be issued to guarantee confidentiality and privacy. In addition, the Secretary and the Attorney General would provide guidance to health care providers through the issuance of safe harbors, advisory opinions and special fraud alerts.

B. Medicare Integrity Program

1. Previous Law

The Medicare integrity program responsibilities fit within the general budget, and is not the subject of special legislation.

2. HIPAA Requirements

The Secretary is directed to contract with private companies to review the activities of private service providers, audit cost reports, evaluate accuracy of payments, educate providers, and develop and maintain an updated list of durable medical equipment providers.

C. Beneficiary Incentive Provisions

1. Previous Law

No provision.

2. HIPAA Requirements

The Secretary is required to provide an explanation of Medicare benefits, and to establish programs to encourage submission of suggestions to improve the Medicare program's efficiency and to encourage reporting of individuals and entities who are engaging in or who have engaged in acts or omissions that constitute grounds for sanctions. For each individual who provides information that leads to a collection of at least $100, the Secretary has the discretion to pay a portion to the informant.

D. Extension of Fraud and Abuse Criminal Sanctions

1. Previous Law

Criminal penalties apply in certain cases of Medicare, Medicaid and state health care program fraud.

2. HIPAA Requirements

The criminal penalties currently applicable in certain cases of Medicare, Medicaid and state health care program fraud are extended to other federal health care programs funded in whole or in part by the United States government and to additional state health care programs funded through federal block grants.

E. Guidance Regarding Sanctions

1. Previous Law

Various payment practices which might be considered violations of the anti-kickback rules are protected from criminal or civil sanctions by federal statute. In addition, the Secretary has the authority to promulgate safe harbors with respect to payment practices that will insulate such practices from fraud and abuse sanctions.

2. HIPAA Requirements

The Secretary will solicit proposals in the Federal Register for new safe harbors and for modifications to existing safe harbors on an annual basis. In consultation with the Attorney General, the Secretary will consider a variety of factors in determining whether or not to adopt or modify any of the proposed safe harbors. In addition, the Act establishes a demonstration program under which the Secretary will issue written advisory opinions binding on the Secretary and the requesting party within sixty days of an advisory opinion request as to what constitutes a violation of the Medicare program with respect to prohibited remuneration or inducements to reduce or limit services unlawfully. The advisory opinions also will specify whether the activity constitutes grounds for civil or criminal sanctions. Only requests made after February 21, 1997 and before August 21, 2000 will be honored. The Secretary also is authorized to issue special fraud alerts in the Federal Register to inform the public of dubious practices under the Medicare or a state health care program.

F. Mandatory Exclusion from Program Participation

1. Previous Law

The Secretary must exclude for a minimum of five years any person or entity from participation in the Medicare and Medicaid programs and in programs funded through the Maternal and Child Health Service or Social Services Block Grants if the person or entity is convicted of criminal offenses related to (a) the delivery of health care services under Medicare or a state health care program or (b) patient abuse in connection with the delivery of health care services. The Secretary has the discretion to exclude persons or entities from participation for offenses such as fraud, kickbacks, obstruction of an investigation, and controlled substances, license revocations or suspensions, and claims for excessive charges or unnecessary services. In addition, an individual convicted of a health care program related felony may be fined up to $25,000 or imprisoned for up to five years or both. An individual or entity submitting false or fraudulent claims for reimbursement is subject to civil monetary penalties.

2. HIPAA Requirements

Mandatory exclusions for at least five years are expanded to include individuals and entities convicted of felony offenses relating to health care fraud or controlled substances. The Secretary's discretionary exclusion authority is expanded to include individuals convicted of (a) misdemeanor criminal health care fraud offenses, and (b) criminal offenses involving financial misconduct with respect to programs other than health care programs funded in whole or in part by federal, state or local agencies.

Unless the Secretary makes a determination otherwise, a three year exclusion must be imposed upon any individual convicted of misdemeanor criminal fraud offensesregarding health care programs, non-health care government programs, obstruction of health care fraud investigations, and controlled substances. Exclusions due to the revocation or suspension of a health care license, professional competence or financial integrity must be at least equal to the period of the revocation or suspension. Exclusions due to providing excessive services or services which fail to meet professionally recognized standards must be for at least one year. The Secretary has discretionary authority to exclude an individual who has a direct or indirect ownership or control interest, or is an officer or employee of, a sanctioned entity and knows or should have known the basis for the sanctioned activity. The Secretary has discretionary authority to exclude for at least one year a practitioner or person who has failed to comply with certain statutory obligations relating to the quality of health care regardless of whether the individual was unwilling or unable to meet the obligation.

G. Intermediate Medicare HMO Sanctions

1. Previous Law

The Secretary generally enters into one-year contracts with Medicare HMO providers with options for automatic renewal. Upon notice and hearing, the Secretary may terminate the contract for failure to perform contract terms, inefficiency and ineffectiveness in carrying out Social Security Act requirements, or failure to meet statutory requirements.

2. HIPAA Requirements

Pursuant to a formal investigation, reasonable opportunity to cure, notice and an opportunity for a hearing, the Secretary is authorized to impose intermediate sanctions; *i.e.*, sanctions such as civil fines that stop short of termination.

VII. New Administrative Simplification Provisions

A. Electronic Data Transmission Standards

1. Previous Law

Under previous law, no federal standards for the transmission of electronic data were promulgated.

2. Promulgation of Standards

By February 1998, the Secretary of Health and Human Services is directed to promulgate uniform standards for the transmission of transaction information in the health care system regarding claims and claims status, attachments, enrollment and disenrollment, eligibility, health care payment and remittance advice, premium payments, injury reports, and referrals. In connection with the promulgation of these standards, the Secretary is to implement a health identifier system similar to the taxpayer identification number utilized by the Internal Revenue Service. The Secretary also is directed to establish uniform standards for coordinating benefits between two or more health care providers. Civil penalties are imposed for failure to comply with the standards two years after promulgation. The Secretary also is directed to establish a national health care fraud and abuse data collection program for reporting final adverse actions against health care providers, suppliers, or practitioners.

B. Future Privacy Regulations

1. Previous Law

Under previous law, no federal standards for maintaining the security and privacy of individually identifiable health information were promulgated.

2. Security and Privacy of Individually Identifiable Information

The Secretary is directed to promulgate standards for protecting the security and privacy of individually identifiable health information. Civil and, in the case of wrongful disclosure, criminal penalties are imposed for disclosure of individually identifiable health information.

VIII. Tax Changes

A. Self-Employed Deduction

1. Previous Law

A self-employed individual was permitted to deduct thirty percent of the amount paid for health insurance, including the cost of insurance for a spouse and dependents. The benefits, however, were included in income.

2. HIPAA Requirements

The self-employed deduction is increased to forty percent in 1997, forty-five percent in 1998 through 2002, fifty percent in 2003, sixty percent in 2004, seventy percent in 2005, and eighty percent thereafter. In addition, the Act clarifies that benefits are excluded to the same extent as benefits under an insured plan so long as the self-insured arrangement is insurance and not merely reimbursement. Payments for personal injury or sickness through an arrangement having the effect of insurance are excluded from income as are payments from arrangements other than insurance which have the effect of insurance.

B. Corporate-Owned Life Insurance (COLI)

1. Previous Law

In general, no income tax is imposed upon a life insurance policyholder with respect to earnings under a life insurance contract, or upon amounts received by a beneficiary due to the death of the insured. In addition, a policyholder generally may borrow against a life insurance contract without affecting either income tax exclusion. However, an employer cannot deduct interest on indebtedness with respect to life insurance contracts covering the life of an officer, employee or other individual with a financial interest in the company to the extent that the total indebtedness incurred with respect to the such individual exceeds $50,000. This type of life insurance in which the corporate employer incurs indebtedness is known as a "leveraged COLI."

2. HIPAA Requirements

The Act substantially reduces the individuals in a company with respect to whom a deduction is available in a leveraged COLI to "key persons." A key person is defined to include persons on whose lives insurance contracts were purchased on or before June 20, 1986, and who are either an officer or a twenty-percent owner of the employer. The total number of key persons cannot exceed the greater of (a) five individuals or (b) the lesser of five percent of the total number of officers and employees of the taxpayer or twenty individuals–a formula which assures that no more than twenty persons can be included as key persons. In addition, deductible interest indebtedness cannot exceed the rate of interest specified in the Moody's Corporate Bond Yield Average. The COLI provisions of the Act are effective with respect to interest paid or accrued after December 31, 1996, subject to certain phase-out rules.

C. Viatical Insurance (Life Insurance Living Benefits)

1. Previous Law

As described in Section B.1 above, income tax is not imposed upon a life insurance policyholder with respect to earnings under a life insurance contract, nor upon amounts received by a beneficiary due to the death of the insured. However, amounts in excess of the taxpayer's investment in a life insurance contract that are received prior to death are taxable. The Department of the Treasury has issued proposed regulations under which certain "qualified accelerated death benefits" paid by reason of the terminal illness of an insured would be treated as paid by reason of the death of the insured and be excluded from income. The proposed regulations do not apply to viatical settlements.

2. HIPAA Requirements

The Act codifies the proposed regulations and provides that life insurance proceeds received prior to death will be tax-free if received under a contract of an individual who is "terminally ill" or "chronically ill." The Act also extends the period of time in which a person will be considered "terminally ill" to an expectation of death in twenty-four months, and expands eligibility to "chronically ill" persons even if such persons are not confined to a nursing home or other similar facility. In addition, the Act provides that amounts received upon the sale or assignment of a life insurance contract by a terminally or chronically ill person to a viatical settlement company are treated as a death benefit that is excluded from tax. The rules for daily benefit limits and other requirements for "chronically ill" individuals are similar to the new rules for long-term care conracts (see below).

3. Action Necessary for Compliance

Employers should consider modifying existing life insurance benefits to provide for accelerated death benefits, and notify employees of the availability of tax-free viatical settlements.

D. Long-term Care

1. Previous Law

Previous law did not explicitly provide tax treatment rules for long-term care insurance contracts or services that were comparable to the rules for medical expenses and accident and health insurance. Under previous and current law, taxpayers generally may deduct medical expenses in excess of 7.5 percent of adjusted gross income, and amounts received by a taxpayer under accident or health insurance contracts generally are not included in gross income even if such amounts are paid pursuant to a contract purchased by the beneficiary's employer. In addition, the employer generally is required to make health plan coverage available to employees for at least eighteen months following termination of employment (see discussion of COBRA in Section II.H.).

2. HIPAA Requirements

The Act generally provides the same tax treatment for qualified long-term care and insurance contracts as for health care and insurance contracts. Qualified long-term care services are included in the definition of medical expenses for purposes of the medical expense deduction, and qualified long-term care insurance contract premiums also are included subject to age-related limits ranging from $200 for an individual who is forty years of age or younger to $2,500 for a person who is over seventy years of age. A qualified long-term care insurance contract is treated like an accident or health insurance contract for purposes of excluding from gross income benefits received under employer-paid coverage and for treating amounts received as reimbursement for expenses actually incurred for medical care. The Act also exempts coverage under a qualified long-term care insurance contract from the COBRA rules. To be treated as a qualified long-term care insurance contract, issuers must comply with National Association of Insurance Commissioners consumer protection standards. The Act permits per diem or periodic payment of benefits regardless of the actual expenses incurred, but does subject periodic payments in excess of $175 per day to tax unless such payments represent reimbursement for actual expenses incurred.

3. Action Necessary for Compliance

Employers currently providing long-term care insurance should make certain that the coverage is consistent with the provisions of the Act. Employers who do not provide long-term care insurance should consider whether to do so in light of the favorable tax treatment available under the Act.

E. Penalty-free Withdrawals from IRAs for Medical Expenses

1. Previous Law

Amounts withdrawn from IRAs or employer-sponsored pension plans prior to age 59½ generally are included in income and subject to a ten percent penalty tax.

2. HIPAA Requirements

To the extent that amounts withdrawn from IRAs prior to age 59½ are used for medical expenses in excess of 7.5 percent of adjusted gross income, the ten percent excise tax that otherwise applies to early withdrawals from IRAs does not apply.

Appendix C
GROUP COORDINATION OF BENEFITS MODEL REGULATION

(Model Regulation Service—January 1996)

From the NAIC *Model Laws, Regulations and Guidelines.* Reprinted with permission of the National Association of Insurance Commissioners.

Table of Contents

Section 1.	Authority
Section 2.	Purpose and Applicability
Section 3.	Definitions
Section 4.	Model COB Contract Provisions
Section 5.	Rules for Coordination of Benefits
Section 6.	Procedure to be Followed by Secondary Plan
Section 7.	Notice to Covered Persons
Section 8.	Miscellaneous Provisions
Section 9.	Effective Date; Existing Contracts
Appendix A.	Model COB Contract Provisions
Appendix B.	Consumer Explanatory Booklet

Section 1. Authority

This regulation is adopted and promulgated by the Commissioner of Insurance pursuant to Section [insert section] of the Insurance Code.

Section 2. Purpose and Applicability

The purpose of this regulation is to:

   A. Permit, but not require, plans to include a coordination of benefits (COB) provision unless prohibited by federal law;

   B. Establish a uniform order of benefit determination under which plans pay claims;

   C. Provide authority for the orderly transfer of necessary information and funds between plans;

   D. Reduce duplication of benefits by permitting a reduction of the benefits to be paid by plans that, pursuant to rules established by this regulation, do not have to pay their benefits first;

   E. Reduce claims payment delays; and

   F. Require that COB provisions be consistent with this regulation.

MEDICAL EXPENSE INSURANCE

Section 3.   Definitions

As used in this regulation, these words and terms have the following meanings, unless the context clearly indicates otherwise:

- A.   "Allowable expense" means a health care service or expense including deductibles, coinsurance or copayments, that is covered in full or in part by any of the plans covering the person, except as set forth below or where a statute requires a different definition. This means that an expense or service or a portion of an expense or service that is not covered by any of the plans is not an allowable expense.

    (1)   The following are examples of expenses or services that are not an allowable expense:

    (a)   If a covered person is confined in a private hospital room, the difference between the cost of a semi-private room in the hospital and the private room, (unless the patient's stay in the private hospital room is medically necessary in terms of generally accepted medical practice, or one of the plans routinely provides coverage for private hospital rooms) is not an allowable expense.

    (b)   If a person is covered by two (2) or more plans that compute their benefit payments on the basis of usual and customary fees, any amount in excess of the highest of the usual and customary fee for a specified benefit is not an allowable expense.

    (c)   If a person is covered by two (2) or more plans that provide benefits or services on the basis of negotiated fees, any amount in excess of the highest of the negotiated fees is not an allowable expense.

    (d)   If a person is covered by one plan that calculates its benefits or services on the basis of usual and customary fees and another plan that provides its benefits or services on the basis of negotiated fees, the primary plan's payment arrangement shall be the allowable expense for all plans.

Drafting Note: Many plans negotiate rates with physicians, hospitals and other providers that are lower than the providers' usual and customary charges. Since the provider has agreed to accept the negotiated payment, less any required deductibles, coinsurance or copayments for the services, COB is not to be used to increase the provider payment. This provision limits COB allowable expense to the negotiated rate. However, if the provider has contracts with the primary and secondary plan, the provider may bill the higher of the two rates, if the provider's contract permits it to do so. Each plan may determine its responsibility based upon the rate it negotiated with the provider. Plans should include provisions in their provider contracts to account for payments under coordination of benefits.

    (2)   The definition of "allowable expense" may exclude certain types of coverage or benefits such as dental care, vision care, prescription drug or hearing aids. A plan that limits the application of COB to certain coverages or benefits may limit the definition of allowable expenses in its contract to services or expenses that are similar to the services or expenses that it provides. When COB is restricted to specific coverages or benefits in a contract, the definition of allowable expense shall include similar services or expenses to which COB applies.

Drafting Note: The intent of this provision is to permit plans to limit the extent of coordination to plans with similar types of coverages or benefits, e.g., coordination of health plans with health plans or dental plans with dental plans, etc.

APPENDIX C

(3) When a plan provides benefits in the form of services, the reasonable cash value of each service will be considered an allowable expense and a benefit paid.

(4) The amount of the reduction may be excluded from allowable expense when a covered person's benefits are reduced under a primary plan:

    (a) Because the covered person does not comply with the plan provisions concerning second surgical opinions or precertification of admissions or services; or

    (b) Because the covered person has a lower benefit because he or she did not use a preferred provider.

(5) If the primary plan is a closed panel plan and the secondary plan is not a closed panel plan, the secondary plan shall pay or provide benefits as if it were primary when a covered person uses a non-panel provider, except for emergency services or authorized referrals that are paid or provided by the primary plan.

B. "Claim" means a request that benefits of a plan be provided or paid. The benefits claimed may be in the form of:

(1) Services (including supplies);

(2) Payment for all or a portion of the expenses incurred;

(3) A combination of Paragraphs (1) and (2) above; or

(4) An indemnification.

C. "Claim determination period" means a period of not less than twelve (12) consecutive months, over which allowable expenses shall be compared with total benefits payable in the absence of COB, to determine whether overinsurance exists and how much each plan will pay or provide.

(1) The claim determination period is usually a calendar year, but a plan may use some other period of time that fits the coverage of the group contract. A person is covered by a plan during a portion of a claim determination period if that person's coverage starts or ends during the claim determination period.

(2) As each claim is submitted, each plan determines its liability and pays or provides benefits based upon allowable expenses incurred to that point in the claim determination period. That determination is subject to adjustment as later allowable expenses are incurred in the same claim determination period.

D. "Closed panel plan" means a health maintenance organization (HMO), preferred provider organization (PPO), exclusive provider organization (EPO), or other plan that provides health benefits to covered persons primarily in the form of services through a panel of providers that have contracted with or are employed by the plan, and that limits or excludes benefits for services provided by other providers, except in cases of emergency or referral by a panel member.

E. "Coordination of benefits" means a provision establishing an order in which plans pay their claims, and permitting secondary plans to reduce their benefits so that the combined benefits of all plans do not exceed total allowable expenses.

MEDICAL EXPENSE INSURANCE

F. "Custodial parent" means the parent awarded custody of a child by a court decree. In the absence of a court decree, the parent with whom the child resides more than one half of the calendar year without regard to any temporary visitation is the custodial parent.

G. "Hospital indemnity benefits" means benefits not related to expenses incurred. The term does not include reimbursement-type benefits even if they are designed or administered to give the insured the right to elect indemnity-type benefits at the time of claim.

H. "Plan" means a form of coverage with which coordination is allowed. The definition of plan in the group contract must state the types of coverage that will be considered in applying the COB provision of that contract. The right to include a type of coverage is limited by the rest of this definition. Separate parts of a plan for members of a group that are provided through alternative contracts that are intended to be part of a coordinated package of benefits are considered one plan and there is no COB among the separate parts of the plan.

Drafting Note: A state may choose to allow coordination by and with nongroup coverages within its COB rules. In that case a state may choose to exempt certain coverages from the definition of "plan" in Section 3H(4): supplemental coverages sold on a non-group basis, such as accident only, specified disease, hospital indemnity, disability income; or coverages issued to supplement liability insurance, workers' compensation or similar insurance; or other limited benefit health coverages.

(1) The definition shown in the model COB provision in Appendix A is an example but any definition that satisfies this subsection may be used.

(2) This regulation uses the term "plan." However, a contract may use "program" or some other term.

(3) Plan may include:

(a) Group insurance contracts and group subscriber contracts;

(b) Uninsured arrangements of group or group-type coverage;

(c) Group or group-type coverage through closed panel plans;

(d) Group-type contracts. Group-type contracts are contracts which are not available to the general public and can be obtained and maintained only because of membership in or connection with a particular organization or group, including franchise or blanket coverage. Individually underwritten and issued guaranteed renewable policies are not "group-type" even if purchased through payroll deduction at a premium savings to the insured since the insured would have the right to maintain or renew the policy independently of continued employment with the employer.

Note: The intent of this provision is to identify certain plans of coverage that may utilize other than a group contract but are administered on a basis more characteristic of group insurance. These "group-type" contracts are distinguished by two factors: (1) they are not available to the general public, but may be obtained only through membership in, or connection with, the particular organization or group through which they are marketed (for example: through an employer payroll withholding system), and (2) they can be obtained only through such affiliation (for example: the contracts might provide that they cannot be renewed if the insured leaves the particular employer or organization.) On the other hand, if such contracts are guaranteed renewable, thereby allowing the insured the right to renew regardless of continued employment with the particular employer or affiliation with the organization, they would not be considered "group-type."

(e) The amount by which group or group-type hospital indemnity benefits exceed $200 per day;

        (f)   The medical care components of group long-term care contracts, such as skilled nursing care;

        (g)   The medical benefits coverage in group, group-type and individual automobile "no fault" and traditional automobile "fault" type contracts; and

        (h)   Medicare or other governmental benefits, as permitted by law, except as provided in Paragraph (4)(i) below. That part of the definition of plan may be limited to the hospital, medical and surgical benefits of the governmental program.

(4)   Plan shall not include:

        (a)   Individual or family insurance contracts;

        (b)   Individual or family subscriber contracts;

        (c)   Individual or family coverage through closed panel plans;

        (d)   Individual or family coverage under other prepayment, group practice and individual practice plans;

        (e)   Group or group-type hospital indemnity benefits of $200 per day or less;

        (f)   School accident-type coverages. These contracts cover students for accidents only, including athletic injuries, either on a twenty-four-hour basis or on a "to and from school" basis;

        (g)   Benefits provided in group long-term care insurance policies for non-medical services, for example, personal care, adult day care, homemaker services, assistance with activities of daily living, respite care and custodial care or for contracts that pay a fixed daily benefit without regard to expenses incurred or the receipt of services;

        (h)   Medicare supplement policies;

        (i)   A state plan under Medicaid; or

        (j)   A governmental plan which, by law, provides benefits that are in excess of those of any private insurance plan or other non-governmental plan.

I.   "Primary plan" means a plan whose benefits for a person's health care coverage must be determined without taking the existence of any other plan into consideration. A plan is a primary plan if either of the following is true:

(1)   The plan either has no order of benefit determination rules, or its rules differ from those permitted by this regulation; or

(2)   All plans that cover the person use the order of benefit determination rules required by this regulation, and under those rules the plan determines its benefits first.

J. "Secondary plan" means a plan that is not a primary plan. If a person is covered by more than one secondary plan, the order of benefit determination rules of this regulation decide the order in which secondary plans benefits are determined in relation to each other. Each secondary plan shall take into consideration the benefits of the primary plan or plans and the benefits of any other plan which, under the rules of this regulation, has its benefits determined before those of that secondary plan.

K. "This plan" means, in a COB provision, the part of the group contract providing the health care benefits to which the COB provision applies and which may be reduced because of the benefits of other plans. Any other part of the group contract providing health care benefits is separate from this plan. A group contract may apply one COB provision to certain of its benefits (such as dental benefits), coordinating only with similar benefits, and may apply another COB provision to coordinate with other benefits.

Section 4. Use of Model COB Contract Provision

A. Appendix A contains a model COB provision for use in group contracts. That use is subject to the provisions of Subsections B, C and D below and to the provisions of Section 5.

B. Appendix B is a plain language description of the COB process that explains to the covered person how insurers will implement coordination of benefits. It is not intended to replace or change the provisions that are set forth in the contract. Its purpose is to explain the process by which the two (or more) plans will pay for or provide benefits, how the benefit reserve is accrued and how the covered person may use the benefit reserve.

C. The COB provision (Appendix A) and the plain language explanation (Appendix B) do not have to use the specific words and format shown in Appendix A or Appendix B. Changes may be made to fit the language and style of the rest of the group contract or to reflect differences among plans that provide services, that pay benefits for expenses incurred and that indemnify. No substantive changes are permitted.

D. A COB provision may not be used that permits a plan to reduce its benefits on the basis that:

   (1) Another plan exists and the covered person did not enroll in that plan;

   (2) A person is or could have been covered under another plan, except with respect to Part B of Medicare; or

   (3) A person has elected an option under another plan providing a lower level of benefits than another option that could have been elected.

E. No plan may contain a provision that its benefits are "always excess" or "always secondary" except in accord with the rules permitted by this regulation.

F. Under the terms of a closed panel plan, benefits are not payable if the covered person does not use the services of a closed panel provider. In most instances, COB does not occur if a covered person is enrolled in two (2) or more closed panel plans and obtains services from a provider in one of the closed panel plans because the other closed panel plan (the one whose providers were not used) has no liability. However, COB

APPENDIX C

may occur during the claim determination period when the covered person receives emergency services that would have been covered by both plans. Then the secondary plan must use the benefit reserve to pay any unpaid allowable expense.

Section 5. Rules for Coordination of Benefits

When a person is covered by two (2) or more plans, the rules for determining the order of benefit payments are as follows:

- A. The primary plan must pay or provide its benefits as if the secondary plan or plans did not exist.

- B. A plan that does not contain a coordination of benefits provision that is consistent with this regulation is always primary. There is one exception: coverage that is obtained by virtue of membership in a group and designed to supplement a part of a basic package of benefits may provide that the supplementary coverage shall be excess to any other parts of the plan provided by the contract holder. Examples of these types of situations are major medical coverages that are superimposed over base plan hospital and surgical benefits, and insurance type coverages that are written in connection with a closed panel plan to provide out-of-network benefits.

- C. A plan may consider the benefits paid or provided by another plan only when it is secondary to that other plan.

- D. Order of Benefit Determination

    The first of the following rules that describes which plan pays its benefits before another plan is the rule to use:

    (1) Non-Dependent or Dependent

    The plan that covers the person other than as a dependent, for example as an employee, member, subscriber or retiree, is primary and the plan that covers the person as a dependent is secondary. However, if the person is a Medicare beneficiary, and, as a result of the provisions of Title XVIII of the Social Security Act and implementing regulations, Medicare is:

    (a) Secondary to the plan covering the person as a dependent; and

    (b) Primary to the plan covering the person as other than a dependent (e.g. a retired employee),

    then the order of benefits is reversed so that the plan covering the person as an employee, member, subscriber or retiree is secondary and the other plan is primary.

    (2) Child Covered Under More Than One Plan

    (a) The primary plan is the plan of the parent whose birthday is earlier in the year if:

    (i) The parents are married;

MEDICAL EXPENSE INSURANCE

(ii) The parents are not separated (whether or not they ever have been married); or

(iii) A court decree awards joint custody without specifying that one parent has the responsibility to provide health care coverage.

(b) If both parents have the same birthday, the plan that has covered either of the parents longer is primary.

(c) If the specific terms of a court decree state that one of the parents is responsible for the child's health care expenses or health care coverage and the plan of that parent has actual knowledge of those terms, that plan is primary. If the parent with financial responsibility has no coverage for the child's health care services or expenses, but that parent's spouse does, the spouse's plan is primary. This subparagraph shall not apply with respect to any claim determination period or plan year during which benefits are paid or provided before the entity has actual knowledge.

(d) If the parents are not married or are separated (whether or not they ever were married) or are divorced, and there is no court decree allocating responsibility for the child's health care services or expenses, the order of benefit determination among the plans of the parents and the parents' spouses (if any) is:

(i) The plan of the custodial parent;

(ii) The plan of the spouse of the custodial parent;

(iii) The plan of the noncustodial parent; and then

(iv) The plan of the spouse of the noncustodial parent.

(3) Active or Inactive Employee

The plan that covers a person as an employee who is neither laid off nor retired (or as that employee's dependent) is primary. If the other plan does not have this rule; and if, as a result, the plans do not agree on the order of benefits, this rule is ignored. Coverage provided an individual as a retired worker and as a dependent of that individual's spouse as an active worker will be determined under Subsection D(1).

Drafting Note: This rule covers the situation where one individual is covered under one policy as an active worker and under another policy as a retired worker. It would also apply to an individual covered as a dependent under both of those policies.

(4) Continuation Coverage

If a person whose coverage is provided under a right of continuation pursuant to federal or state law also is covered under another plan, the plan covering the person as an employee, member, subscriber or retiree (or as that person's dependent) is primary and the continuation coverage is secondary.

APPENDIX C

> If the other plan does not have this rule, and if, as a result, the plans do not agree on the order of benefits, this rule is ignored.

Drafting Note: The Consolidated Omnibus Budget Reconciliation Act of 1987 (COBRA) originally provided that coverage under a new group health plan caused the COBRA coverage to end. An amendment passed as part of P.L. 101-239, the Omnibus Budget Reconciliation Act of 1989 (OBRA 89) allows the COBRA coverage to continue if the new group plan contains any preexisting condition limitation. In this instance two group plans will cover an individual, and the rule above will be used to determine which of them assumes the primary position. In addition, some states have continuation provisions comparable to the federal law.

    (5)   Longer or Shorter Length of Coverage

> If the preceding rules do not determine the order of benefits, the plan that covered the person for the longer period of time is primary.

        (a)   To determine the length of time a person has been covered under a plan, two plans shall be treated as one if the covered person was eligible under the second within twenty-four (24) hours after the first ended.

        (b)   The start of a new plan does not include:

            (i)   A change in the amount of scope of a plan's benefits;

            (ii)   A change in the entity that pays, provides or administers the plan's benefits; or

            (iii)   A change from one type of plan to another (such as, from a single employer plan to that of a multiple employer plan).

        (c)   The person's length of time covered under a plan is measured from the person's first date of coverage under that plan. If that date is not readily available for a group plan, the date the person first became a member of the group shall be used as the date from which to determine the length of time the person's coverage under the present plan has been in force.

    (6)   If none of the preceding rules determines the primary plan, the allowable expenses shall be shared equally between the plans.

Section 6.   **Procedure to be Followed by Secondary Plan**

A.   (1)   When a plan is secondary, it shall reduce its benefits so that the total benefits paid or provided by all plans during a claim determination period are not more than 100 percent of total allowable expenses. The secondary plan shall calculate its savings by subtracting the amount that it paid as a secondary plan from the amount it would have paid had it been primary. These savings shall be recorded as a benefit reserve for the covered person and shall be used by the secondary plan to pay any allowable expenses, not otherwise paid, that are incurred by the covered person during the claim determination period. As each claim is submitted, the secondary plan must:

        (a)   Determine its obligation, pursuant to its contract;

(b) Determine whether a benefit reserve has been recorded for the covered person; and

(c) Determine whether there are any unpaid allowable expenses during that claims determination period.

(2) If there is a benefit reserve, the secondary plan shall use the covered person's recorded benefit reserve to pay up to 100 percent of total allowable expenses incurred during the claim determination period. At the end of the claim determination period the benefit reserve returns to zero. A new benefit reserve must be created for each new claim determination period.

Drafting Note: A plan must establish a benefit reserve whenever it is secondary and has either reduced its payments or has collected an amount from the primary plan for the services it has provided. A plan must use the benefit reserve to honor its obligations as a secondary plan according to the rules set forth in this regulation.

B. The benefits of the secondary plan shall be reduced when the sum of the benefits that would be payable for the allowable expenses under the secondary plan in the absence of this COB provision and the benefits that would be payable for the allowable expenses under the other plans, in the absence of provisions with a purpose like that of this COB provision, whether or not a claim is made, exceeds the allowable expenses in a claim determination period. In that case, the benefits of the secondary plan shall be reduced so that they and the benefits payable under the other plans do not total more than the allowable expenses.

(1) When the benefits of a plan are reduced as described above, each benefit is reduced in proportion. It is then charged against any applicable benefit limit of the plan.

(2) The requirements of Paragraph B(1) do not apply if the plan provides only one benefit, or may be altered to suit the coverage provided.

Section 7. Notice to Covered Persons

A plan shall, in its explanation of benefits provided to covered persons, include the following language: "If you are covered by more than one health benefit plan, you should file all your claims with each plan."

Section 8. Miscellaneous Provisions

A. A secondary plan that provides benefits in the form of services may recover the reasonable cash value of the services from the primary plan, to the extent that benefits for the services are covered by the primary plan and have not already been paid or provided by the primary plan. Nothing in this provision shall be interpreted to require a plan to reimburse a covered person in cash for the value of services provided by a plan that provides benefits in the form of services.

B. (1) A plan with order of benefit determination rules that comply with this regulation (complying plan) may coordinate its benefits with a plan that is "excess" or "always secondary" or that uses order of benefit determination rules that are inconsistent with those contained in this regulation (noncomplying plan) on the following basis:

(a) If the complying plan is the primary plan, it shall pay or provide its benefits first;

APPENDIX C

- (b) If the complying plan is the secondary plan, it shall, nevertheless, pay or provide its benefits first, but the amount of the benefits payable shall be determined as if the complying plan were the secondary plan. In such a situation, the payment shall be the limit of the complying plan's liability; and

- (c) If the noncomplying plan does not provide the information needed by the complying plan to determine its benefits within a reasonable time after it is requested to do so, the complying plan shall assume that the benefits of the noncomplying plan are identical to its own, and shall pay its benefits accordingly. If, within two (2) years of payment, the complying plan receives information as to the actual benefits of the noncomplying plan, it shall adjust payments accordingly.

(2) If the noncomplying plan reduces its benefits so that the covered person receives less in benefits than he or she would have received had the complying plan paid or provided its benefits as the secondary plan and the noncomplying plan paid or provided its benefits as the primary plan, and governing state law allows the right of subrogation set forth below, then the complying plan shall advance to or on behalf of the covered person an amount equal to the difference.

(3) In no event shall the complying plan advance more than the complying plan would have paid had it been the primary plan less any amount it previously paid for the same expense or service. In consideration of the advance, the complying plan shall be subrogated to all rights of the covered person against the noncomplying plan. The advance by the complying plan shall also be without prejudice to any claim it may have against a noncomplying plan in the absence of subrogation.

C. COB differs from subrogation. Provisions for one may be included in health care benefits contracts without compelling the inclusion or exclusion of the other.

D. If the plans cannot agree on the order of benefits within thirty (30) calendar days after the plans have received all of the information needed to pay the claim, the plans shall immediately pay the claim in equal shares and determine their relative liabilities following payment, except that no plan shall be required to pay more than it would have paid had it been primary.

Section 9. Effective Date; Existing Contracts

A. This regulation is applicable to every group contract that provides health care benefits and that is issued on or after the effective date of this regulation, which is [insert date].

B. A group contract that provides health care benefits and that was issued before the effective date of this regulation shall be brought into compliance with this regulation by the later of:

(1) The next anniversary date or renewal date of the group contract; or

(2) The expiration of any applicable collectively bargained contract pursuant to which it was written.

APPENDIX A. MODEL COB CONTRACT PROVISIONS

**COORDINATION OF THIS GROUP CONTRACT'S BENEFITS
WITH OTHER BENEFITS**

This coordination of benefits (COB) provision applies when a person has health care coverage under more than one plan. "Plan" is defined below.

The order of benefit determination rules below determine which plan will pay as the primary plan. The primary plan that pays first pays without regard to the possibility that another plan may cover some expenses. A secondary plan pays after the primary plan and may reduce the benefits it pays so that payments from all group plans do not exceed 100% of the total allowable expense.

DEFINITIONS

A. A "plan" is any of the following that provides benefits or services for medical or dental care or treatment. However, if separate contracts are used to provide coordinated coverage for members of a group, the separate contracts are considered parts of the same plan and there is no COB among those separate contracts.

  (1) "Plan" includes: group insurance, closed panel or other forms of group or group-type coverage (whether insured or uninsured); hospital indemnity benefits in excess of $200 per day; medical care components of group long-term care contracts, such as skilled nursing care; medical benefits under group or individual automobile contracts; and Medicare or other governmental benefits, as permitted by law.

  (2) "Plan" does not include: individual or family insurance; closed panel or other individual coverage (except for group-type coverage); amounts of hospital indemnity insurance of $200 or less per day; school accident type coverage, benefits for non-medical components of group long-term care policies; Medicare supplement policies, Medicaid policies and coverage under other governmental plans, unless permitted by law.

  Each contract for coverage under (1) or (2) is a separate plan. If a plan has two parts and COB rules apply only to one of the two, each of the parts is treated as a separate plan.

B. The order of benefit determination rules determine whether this plan is a "primary plan" or "secondary plan" when compared to another plan covering the person.

  When this plan is primary, its benefits are determined before those of any other plan and without considering any other plan's benefits. When this plan is secondary, its benefits are determined after those of another plan and may be reduced because of the primary plan's benefits.

C. "Allowable expense" means a health care service or expense, including deductibles and copayments, that is covered at least in part by any of the plans covering the person. When a plan provides benefits in the form of services, (for example an HMO) the reasonable cash value of each service will be considered an allowable expense and a benefit paid. An expense or service that is not covered by any of the plans is not an allowable expense. The following are examples of expenses or services that are not allowable expenses:

  (1) If a covered person is confined in a private hospital room, the difference between the cost of a semi-private room in the hospital and the private room, (unless the patient's

stay in a private hospital room is medically necessary in terms of generally accepted medical practice, or one of the plans routinely provides coverage for hospital private rooms) is not an allowable expense.

 (2) If a person is covered by 2 or more plans that compute their benefit payments on the basis of usual and customary fees, any amount in excess of the highest of the usual and customary fees for a specific benefit is not an allowable expense.

 (3) If a person is covered by 2 or more plans that provide benefits or services on the basis of negotiated fees, an amount in excess of the highest of the negotiated fees is not an allowable expense.

 (4) If a person is covered by one plan that calculates its benefits or services on the basis of usual and customary fees and another plan that provides its benefits or services on the basis of negotiated fees, the primary plan's payment arrangements shall be the allowable expense for all plans.

 (5) The amount a benefit is reduced by the primary plan because a covered person does not comply with the plan provisions. Examples of these provisions are second surgical opinions, precertification of admissions, and preferred provider arrangements.

D. "Claim determination period" means a calendar year. However, it does not include any part of a year during which a person has no coverage under this plan, or before the date this COB provision or a similar provision takes effect.

E. "Closed panel plan" is a plan that provides health benefits to covered persons primarily in the form of services through a panel of providers that have contracted with or are employed by the plan, and that limits or excludes benefits for services provided by other providers, except in cases of emergency or referral by a panel member.

F. "Custodial parent" means a parent awarded custody by a court decree. In the absence of a court decree, it is the parent with whom the child resides more than one half of the calendar year without regard to any temporary visitation.

ORDER OF BENEFIT DETERMINATION RULES

When two or more plans pay benefits, the rules for determining the order of payment are as follows:

A. The primary plan pays or provides its benefits as if the secondary plan or plans did not exist.

B. A plan that does not contain a coordination of benefits provision that is consistent with this regulation is always primary. There is one exception: coverage that is obtained by virtue of membership in a group that is designed to supplement a part of a basic package of benefits may provide that the supplementary coverage shall be excess to any other parts of the plan provided by the contract holder. Examples of these types of situations are major medical coverages that are superimposed over base plan hospital and surgical benefits, and insurance type coverages that are written in connection with a closed panel plan to provide out-of-network benefits.

C. A plan may consider the benefits paid or provided by another plan in determining its benefits only when it is secondary to that other plan.

D. The first of the following rules that describes which plan pays its benefits before another plan is the rule to use.

MEDICAL EXPENSE INSURANCE

(1) Non-Dependent or Dependent. The plan that covers the person other than as a dependent, for example as an employee, member, subscriber or retiree is primary and the plan that covers the person as a dependent is secondary. However, if the person is a Medicare beneficiary and, as a result of federal law, Medicare is secondary to the plan covering the person as a dependent; and primary to the plan covering the person as other than a dependent (e.g. a retired employee); then the order of benefits between the two plans is reversed so that the plan covering the person as an employee, member, subscriber or retiree is secondary and the other plan is primary.

(2) Child Covered Under More Than One Plan. The order of benefits when a child is covered by more than one plan is:

   (a) The primary plan is the plan of the parent whose birthday is earlier in the year if:

   - The parents are married;
   - The parents are not separated (whether or not they ever have been married); or
   - A court decree awards joint custody without specifying that one party has the responsibility to provide health care coverage.

   If both parents have the same birthday, the plan that covered either of the parents longer is primary.

   (b) If the specific terms of a court decree state that one of the parents is responsible for the child's health care expenses or health care coverage and the plan of that parent has actual knowledge of those terms, that plan is primary. This rule applies to claim determination periods or plan years commencing after the plan is given notice of the court decree.

   (c) If the parents are not married, or are separated (whether or not they ever have been married) or are divorced, the order of benefits is:

   - The plan of the custodial parent;
   - The plan of the spouse of the custodial parent;
   - The plan of the noncustodial parent; and then
   - The plan of the spouse of the noncustodial parent.

(3) Active or inactive employee. The plan that covers a person as an employee who is neither laid off nor retired, is primary. The same would hold true if a person is a dependent of a person covered as a retiree and an employee. If the other plan does not have this rule, and if, as a result, the plans do not agree on the order of benefits, this rule is ignored. Coverage provided an individual as a retired worker and as a dependent of an actively working spouse will be determined under the rule labeled B(1).

(4) Continuation coverage. If a person whose coverage is provided under a right of continuation provided by federal or state law also is covered under another plan, the plan covering the person as an employee, member, subscriber or retiree (or as

APPENDIX C

that person's dependent) is primary, and the continuation coverage is secondary. If the other plan does not have this rule, and if, as a result, the plans do not agree on the order of benefits, this rule is ignored.

(5) Longer or shorter length of coverage. The plan that covered the person as an employee, member, subscriber or retiree longer is primary.

(6) If the preceding rules do not determine the primary plan, the allowable expenses shall be shared equally between the plans meeting the definition of plan under this regulation. In addition, this plan will not pay more than it would have paid had it been primary.

EFFECT ON THE BENEFITS OF THIS PLAN

A. When this plan is secondary, it may reduce its benefits so that the total benefits paid or provided by all plans during a claim determination period are not more than 100 percent of total allowable expenses. The difference between the benefit payments that this plan would have paid had it been the primary plan, and the benefit payments that it actually paid or provided shall be recorded as a benefit reserve for the covered person and used by this plan to pay any allowable expenses, not otherwise paid during the claim determination period. As each claim is submitted, this plan will:

(1) Determine its obligation to pay or provide benefits under its contract;

(2) Determine whether a benefit reserve has been recorded for the covered person; and

(3) Determine whether there are any unpaid allowable expenses during that claims determination period.

If there is a benefit reserve, the secondary plan will use the covered person's benefit reserve to pay up to 100% of total allowable expenses incurred during the claim determination period. At the end of the claims determination period, the benefit reserve returns to zero. A new benefit reserve must be created for each new claim determination period.

B. If a covered person is enrolled in two or more closed panel plans and if, for any reason, including the provision of service by a non-panel provider, benefits are not payable by one closed panel plan, COB shall not apply between that plan and other closed panel plans.

RIGHT TO RECEIVE AND RELEASE NEEDED INFORMATION

Certain facts about health care coverage and services are needed to apply these COB rules and to determine benefits payable under this plan and other plans. [Organization responsibility for COB administration] may get the facts it needs from or give them to other organizations or persons for the purpose of applying these rules and determining benefits payable under this plan and other plans covering the person claiming benefits. [Organization responsibility for COB administration] need not tell, or get the consent of, any person to do this. Each person claiming benefits under this plan must give [Organization responsibility for COB administration] any facts it needs to apply those rules and determine benefits payable.

FACILITY OF PAYMENT

A payment made under another plan may include an amount that should have been paid under this plan. If it does, [Organization responsibility for COB administration] may pay that amount to the organization that made that payment. That amount will then be treated as though it were a benefit

MEDICAL EXPENSE INSURANCE

paid under this plan. [Organization responsibility for COB administration] will not have to pay that amount again. The term "payment made" includes providing benefits in the form of services, in which case "payment made" means reasonable cash value of the benefits provided in the form of services.

RIGHT OF RECOVERY

If the amount of the payments made by [Organization responsibility for COB administration] is more than it should have paid under this COB provision, it may recover the excess from one or more of the persons it has paid or for whom it has paid; or any other person or organization that may be responsible for the benefits or services provided for the covered person. The "amount of the payments made" includes the reasonable cash value of any benefits provided in the form of services.

APPENDIX B. CONSUMER EXPLANATORY BOOKLET

COORDINATION OF BENEFITS

IMPORTANT NOTICE

This is a summary of only a few of the provisions of your health plan to help you understand coordination of benefits, which can be very complicated. This is not a complete description of all of the coordination rules and procedures, and does not change or replace the language contained in your insurance contract, which determines your benefits.

Double Coverage

It is common for family members to be covered by more than one health care plan. This happens, for example, when a husband and wife both work and choose to have family coverage through both employers.

When you are covered by more than one group health plan, state law permits your insurers to follow a procedure called "coordination of benefits" to determine how much each should pay when you have a claim. The aim is to make sure that the combined payments of all plans do not add up to more than your covered health care expenses.

Coordination of benefits (COB) is complicated, and covers a wide variety of circumstances. This is only an outline of some of the most common ones. If your situation is not described, read your evidence of coverage or contact your state insurance department.

Primary or Secondary?

You will be asked to identify all the plans that cover family members. We need this information to determine whether we are "primary" or "secondary." The primary plan always pays first.

Any plan which does not contain your state's coordination of benefits rules will always be primary.

When This Plan is Primary

If you or a family member are covered under another plan in addition to this one, we will be primary when;

254

Your Own Expenses
- The claim is for your own health care expenses, unless you are covered by Medicare and both you and your spouse are retired.

Your Spouse's Expenses
- The claim is for your spouse, who is covered by Medicare, and you are not both retired.

Your Child's Expenses

- The claim is for the health care expenses of a child covered by this plan and

    - your birthday is earlier in the year than your spouse's. This is known as the "birthday rule";
        or
    - you are not married and you have informed us of a court decree that makes you responsible for the child's health care expenses;
        or
    - there is no court decree, but you have custody of the child.

Other Situations
We will be primary when any other provisions of state or federal law require us to be.

How We Pay Claims When We Are Primary
When we are the primary plan, we will pay the benefits provided by your contract, just as if you had no other coverage.

How We Pay Claims When We Are Secondary
We will be secondary whenever the rules do not require us to be primary.

How We Pay Claims When We Are Secondary
When we are the secondary plan, we do not pay until after the primary plan has paid its benefits. We will then pay part or all of the allowable expenses left unpaid. An "allowable expense" is a health care service or expense covered by one of the plans, including copayments and deductibles.

- If there is a difference between the amount the plans allow, we will base our payment on the higher amount. However, if the primary plan has a contract with the provider, our combined payments will not be more than the contract calls for. Health maintenance organizations (HMO) and preferred provider organizations (PPO) usually have contracts with their providers.

- We will determine our payment by subtracting the amount the primary plan paid from the amount we would have paid if we had been primary. We will use any savings to pay the balance of any unpaid allowable expenses covered by either plan.

- If the primary plan covers similar kinds of health care, but allows expenses that we do not cover, we will pay for those items as long as there is a balance in your benefit reserve, as explained below.

- We will not pay an amount the primary plan didn't cover because you didn't follow its rules and procedures. For example, if your plan has reduced its benefit because you did not obtain pre-certification, we will not pay the amount of the reduction, because it is not an allowable expense.

Benefit Reserve

When we are secondary we often will pay less than we would have paid if we had been primary. Each time we "save" by paying less, we will put that savings into a benefit reserve. Each family member covered by this plan has a separate benefit reserve.

- We use the benefit reserve to pay allowable expenses that are covered only partially by both plans. To obtain a reimbursement, you must show us what the primary plan has paid so we can calculate the savings.

- To make sure you receive the full benefit or coordination, you should submit all claims to each of your plans.

- Savings can build up in your reserve for one year. At the end of the year any balance is erased, and a fresh benefit reserve begins for each person the next year as soon as there are savings on their claims.

Questions About Coordination of Benefits?
Contact Your State Insurance Department

Legislative history (all references are to the Proceedings of the NAIC).

1971 Proc. I 54, 58, 208, 225, 226-230 (adopted).
1980 Proc. II 22, 26, 588, 592-593 (added section on divorced parents).
1983 Proc. I 6, 35, 644, 693, 699 (added section on laid-off and retired employees).
1984 Proc. II 9, 20, 536, 616, 625-636 (revised and added birthdate rule and reprinted).
1985 Proc. II 11, 23, 609, 615, 627-638 (adopted easy-to-read version).
1986 Proc. I 9-10, 23, 665, 673 (footnote added).
1988 Proc. I 9, 20-21, 630, 713, 715-728 (amended and reprinted).
1989 Proc. I 9, 24-25, 703-704, 839, 843-846 (amended).
1990 Proc. II 7, 16, 600, 676-677, 678-683 (amended).
1991 Proc. I 9, 17-18, 609, 648-652 (amended).
1995 Proc. 3rd Quarter 4, 18, 692, 696, 703-717 (amended and reprinted).

Appendix D
GROUP COVERAGE DISCONTINUANCE AND REPLACEMENT MODEL REGULATION

(Model Regulation Service—April 1996)

From the NAIC *Model Laws, Regulations and Guidelines.* Reprinted with permission of the National Association of Insurance Commissioners.

Table of Contents

Section 1.	Authority
Section 2.	Scope
Section 3.	Definition
Section 4.	Effective Date of Discontinuance for Non-Payment of Premium or Subscription Charges
Section 5.	Requirements for Notice of Discontinuance
Section 6.	Extension of Benefits
Section 7.	Continuance of Coverage in Situations Involving Replacement of One Carrier by Another
Section 8.	Effective Date

Section 1.   Authority

This regulation is adopted and promulgated by [title of supervisory authority] pursuant to Section [insert applicable section] of the [insert state] Insurance Code.

Section 2.   Scope

This regulation is applicable to all insurance policies and subscriber contracts issued or provided by an insurance company or a nonprofit service corporation on a group or group-type basis covering persons as employees of employers or as members of unions [or associations].

Section 3.   Definition

The term "group-type basis" means a benefit plan, other than "salary budget" plans utilizing individual insurance policies or subscriber contracts, which meets the following conditions:

- A. Coverage is provided through insurance policies or subscriber contracts to classes of employees or members defined in terms of conditions pertaining to employment or membership;

- B. The coverage is not available to the general public and can be obtained and maintained only because of the covered person's membership in or connection with the particular organization or group;

- C. There are arrangements for bulk payment of premiums or subscription charges to the insurer or nonprofit service corporation; and

- D. There is sponsorship of the plan by the employer, union [or association].

MEDICAL EXPENSE INSURANCE

Section 4. **Effective Date of Discontinuance for Non-Payment of Premiu Subscription Charges**

A. If a policy or contract subject to this regulation provides for automatic disconti of the policy or contract after a premium or subscription charge has remained through the grace period allowed for payment, the carrier shall be liable fo claims for covered losses incurred prior to the end of the grace period.

B. If the actions of the carrier after the end of the grace period indicate that it considers the policy or contract as continuing in force beyond the end of the grace period (such as, by continuing to recognize claims subsequently incurred), the carrier shall be liable for valid claims for losses beginning prior to the effective date of written notice of discontinuance to the policyholder or other entity responsible for making payments or submitting subscription charges to the carrier. The effective date of discontinuance shall not be prior to midnight at the end of the third scheduled workday after the date upon which the notice is delivered.

Section 5. **Requirements for Notice of Discontinuance**

A. A notice of discontinuance given by the carrier shall include a request to the group policyholder or other entity involved to notify employees covered under the policy or subscriber contract of the date on which the group policy or contract will discontinue and to advise that, unless otherwise provided in the policy or contract, the carrier shall not be liable for claims for losses incurred after that date. Notice of discontinuance shall also advise, in any instance in which the plan involves employee contributions, that if the policyholder or other entity continues to collect contributions for the coverage beyond the date of discontinuance, the policyholder or other entity may be held solely liable for the benefits with respect to which the contributions have been collected.

B. The carrier will prepare and furnish to the policyholder or other entity at the same time a supply of notice forms to be distributed to the employees or members concerned, indicating the discontinuance and the effective date thereof, and urging the employees or members to refer to their certificates or contracts in order to determine what rights, if any, are available to them upon discontinuance.

Section 6. **Extension of Benefits**

A. Every group policy or other contract subject to these rules and regulations hereafter issued, or under which the level of benefits is hereafter altered, modified or amended, shall provide a reasonable provision for extension of benefits in the event of total disability at the date of discontinuance of the group policy or contract, as required by the following subsections of this section.

B. In the case of a group life plan which contains a disability benefit extension of any type (e.g., premium waiver extension, extended death benefit in event of total disability, or payment of income for a specified period during total disability), the discontinuance of the group policy shall not operate to terminate the extension.

C. In the case of a group plan providing benefits for loss of time from work or specific indemnity during hospital confinement, discontinuance of the policy during a disability shall have no effect on benefits payable for that disability or confinement.

D. In the case of hospital or medical expense coverages other than dental and maternity expense, a reasonable extension of benefits or accrued liability provision is required.

APPENDIX D

A provision will be considered "reasonable" if it provides an extension of at least twelve (12) months under "major medical" and "comprehensive medical" type coverages, and under other types of hospital or medical expense coverages provides either an extension of at least ninety (90) days or an accrued liability for expenses incurred during a period of disability or during a period of at least ninety (90) days starting with a specific event which occurred while coverage was in force (e.g., an accident).

E. Any applicable extension of benefits or accrued liability shall be described in any policy or contract involved as well as in group insurance certificates. The benefits payable during any period of extension or accrued liability may be subject to the policy's or contract's regular benefit limits (e.g., benefits ceasing at exhaustion of a benefit period or of maximum benefits).

Section 7. Continuance of Coverage in Situations Involving Replacement of One Carrier by Another

A. This section shall indicate the carrier responsible for liability in those instances in which one carrier's contract replaces a plan of similar benefits of another.

B. Liability of prior carrier. The prior carrier remains liable only to the extent of its accrued liabilities and extensions of benefits. The position of the prior carrier shall be the same whether the group policyholder or other entity secures replacement coverage from a new carrier, self-insures or foregoes the provision of coverage.

C. Liability of Succeeding Carrier.

(1) Each person who is eligible for coverage in accordance with the succeeding carrier's plan of benefits (in respect of classes eligible and actively at work and non-confinement rules) shall be covered by that carrier's plan of benefits.

(2) Each person not covered under the succeeding carrier's plan of benefits in accordance with Paragraph (1) above shall nevertheless be covered by the succeeding carrier in accordance with the following rules if the individual was validly covered (including benefit extension) under the prior plan on the date of discontinuance and if the individual is a member of the class or classes of individuals eligible for coverage under the succeeding carrier's plan. Any reference in the following rules to an individual who was or was not totally disabled is a reference to the individual's status immediately prior to the date the succeeding carrier's coverage becomes effective.

(a) The minimum level of benefits to be provided by the succeeding carrier shall be the applicable level of benefits of the prior carrier's plan reduced by any benefits payable by the prior plan.

(b) Coverage must be provided by the succeeding carrier until at least the earliest of the following dates:

(i) The date the individual becomes eligible under the succeeding carrier's plan as described in Paragraph (1) above.

(ii) For each type of coverage, the date the individual's coverage would terminate in accordance with the succeeding carrier's plan provisions applicable to individual termination of coverage (e.g., at termination of employment or ceasing to be an eligible dependent, as the case may be).

(iii) In the case of an individual who was totally disabled, and in the case of a type of coverage for which Section 6 requires an extension of accrued liability, the end of any period of extension or accrued liability which is required of the prior carrier by Section 6, or if the prior carrier's policy or contract is not subject to that section, would have been required of that carrier had its policy or contract been subject to Section 6 at the time the prior plan was discontinued and replaced by the succeeding carrier's plan.

(3) In the case of a preexisting conditions limitation included in the succeeding carrier's plan, the level of benefits applicable to preexisting conditions of persons becoming covered by the succeeding carrier's plan in accordance with this paragraph during the period of time this limitation applies under the new plan shall be the lessor of:

(a) The benefits of the new plan determined without application of the preexisting conditions limitation; or

(b) The benefits of the prior plan.

(4) The succeeding carrier, in applying any deductibles or waiting periods in its plan, shall give credit for the satisfaction or partial satisfaction of the same or similar provisions under a prior plan providing similar benefits. In the case of deductible provisions, the credit shall apply for the same or overlapping benefit periods and shall be given for expenses actually incurred and applied against the deductible provisions of the prior carrier's plan during the ninety (90) days preceding the effective date of the succeeding carrier's plan but only to the extent these expenses are recognized under the terms of the succeeding carrier's plan and are subject to a similar deductible provision.

(5) In a situation where a determination of the prior carrier's benefit is required by the succeeding carrier, at the succeeding carrier's request the prior carrier shall furnish a statement of the benefits available or pertinent information, sufficient to permit verification of the benefit determination or the determination itself by the succeeding carrier. For the purposes of this paragraph, benefits of the prior plan will be determined in accordance with all of the definitions, conditions and covered expense provisions of the prior plan rather than those of the succeeding plan. The benefit determination will be made as if coverage had not been replaced by the succeeding carrier.

Section 8.   Effective Date

This regulation shall take effect on [insert a date at least 120 days after promulgation].

Legislative History (all references are to the Proceedings of the NAIC).

1972 Proc. II 10, 13, 410, 483, 484-487 (adopted).

Appendix E
RULES GOVERNING ADVERTISEMENTS OF ACCIDENT AND SICKNESS INSURANCE WITH INTERPRETIVE GUIDELINES

(Model Regulation Service—July 1989)

From the NAIC *Model Laws, Regulations and Guidelines*. Reprinted with permission of the National Association of Insurance Commissioners.

Table of Contents

Preamble
Section 1.   Purpose
Section 2.   Applicability
Section 3.   Definitions
Section 4.   Method of Disclosure of Required Information
Section 5.   Form and Content of Advertisements
Section 6.   Advertisement of Benefits Payable, Losses Covered by Premiums Payable
Section 7.   Necessity for Disclosing Policy Provisions Relating to Renewability, Cancellability and Termination
Section 8.   Testimonials or Endorsements by Third Parties
Section 9.   Use of Statistics
Section 10. Identification of Plan or Number of Policies
Section 11. Disparaging Comparisons and Statements
Section 12. Jurisdictional Licensing and Status of Insurer
Section 13. Identity of Insurer
Section 14. Group or Quasi-Group Implications
Section 15. Introductory, Initial or Special Offers
Section 16. Statements About an Insurer
Section 17. Enforcement Procedures
Section 18. Severability Provision
Section 19. Filing for Prior Review
Appendix   Interpretive Guidelines

Preamble

The proper expansion of accident and sickness coverage is in the public interest. Appropriate advertising can broaden the distribution of insurance and coverage under health maintenance organizations and other prepaid plans among various segments of the public. These rules, while referencing insurance, are intended to apply to the advertisement of accident and sickness benefits whether provided on an indemnity, reimbursement, service or prepaid basis. Advertising can increase public awareness of new and beneficial forms of coverage and thereby encourage product competition. Advertising can also provide the insurance-buying public with the means by which it can compare the advantages of competing forms of coverage.

Insurance advertising has become increasingly important in the years since the 1956 Rules Governing Advertising of Accident and Sickness Insurance were developed. The increasing

MEDICAL EXPENSE INSURANCE

availability of coverage under group insurance plans and the advent of governmental benefit programs have complicated the decisions the insurance-buying public must make to avoid duplication of benefits and gaps in coverage. The consequent need for detailed information about insurance products is reflected in the requirements for disclosure established by the 1972 Rules (as amended in 1977) Governing Advertisements of Accident and Sickness Insurance. This need for detailed disclosure is especially critical in helping to assure that the insurance-buying public receives full and truthful advertising for accident and sickness insurance. In 1987 the NAIC adopted the Model Rules Governing Advertisements of Medicare Supplement Insurance With Interpretive Guidelines to separately address Medicare supplement insurance advertising. The NAIC has now determined that while the 1972 Rules (as amended in 1977) Governing Advertisements of Accident and Sickness Insurance did address accident and sickness insurance, these new Rules and Interpretive Guidelines revise the previous 1972 Rules and Interpretive Guidelines with respect to accident and sickness insurance advertising and eliminate duplicative or inconsistent regulation of Medicare supplement insurance advertising.

Although modern insurance advertising patterns much of its design after advertising for other goods and services, the uniqueness of insurance as a product must always be kept in mind in developing advertising of accident and sickness insurance. By the time an insured discovers that a particular insurance product is unsuitable for his needs, it may be too late for him to return to the marketplace to find a more satisfactory product.

Hence, the insurance-buying public should be afforded a means by which it can determine, in advance of purchase, the desirability of the competing insurance products proposed to be sold. This can be accomplished by advertising which accurately describes the advantages and disadvantages of the insurance product without either exaggerating the benefits or minimizing the limitations. Properly designed advertising can provide such description and disclosure without sacrificing the sales appeal which is essential to its usefulness to the insurance-buying public and the insurance business. The purpose of the new Rules Governing Advertisements of Accident and Sickness Insurance is to establish minimum criteria to assure proper and accurate description and disclosure.

Section 1. Purpose

The purpose of these rules is to protect prospective purchasers with respect to the advertisement of accident and sickness insurance in the same manner as the rules governing advertisements of Medicare supplement insurance. The rules assure the clear and truthful disclosure of the benefits, limitations and exclusions of policies sold as accident and sickness insurance. This is intended to be accomplished by the establishment of guidelines and permissible and impermissible standards of conduct in the advertising of accident and sickness insurance in a manner which prevents unfair, deceptive and misleading advertising and is conducive to accurate presentation and description to the insurance-buying public through the advertising media and material used by insurance agents and companies.

Section 2. Applicability

A. These rules shall apply to any accident and sickness (except Medicare supplement insurance) "advertisement," as that term is defined herein unless otherwise specified in these rules, which the insurer knows or reasonably should know is intended for presentation, distribution or dissemination in this State when such presentation, distribution or dissemination is made either directly or indirectly by or on behalf of an insurer, agent, broker, producer or solicitor, as those terms are defined in the Insurance Code of this State.

APPENDIX E

B. Every insurer shall establish and at all times maintain a system of control over the content, form and method of dissemination of all advertisements of its policies. All such advertisements, regardless of by whom written, created, designed or presented, shall be the responsibility of the insurer whose policies are so advertised.

C. Advertising materials which are reproduced in quantity shall be identified by form numbers or other identifying means. Such identification shall be sufficient to distinguish an advertisement from any other advertising materials, policies, applications or other materials used by the insurer.

Section 3. Definitions

A. (1) An advertisement for the purpose of these rules shall include:

    (a) Printed and published material, audio visual material, and descriptive literature of an insurer used in direct mail, newspapers, magazines, radio scripts, TV scripts, billboards and similar displays; and

    (b) Descriptive literature and sales aids of all kinds issued by an insurer, agent, producer, broker or solicitor for presentation to members of the insurance-buying public, including but not limited to circulars, leaflets, booklets, depictions, illustrations, form letters and lead-generating devices of all kinds as herein defined; and

    (c) Prepared sales talks, presentations and material for use by agents, brokers, producers and solicitors whether prepared by the insurer or the agent, broker, producer or solicitor.

(2) The definition of "advertisement" includes advertising material included with a policy when the policy is delivered and material used in the solicitation of renewals and reinstatements.

(3) The definition of "advertisement" does not include:

    (a) Material to be used solely for the training and education of an insurer's employees, agents or brokers;

    (b) Material used in-house by insurers;

    (c) Communications within an insurer's own organization not intended for dissemination to the public;

    (d) Individual communications of a personal nature with current policyholders other than material urging such policyholders to increase or expand coverages;

    (e) Correspondence between a prospective group or blanket policyholder and an insurer in the course of negotiating a group or blanket contract;

    (f) Court-approved material ordered by a court to be disseminated to policyholders; or

    (g) A general announcement from a group or blanket policyholder to eligible individuals on an employment or membership list that a contract or program has been written or arranged; provided, the announcement clearly indicates that it is preliminary to the issuance of a booklet.

MEDICAL EXPENSE INSURANCE

B. "Accident and Sickness Insurance Policy" for the purpose of these rules shall include any policy, plan, certificate, contract, agreement, statement of coverage, rider or endorsement which provides accident or sickness benefits or medical, surgical or hospital expense benefits, whether on an indemnity, reimbursement, service or prepaid basis, except when issued in connection with another kind of insurance other than life and except disability, waiver of premium and double indemnity benefits included in life insurance and annuity contracts. Accident and sickness insurance policy shall not include any Medicare supplement insurance policy.

C. "Certificate" means for the purpose of these rules, any certificate issued under a group accident and sickness insurance policy, which certificate has been delivered or issued for delivery in this State.

D. "Insurer" for the purpose of these rules shall include any individual, corporation, association, partnership, reciprocal exchange, inter-insurer, Lloyds, fraternal benefit society, health maintenance organization, hospital service corporation, medical service corporation, prepaid health plan and any other legal entity which is defined as an "insurer" in the Insurance Code of this State and is engaged in the advertisement of itself, or an accident and sickness insurance policy.

E. "Exception" for the purpose of these rules shall mean any provision in a policy whereby coverage for a specified hazard is entirely eliminated; it is a statement of a risk not assumed under the policy.

F. "Reduction" for the purpose of these rules shall mean any provision which reduces the amount of the benefit; a risk of loss is assumed but payment upon the occurrence of such loss is limited to some amount or period less than would be otherwise payable and such reduction has not been used.

G. "Limitation" for the purpose of these rules shall mean any provision which restricts coverage under the policy other than an exception or a reduction.

H. "Institutional Advertisement" for the purpose of these rules shall mean an advertisement having as its sole purpose the promotion of the reader's, viewer's or listener's interest in the concept of accident and sickness insurance, or the promotion of the insurer as a seller of accident and sickness insurance.

I. "Invitation to Inquire" for the purpose of these rules shall mean an advertisement having as its objective the creation of a desire to inquire further about accident and sickness insurance and which is limited to a brief description of coverage, and which shall contain a provision in the following or substantially similar form:

"This policy has [exclusions] [limitations] [reduction of benefits] [terms under which the policy may be continued in force or discontinued]. For costs and complete details of the coverage, call [or write] your insurance agent or the company [whichever is applicable]."

J. "Invitation to Contract" for the purpose of these rules shall mean an advertisement which is neither an invitation to inquire nor an institutional advertisement.

K. "Person" for the purpose of these rules shall mean any natural person, association, organization, partnership, trust, group, discretionary group, corporation or any other entity.

L. "Lead-Generating Device", for the purpose of these rules, shall mean any communication directed to the public which, regardless of form, content or stated purpose, is intended to result in the compilation or qualification of a list containing names and other personal information to be used to solicit residents of this State for the purchase of accident and sickness insurance.

Section 4. Method of Disclosure of Required Information

All information required to be disclosed by these rules shall be set out conspicuously and in close conjunction with the statements to which such information relates or under appropriate captions of such prominence that it shall not be minimized, rendered obscure or presented in an ambiguous fashion or intermingled with the context of the advertisements so as to be confusing or misleading.

Section 5. Form and Content of Advertisements

A. The format and content of an advertisement of an accident or sickness insurance policy shall be sufficiently complete and clear to avoid deception or the capacity or tendency to mislead or deceive. Whether an advertisement has a capacity or tendency to mislead or deceive shall be determined by the Commissioner of Insurance from the overall impression that the advertisement may be reasonably expected to create upon a person of average education or intelligence, within the segment of the public to which it is directed.

B. Advertisements shall be truthful and not misleading in fact or in implication. Words or phrases, the meaning of which is clear only by implication or by familiarity with insurance terminology, shall not be used.

C. An insurer must clearly identify its accident and sickness insurance policy as an insurance policy. A policy trade name must be followed by the words "Insurance Policy" or similar words clearly identifying the fact that an insurance policy or health benefits product (in the case of health maintenance organizations, prepaid health plans and other direct service organizations) is being offered.

D. No insurer, agent, broker, producer, solicitor or other person shall solicit a resident of this State for the purchase of accident and sickness insurance in connection with or as the result of the use of advertisement by such person or any other persons, where the advertisement:

  (1) Contains any misleading representations or misrepresentations, or is otherwise untrue, deceptive or misleading with regard to the information imparted, the status, character or representative capacity of such person or the true purpose of the advertisement; or

  (2) Otherwise violates the provisions of these rules.

E. No insurer, agent, broker, producer, solicitor or other person shall solicit residents of this State for the purchase of accident and sickness insurance through the use of a true or fictitious name which is deceptive or misleading with regard to the status, character, or proprietary or representative capacity of such person or the true purpose of the advertisement.

Section 6. Advertisements of Benefits Payable, Losses Covered or Premiums Payable

A. Deceptive Words, Phrases or Illustrations Prohibited

  (1) No advertisement shall omit information or use words, phrases, statements, references or illustrations if the omission of such information or use of such words, phrases, statements, references or illustrations has the capacity, tendency or effect of misleading or deceiving purchasers or prospective purchasers as to the nature or extent of any policy benefit payable, loss covered or premium payable. The fact that the policy offered is made available to a prospective insured for inspection prior to consummation of the sale or an offer is made to refund the premium if the purchaser is not satisfied, does not remedy misleading statements.

MEDICAL EXPENSE INSURANCE

(2) No advertisement shall contain or use words or phrases such as "all," "full," "complete," "comprehensive," "unlimited," "up to," "as high as," "this policy will help fill some of the gaps that Medicare and your present insurance leave out," "the policy will help to replace your income," (when used to express loss of time benefits), or similar words and phrases, in a manner which exaggerates any benefits beyond the terms of the policy.

(3) An advertisement which also is an invitation to join an association, trust or discretionary group must solicit insurance coverage on a separate and distinct application which requires separate signatures for each application. The separate and distinct applications required need not be on a separate document or contained in a separate mailing. The insurance program must be presented so as not to mislead or deceive the prospective members that they are purchasing insurance as well as applying for membership, if that is the case.

(4) An advertisement shall not contain descriptions of policy limitations, exceptions or reductions, worded in a positive manner to imply that it is a benefit, such as describing a waiting period as a "benefit builder" or stating "even preexisting conditions are covered after two years." Words and phrases used in an advertisement to describe such policy limitations, exceptions and reductions shall fairly and accurately describe the negative features of such limitations, exceptions and reductions of the policy offered.

(5) An advertisement of accident and sickness insurance sold by direct response shall not state or imply that because "no insurance agent will call and no commissions will be paid to 'agents' that it is 'a low cost plan,'" or use other similar words or phrases because the cost of advertising and servicing such policies is a substantial cost in the marketing by direct response.

(6) No advertisement of a benefit for which payment is conditional upon confinement in a hospital or similar facility shall use words or phrases such as "tax-free," "extra cash," "extra income," "extra pay," or substantially similar words or phrases because such words and phrases have the capacity, tendency or effect of misleading the public into believing that the policy advertised will, in some way, enable them to make a profit from being hospitalized.

(7) No advertisement of a hospital or other similar facility confinement benefit shall advertise that the amount of the benefit is payable on a monthly or weekly basis when, in fact, the amount of the benefit payable is based upon a daily pro rata basis relating to the number of days of confinement unless such statements of such monthly or weekly benefit amounts are in juxtaposition with equally prominent statements of the benefit payable on a daily basis. The term "juxtaposition" means side by side or immediately above or below. When the policy contains a limit on the number of days of coverage provided, such limit must appear in the advertisement.

(8) No advertisement of a policy covering only one disease or a list of specified diseases shall imply coverage beyond the terms of the policy. Synonymous terms shall not be used to refer to any disease so as to imply broader coverage than is the fact.

(9) An advertisement for a policy providing benefits for specified illnesses only, such as cancer, or for specified accidents only, such as automobile accidents, shall clearly and conspicuously in prominent type state the limited nature of the policy. The statement shall be worded in language identical to or substantially similar to the following: "THIS IS A LIMITED POLICY," "THIS IS A CANCER ONLY POLICY," or "THIS IS AN AUTOMOBILE ACCIDENT ONLY POLICY."

B. Exceptions, Reductions and Limitations

   (1) An advertisement which is an invitation to contract shall disclose those exceptions, reductions and limitations affecting the basic provisions of the policy.

   (2) When a policy contains a waiting, elimination, probationary or similar time period between the effective date of the policy and the effective date of coverage under the policy or at a time period between the date a loss occurs and the date benefits begin to accrue for such loss, an advertisement which is subject to the requirements of the preceding paragraph shall disclose the existence of such periods.

   (3) An advertisement shall not use the words "only," "just," "merely," "minimum," "necessary" or similar words or phrases to describe the applicability of any exceptions, reductions, limitations or exclusions such as: "This policy is subject to the following minimum exceptions and reductions."

C. Preexisting Conditions

   (1) An advertisement which is an invitation to contract shall, in negative terms, disclose the extent to which any loss is not covered if the cause of such loss is traceable to a condition existing prior to the effective date of the policy. The use of the term "preexisting condition" without an appropriate definition or description shall not be used.

   (2) When an accident and sickness insurance policy does not cover losses resulting from preexisting conditions, no advertisement of the policy shall state or imply that the applicant's physical condition or medical history will not affect the issuance of the policy or payment of a claim thereunder. This rule prohibits the use of the phrase "no medical examination required" and phrases of similar import, but does not prohibit explaining "automatic issue." If an insurer requires a medical examination for a specified policy, the advertisement if it is an invitation to contract shall disclose that a medical examination is required.

   (3) When an advertisement contains an application form to be completed by the applicant and returned by mail, such application form shall contain a question or statement which reflects the preexisting condition provisions of the policy immediately preceding the blank space for the applicant's signature. For example, such an application form shall contain a question or statement substantially as follows:

   Do you understand that this policy will not pay benefits during the first [insert number] year(s) after the issue date for a disease or physical condition which you now have or have had in the past?   YES

   Or substantially the following statement:

   I understand that the policy applied for will not pay benefits for any loss incurred during the first [insert number] year(s) after the issue date on account of disease or physical condition which I now have or have had in the past.

Section 7.   Necessity for Disclosing Policy Provisions Relating to Renewability, Cancellability and Termination

An advertisement which is an invitation to contract shall disclose the provisions relating to renewability, cancellability and termination and any modification of benefits, losses covered, or premiums because of age or for other reasons, in a manner which shall not minimize or render obscure the qualifying conditions.

MEDICAL EXPENSE INSURANCE

Section 8.   Testimonials or Endorsements by Third Parties

A. Testimonials and endorsements used in advertisements must be genuine, represent the current opinion of the author, be applicable to the policy advertised and be accurately reproduced. The insurer, in using a testimonial or endorsement, makes as its own all of the statements contained therein, and the advertisement, including such statement, is subject to all the provisions of these rules. When a testimonial or endorsement is used more than one year after it was originally given, a confirmation must be obtained.

B. A person shall be deemed a "spokesperson" if the person making the testimonial or endorsement:

   (1) Has a financial interest in the insurer or a related entity as a stockholder, director, officer, employee or otherwise; or

   (2) Has been formed by the insurer, is owned or controlled by the insurer, its employees, or the person or persons who own or control the insurer; or

   (3) Has any person in a policy-making position who is affiliated with the insurer in any of the above described capacities; or

   (4) Is in any way directly or indirectly compensated for making a testimonial or endorsement.

C. The fact of a financial interest or the proprietary or representative capacity of a spokesperson shall be disclosed in an advertisement and shall be accomplished in the introductory portion of the testimonial or endorsement in the same form and with equal prominence thereto. If a spokesperson is directly or indirectly compensated for making a testimonial or endorsement, such fact shall be disclosed in the advertisement by language substantially as follows: "Paid Endorsement." The requirement of this disclosure may be fulfilled by use of the phrase "Paid Endorsement" or words of similar import in a type style and size at least equal to that used for the spokesperson's name or the body of the testimonial or endorsement whichever is larger. In the case of television or radio advertising, the required disclosure must be accomplished in the introductory portion of the advertisement and must be given prominence.

D. The disclosure requirements of this rule shall not apply where the sole financial interest or compensation of a spokesperson, for all testimonials or endorsements made on behalf of the insurer, consists of the payment of union scale wages required by union rules, and if the payment is actually for such scale for TV or radio performances.

E. An advertisement shall not state or imply that an insurer or an accident and sickness insurance policy has been approved or endorsed by any individual, group of individuals, society, association or other organizations, unless such is the fact, and unless any proprietary relationship between an organization and the insurer is disclosed. If the entity making the endorsement or testimonial has been formed by the insurer or is owned or controlled by the insurer or the person or persons who own or control the insurer, such fact shall be disclosed in the advertisement. If the insurer or an officer of the insurer formed or controls the association, or holds any policy-making position in the association, that fact must be disclosed.

F. When a testimonial refers to benefits received under an accident and sickness insurance policy, the specific claim data, including claim number, date of loss and other pertinent information shall be retained by the insurer for inspection for a period of four years or until the filing of the next regular report of examination of the insurer, whichever is the longer period of time. The use of testimonials which do not correctly reflect the present practices of the insurer or which are not applicable to the policy or benefit being advertised is not permissible.

Section 9. Use of Statistics

A. An advertisement relating to the dollar amounts of claims paid, the number of persons insured, or similar statistical information relating to any insurer or policy shall not use irrelevant facts, and shall not be used unless it accurately reflects all of the relevant facts. Such an advertisement shall not imply that such statistics are derived from the policy advertised unless such is the fact, and when applicable to other policies or plans shall specifically so state.

   (1) An advertisement shall specifically identify the accident and sickness insurance policy to which statistics relate and where statistics are given which are applicable to a different policy, it must be stated clearly that the data do not relate to the policy being advertised.

   (2) An advertisement using statistics which describe an insurer, such as assets, corporate structure, financial standing, age, product lines or relative position in the insurance business, may be irrelevant and, if used at all, must be used with extreme caution because of the potential for misleading the public. As a specific example, an advertisement for accident and sickness insurance which refers to the amount of life insurance which the company has in force or the amounts paid out in life insurance benefits is not permissible unless the advertisement clearly indicates the amount paid out for each line of insurance.

B. An advertisement shall not represent or imply that claim settlements by the insurer are "liberal" or "generous," or use words of similar import, or that claim settlements are or will be beyond the actual terms of the contract. An unusual amount paid for a unique claim for the policy advertised is misleading and shall not be used.

C. The source of any statistics used in an advertisement shall be identified in such advertisement.

Section 10. Identification of Plan or Number of Policies

A. When a choice of the amount of benefits is referred to, an advertisement which is an invitation to contract shall disclose that the amount of benefits provided depends upon the plan selected and that the premium will vary with the amount of the benefits selected.

B. When an advertisement which is an invitation to contract refers to various benefits which may be contained in two or more policies, other than group master policies, the advertisement shall disclose that such benefits are provided only though a combination of such policies.

Section 11. Disparaging Comparisons and Statements

An advertisement shall not directly or indirectly make unfair or incomplete comparisons of policies or benefits or comparisons of non-comparable policies of other insurers, and shall not disparage competitors, their policies, services or business methods, and shall not disparage or unfairly minimize competing methods of marketing insurance.

   A. An advertisement shall not contain statements such as "no red tape" or "here is all you do to receive benefits."

MEDICAL EXPENSE INSURANCE

B. Advertisements which state or imply that competing insurance coverages customarily contain certain exceptions, reductions or limitations not contained in the advertised policies are unacceptable unless such exceptions, reductions or limitations are contained in a substantial majority of such competing coverages.

C. Advertisements which state or imply that an insurer's premiums are lower or that its loss ratios are higher because its organizational structure differs from that of competing insurers are unacceptable.

Section 12. Jurisdictional Licensing and Status of Insurer

A. An advertisement which is intended to be seen or heard beyond the limits of the jurisdiction in which the insurer is licensed shall not imply licensing beyond those limits.

B. An advertisement shall not create the impression directly or indirectly that the insurer, its financial condition or status, or the payment of its claims, or the merits, desirability, or advisability of its policy forms or kinds or plans of insurance are approved, endorsed or accredited by any division or agency of this State or the United States Government.

C. An advertisement shall not imply that approval, endorsement or accreditation of policy forms or advertising has been granted by any division or agency of the state or federal government. "Approval" of either policy forms or advertising shall not be used by an insurer to imply or state that a governmental agency has endorsed or recommended the insurer, its policies, advertising or its financial condition.

Section 13. Identity of Insurer

A. The name of the actual insurer shall be stated in all of its advertisements. The form number or numbers of the policy advertised shall be stated in an advertisement which is an invitation to contract. An advertisement shall not use a trade name, any insurance group designation, name of the parent company of the insurer, name of a particular division of the insurer, service mark, slogan, symbol or other device which without disclosing the name of the actual insurer would have the capacity and tendency to mislead or deceive as to the true identity of the insurer.

B. No advertisement shall use any combination of words, symbols, or physical materials which by their content, phraseology, shape, color or other characteristics are so similar to combination of words, symbols or physical materials used by agencies of the federal government or of this State, or otherwise appear to be of such a nature that it tends to confuse or mislead prospective insureds into believing that the solicitation is in some manner connected with an agency of the municipal, state or federal government.

C. Advertisements, envelopes or stationery which employ words, letters, initials, symbols or other devices which are so similar to those used in governmental agencies or by other insurers are not permitted if they may lead the public to believe:

  (1) That the advertised coverages are somehow provided by or are endorsed by such governmental agencies or such other insurers;

  (2) That the advertiser is the same as, is connected with or is endorsed by such governmental agencies or such other insurers.

D. No advertisement shall use the name of a state or political subdivision thereof in a policy name or description.

E. No advertisement in the form of envelopes or stationery of any kind may use any name, service mark, slogan, symbol or any device in such a manner that implies that the insurer or the policy advertised, or that any agent who may call upon the consumer in response to the advertisement is connected with a governmental agency, such as the Social Security Administration.

F. No advertisement may incorporate the word "Medicare" in the title of the plan or policy being advertised unless, wherever it appears, said word is qualified by language differentiating it from Medicare. Such an advertisement, however, shall not use the phrase "[   ] Medicare Department of the [   ] Insurance Company," or language of similar import.

G. No advertisement may imply that the reader may lose a right or privilege or benefit under federal, state or local law if he fails to respond to the advertisement.

H. The use of letters, initials, or symbols of the corporate name or trademark that would have the tendency or capacity to mislead or deceive the public as to the true identity of the insurer is prohibited unless the true, correct and complete name of the insurer is in close conjunction and in the same size type as the letters, initials or symbols of the corporate name or trademark.

I. The use of the name of an agency or "[   ] Underwriters" or "[   ] Plan" in type, size and location so as to have the capacity and tendency to mislead or deceive as to the true identity of the insurer is prohibited.

J. The use of an address so as to mislead or deceive as to true identity of the insurer, its location or licensing status is prohibited.

K. No insurer may use, in the trade name of its insurance policy, any terminology or words so similar to the name of a governmental agency or governmental program as to have the tendency to confuse, deceive or mislead the prospective purchaser.

L. All advertisements used by agents, producers, brokers or solicitors of an insurer must have prior written approval of the insurer before they may be used.

M. An agent who makes contact with a consumer, as a result of acquiring that consumer's name from a lead-generating device, must disclose such fact in the initial contact with the consumer.

Section 14.   Group or Quasi-Group Implications

A. An advertisement of a particular policy shall not state or imply that prospective insureds become group or quasi-group members covered under a group policy and as such enjoy special rates or underwriting privileges, unless such is the fact.

B. This rule prohibits the solicitations of a particular class, such as governmental employees, by use of advertisements which state or imply that their occupational status entitles them to reduced rates on a group or other basis when, in fact, the policy being advertised is sold only on an individual basis at regular rates.

Section 15.   Introductory, Initial or Special Offers

A. (1) An advertisement of an individual policy shall not directly or by implication represent that a contract or combination of contracts is an introductory, initial or special offer, or

MEDICAL EXPENSE INSURANCE

that applicants will receive substantial advantages not available at a later date, or that the offer is available only to a specified group of individuals, unless such is the fact. An advertisement shall not contain phrases describing an enrollment period as "special," "limited," or similar words or phrases when the insurer uses such enrollment periods as the usual method of advertising accident and sickness insurance.

(2) An enrollment period during which a particular insurance product may be purchased on an individual basis shall not be offered within this State unless there has been a lapse of not less than [insert number] months between the close of the immediately preceding enrollment period for the same product and the opening of the new enrollment period. The advertisement shall indicate the date by which the applicant must mail the application, which shall be not less than ten days and not more than forty days from the date that such enrollment period is advertised for the first time. This rule applies to all advertising media, i.e., mail, newspapers, radio, television, magazines and periodicals, by any one insurer. It is inapplicable to solicitations of employees or members of a particular group or association which otherwise would be eligible under specific provisions of the Insurance Code for group, blanket or franchise insurance. The phrase "any one insurer" includes all the affiliated companies of a group of insurance companies under common management or control.

NOTE: The number of months was left blank in this rule because several states currently permit six months, several states allow three months, and other states currently prohibit such periods of enrollment. Whether such enrollment periods should be permissible and the period of time between enrollment are items on which each state should make its own decision. Each state should modify the time limit in this guideline to comply with the rule adopted by the particular state.

(3) This rule prohibits any statement or implication to the effect that only a specific number of policies will be sold, or that a time is fixed for the discontinuance of the sale of the particular policy advertised because of special advantages available in the policy, unless such is the fact.

(4) The phrase "a particular insurance product" in Paragraph (2) of this section means an insurance policy which provides substantially different benefits than those contained in any other policy. Different terms of renewability; an increase or decrease in the dollar amounts of benefits; an increase or decrease in any elimination period or waiting period from those available during an enrollment period for another policy shall not be sufficient to constitute the product being offered as a different product eligible for concurrent or overlapping enrollment periods.

B. An advertisement shall not offer a policy which utilizes a reduced initial premium rate in a manner which overemphasizes the availability and the amount of the initial reduced premium. When an insurer charges an initial premium that differs in amount from the amount of the renewal premium payable on the same mode, the advertisement shall not display the amount of the reduced initial premium either more frequently or more prominently than the renewal premium, and both the initial reduced premium and the renewal premium must be stated in juxtaposition in each portion of the advertisement where the initial reduced premium appears.

NOTE: Some states prohibit a reduced initial premium. Section 15B does not imply that the states which prohibit such initial premium are not in conformity with the NAIC Rules. This item is indicated in the rule as an item to be decided on a state-by-state basis.

C. Special awards, such as a "safe drivers' award" shall not be used in connection with advertisements of accident and sickness insurance.

Section 16. Statements About an Insurer

An advertisement shall not contain statements which are untrue in fact, or by implication misleading, with respect to the assets, corporate structure, financial standing, age or relative position of the insurer in the insurance business. An advertisement shall not contain a recommendation by any commercial rating system unless it clearly indicates the purpose of the recommendation and the limitations of the scope and extent of the recommendations.

Section 17. Enforcement Procedures

A. Advertising File. Each insurer shall maintain at its home or principal office a complete file containing every printed, published or prepared advertisement of its individual policies and typical printed, published or prepared advertisements of its blanket, franchise and group policies hereafter disseminated in this or any other state, whether or not licensed in such other state, with a notation attached to each such advertisement which shall indicate the manner and extent of distribution and the form number of any policy advertised. Such file shall be subject to regular and periodical inspection by this Department. All such advertisements shall be maintained in said file for a period of either four years or until the filing of the next regular report on examination of the insurer, whichever is the longer period of time.

B. Certificate of Compliance. Each insurer required to file an Annual Statement which is now or which hereafter becomes subject to the provisions of these rules must file with this Department, with its annual statement, a certificate of compliance executed by an authorized officer of the insurer wherein it is stated that, to the best of his knowledge, information and belief, the advertisements which were disseminated by the insurer during the preceding statement year complied or were made to comply in all respects with the provisions of these rules and the insurance laws of this State as implemented and interpreted by these rules.

NOTE: Where the rules were adopted on other than January 1 of the year, the required certification that all advertisements used in the preceding annual statement year complied with these rules cannot be given. The respective insurance departments should consider remedying the problem in the Certificate of Compliance used for the calendar year in which the rules were adopted.

Section 18. Severability Provision

If any section or portion of a section of these rules, or the applicability thereof to any person or circumstance is held invalid by a court, the remainder of the rules, or the applicability of such provision to other persons or circumstances, shall not be affected thereby.

Section 19. Filing for Prior Review

The Commissioner may, at his discretion, require the filing with the Department, for review prior to use, of any accident and sickness insurance advertising material. Such advertising material must be filed by the insurer with the Department not less than thirty days prior to the date the insurer desires to use the advertisement.

NOTES

1. Health Insurance Association of America. 1996. *Source Book of Health Insurance Data—1996.* Washington, DC: Health Insurance Association of America.
2. Koob Cannie, Joan. 1995. *Seeking Customers for Life.* New York, NY: AMACOM.
3. The Principal Financial Group memorandum, November 1996.
4. Health Insurance Association of America. 1996. *Source Book of Health Insurance Data—1996.* Washington, DC: Health Insurance Association of America.
5. Jensen, Gail A. et al. 1997. "The New Dominance of Managed Care: Insurance Trends in the 1990s." *Health Affairs* (January-February).
6. Butler, Patricia, and Karl Polzer. 1996. "Private-Sector Health Coverage: Variations in Consumer Protections Under ERISA and State Law." Washington, DC: The George Washington University (June).
7. Center for Studying Health System Change. 1997. "Tracking Health Care Costs: A Slowing Down of the Rate of Increase." *Issue Brief* (6).
8. *Ibid*.
9. Jensen, *op.cit*.
10. Liu, John C., and Robert E. Moffit. 1995. "A Taxpayer's Guide to the Medicare Crisis." Washington, DC: The Heritage Foundation (Sept. 7).

GLOSSARY

A

ACTUARY   An accredited insurance mathematician who calculates premium rates, dividends, and reserves, and prepares statistical studies and reports.

ADMINISTRATION   The handling of all functions related to the operation of the group insurance plan once it becomes effective. The claim function may or may not be included.

ADMINISTRATION MANUAL   A book of instructions given to the policyholder by the insurer that outlines and explains the duties of the plan administrator.

ADMINISTRATIVE SERVICES ONLY (ASO) AGREEMENT   A contract for the provision of certain services to a group employer, eligible group, trustee, and so forth by an insurer or its subsidiary. Such services often include actuarial activities, benefit plan design, claim processing, data recovery and analysis, employee benefits communication, financial advice, medical care conversions, preparation of data for reports to governmental units, and stop-loss coverage.

ADMINISTRATOR   The individual or third-party firm responsible for the administration of a group insurance program. Accounting, certificate issuance, and claims settlement may be included activities.

ADVERSE SELECTION   The actions of individuals, acting for themselves or for others, who are motivated directly or indirectly to take financial advantage of the risk classification system.

AGENT   A state-licensed insurance company representative who solicits, negotiates, or effects contracts of insurance, and services the policyholder for the insurer.

ALL CAUSE DEDUCTIBLE   A policy provision under which the deductible amount is met by the accumulation of all eligible expenses for any variety of covered claims.

ALLOCATED BENEFITS   Benefits for which the maximum amount payable for specific services is itemized in the contract.

AMBULATORY CARE   Medical services provided on an outpatient (non-hospitalized) basis. Services may include diagnosis, treatment, surgery, and rehabilitation.

ANCILLARY CHARGES Miscellaneous hospital expenses, other than room and board, including medications, radiology services, laboratory services, surgical and medical supplies, equipment fees, and operating room fees.

APPLICATION Statement of relevant facts signed by an individual who is seeking insurance or by a prospective group policyholder; the application is the basis for the insurer's decision to issue a policy. The application usually is incorporated into the policy.

B

BASE PLAN Any basic medical care plan that provides limited first-dollar hospital, surgical, or medical benefits, as contrasted with major medical benefit plans that provide comprehensive hospital, surgical, and medical benefits.

BASIC COVERAGE Refers to base plan benefits over which major medical benefits may be superimposed.

BENEFIT The amount payable by the insurer to a claimant, assignee, or beneficiary when the insured suffers a loss covered by the policy.

BENEFIT MAXIMUM The maximum amount for which benefits are payable under an insurance contract.

BENEFIT PERIOD The period of time for which benefits are payable under an insurance contract.

BENEFIT PROVISION The promises made by the insurer, explained in detail in the contract.

BENEFIT WAITING PERIOD The period of time that must elapse before benefits are payable under a group insurance contract.

BLUE CROSS A nonprofit membership corporation providing protection against the costs of hospital care in a limited geographic area.

BLUE SHIELD A nonprofit membership corporation providing protection against the costs of surgery and other items of medical care in a limited geographic area.

BROKER A state-licensed person who places business with several insurers and who represents the insurance buyer rather than the insurance company, even though paid commissions by the insurer.

C

CANCELLABLE CONTRACT A contract of health insurance that may be canceled during the policy term by the insurer.

CAPITATION   A method of payment for health services in which a physician or hospital is paid a fixed amount for each person served regardless of the actual number or nature of services provided to each person.

CARRIER   A term sometimes used to identify the party (insurer) to the group contract that agrees to underwrite (carry the risk) and provide certain types of coverage and service.

CASE   The term used to refer to the entire group plan of a policyholder.

CEDE   Activity of an insurer under a reinsurance treaty.

CEDING INSURER   The insurer that insures part of a financial risk with another insurer, called the reinsurer.

CERTIFICATE HOLDER   The insured person under a group plan who has been issued a certificate of insurance.

CERTIFICATE OF INSURANCE   The document delivered to an individual that summarizes the benefits and principal provisions of a group insurance contract. May be distributed in booklet form.

CHARGE   The term used when referring to dollar amounts or fees (e.g., for the services provided by a physician).

CLASS   The category into which insureds are placed to determine the amount of coverage for which they are eligible under the policy.

CLAIM   A demand to the insurer by, or on behalf of, the insured person for the payment of benefits under a policy.

CLAIMANT   The insured or beneficiary exercising the right to receive benefits.

CLAIM RESERVES   Funds retained by an insurer to settle incurred but unpaid claims that may also include reserves for potential claim fluctuation.

COINSURANCE   The arrangement by which the insurer and the insured share a percentage of covered losses after the deductible is met.

COMMISSION   The part of an insurance premium an insurer pays an agent or broker for services in procuring and servicing insurance.

COMPLIANCE   In insurance, the act of conforming to or observing regulatory requirements.

COMPLICATION OF PREGNANCY   A condition of pregnancy that substantially increases the level of medical care and treatment required for the management of the pregnancy.

MEDICAL EXPENSE INSURANCE

COMPREHENSIVE MEDICAL EXPENSE INSURANCE A form of health insurance that provides, in one policy, protection for both basic hospital expense and major medical expense coverage.

CONTESTABLE PERIOD That time allowed an insurer after a policy is issued to investigate possible misrepresentation in the application and contest the policy's validity. (See "Rescission.")

CONTRACT A binding agreement between two or more parties. A contract of insurance is a written document called the policy.

CONTRACT RATE The premium rate for a group insurance coverage that is specified in a master policy.

CONTRIBUTION That part of the insurance premium paid by either the policyholder or the insured or both.

CONTRIBUTORY PLAN A group insurance plan under which the employer requires employees to share in its cost. In a fully contributory plan, employees pay 100 percent of the premium.

CONVERSION PRIVILEGE The right given to an insured person under a group insurance contract to change coverage, without evidence of medical insurability, to an individual policy upon termination of the group coverage.

COORDINATION OF BENEFITS (COB) A method of integrating benefits payable under more than one group health insurance plan so that the insured's benefits from all sources do not exceed 100 percent of allowable medical expenses.

COPAYMENT The arrangement by which the insured pays a specified charged for a specified service (e.g., $10 for an office visit).

CORRIDOR DEDUCTIBLE A fixed out-of-pocket amount (e.g., $100) that the insured must pay above covered benefits of a basic plan before supplemental major medical plan benefits are payable.

COSMETIC SURGERY Surgery done to alter the texture or configuration of the skin or the configuration or relationship of contiguous structures of any feature of the human body for primarily personal reasons.

COST MANAGEMENT Efforts by medical providers, insurance companies, insureds, or other interested groups to control health care costs.

COST SHARING Policy provisions that require insureds to pay, through deductibles and coinsurance, a portion of their health insurance expenses.

COVERAGE A major classification of benefits provided by a policy (i.e., short-term disability, major medical), or the amount of insurance or benefit stated in the policy for which an insured is eligible.

COVERED CHARGES Charges for medical care or supplies, which, if incurred by an insured or other covered person, create a liability for the insurer under the terms of a group policy.

COVERED EXPENSES Those specified health care expenses that an insurer will consider for payment under the terms of a health insurance policy.

COVERED PERSON Any person entitled to benefits under a policy (insured or covered dependent).

D

DAILY BENEFIT A specified daily maximum amount payable for room and board charges under a hospital or major medical benefits policy.

DEDUCTIBLE The amount of covered expenses that must be incurred and paid by the insured before benefits become payable by the insurer.

DELINQUENT PREMIUM Premium due the insurer that has not been paid by the end of the grace period.

DEPENDENT An insured's spouse (wife or husband), not legally separated from the insured, and unmarried child(ren) who meet certain eligibility requirements and who are not otherwise insured under the same group policy. The precise definition of a dependent varies by insurer.

DISTRIBUTION The separation of all insureds (prospective or in force) under a group insurance plan by age, sex, location, income, dependency status, and benefit class for the purpose of computing gross premium rates.

DOMICILE The legal residence of an individual or the jurisdiction in which a corporation maintains its center of corporate affairs.

DUPLICATE COVERAGE Coverage of an insured under two or more policies for the same potential loss.

E

EFFECTIVE DATE The date that insurance coverage goes into effect.

ELIGIBILITY The provisions of the group policy that state the requirements that members of the group and/or their dependents must satisfy to become insured.

ELIGIBILITY DATE The date on which a member of an insured group may apply for insurance.

ELIGIBILITY PERIOD The time following the eligibility date (usually 31 days) during which a member of an insured group may apply for insurance without evidence of insurability.

ELIGIBILITY REQUIREMENTS Underwriting requirements the applicant must satisfy in order to become insured.

ELIGIBLE EMPLOYEES Those employees who have met the eligibility requirements for insurance set forth in the group policy.

ELIGIBLE GROUP A group of persons permitted, under state insurance laws and insurer underwriting practices, to be insured under a group policy; usually includes individual employer groups, multiple employer groups, labor union groups, and certain association groups.

ELIGIBLE MEDICAL EXPENSE A term describing the various types of expense the policy covers. The provision that describes these expenses commonly contains limitations applicable to certain of these expenses.

ELIMINATION PERIOD A specified number of days at the beginning of each period of disability during which no disability income benefits are paid.

EMPLOYEE RETIREMENT INCOME SECURITY ACT OF 1974 (ERISA) Federal legislation that affects pension and profit-sharing plans. It mandates reporting and disclosure requirements for group health and life insurance plans.

EMPLOYER CONTRIBUTION The amount an employer contributes toward the premium costs of the group insurance plan.

EXCLUSIONS (EXCEPTIONS) Specified conditions or circumstances, listed in the policy, for which the policy will not provide benefits.

EXCLUSIVE PROVIDER ORGANIZATION (EPO) Form of managed care in which participants are reimbursed for care received only from affiliated providers.

EXPENSE LOADING That portion of a group insurance premium required to cover acquisition and administration costs.

EXPENSE RATIO A percentage showing the relationship of expenses to earned premiums.

EXPENSES The term used when referring to categories of bills or charges that may or may not be covered under a policy.

EXPERIENCE RATING The process of determining the premium rate for a group risk based wholly or partially on that risk's experience.

F

FEE-FOR-SERVICE A method of charging whereby a physician or other practitioner bills for each visit or service rendered.

FEE SCHEDULE Maximum dollar or unit allowances for health services that apply under a specific contract.

FIRST-DOLLAR COVERAGE A hospital or surgical policy with no deductible amount.

FRANCHISE INSURANCE Individual insurance contracts issued to members of a specific group (such as employees of a common employer or members of an association) under a group-like arrangement in which the employer or association collects and remits premiums and the insurer waives its right to cancel or modify any policy unless done for all persons in the group.

FRATERNAL INSURANCE A cooperative type of insurance provided by social organizations for their members. The social group may pay premiums into a fund and withdraw monies to pay claims upon the death of one of its members.

FREQUENCY A measure of the number of times a claim occurs during a given period.

G

GRACE PERIOD A specified time (usually 31 days) following the premium due date during which the insurance remains in force and a policyholder may pay the premium without penalty.

GROSS PREMIUM The contracted premium before applying any discounts.

GROUP CONTRACT A contract of health insurance made with an employer or other entity that covers a group of persons as a single unit. The entity is the policyholder.

GROUP INSURANCE An arrangement for insuring a number of people under a single, master insurance policy.

GROUP POLICYHOLDER The legal entity to which the master policy is issued.

GROUP REPRESENTATIVE A salaried employee of the insurer whose principal tasks are to assist agents and brokers in developing and soliciting prospects for group insurance and to install and service group contracts.

GUARANTEED RENEWABLE POLICY A contract under which an insured has the right, commonly up to a certain age, to continue the policy in force by the timely payment of premiums. However, the insurer reserves the right to change premium rates by policy class.

H

HEALTH INSURANCE Coverage that provides for the payments of benefits as a result of sickness or injury. Includes insurance for losses from accident, medical expense, disability, or accidental death and dismemberment.

HEALTH INSURANCE PORTABILITY AND ACCOUNTABILITY ACT OF 1996 (HIPAA) Federal legislation to improve portability and continuity of health insurance coverage; to combat waste, fraud, and abuse; to promote the use of medical savings accounts; and to improve access to long-term care services and coverage.

HEALTH INSURANCE PURCHASING COOPERATIVE (HIPC) Privately or state-sponsored groups through which small businesses can offer their employees a choice of medical expense plans, the way large employers do.

HEALTH MAINTENANCE ORGANIZATION (HMO) An organization that provides for a wide range of comprehensive health care services for a specified group at a fixed periodic prepayment.

HOME HEALTH CARE A comprehensive, medically necessary range of health services provided by a recognized provider organization to a patient at home.

HOME OFFICE ADMINISTRATION The method of insurance plan administration in which the insurer maintains the basic records for the persons covered.

HOSPITAL DAILY BENEFIT The maximum amount payable for hospital room and board per day of hospital confinement.

HOSPITAL INDEMNITY INSURANCE A form of health insurance that provides a stipulated daily, weekly, or monthly payment to an insured during hospital confinement, without regard to the actual expense of the confinement.

HOSPITAL-SURGICAL INSURANCE A form of health insurance that provides specific benefits for hospital services, including daily room and board and surgery, during a hospital confinement.

I

IDENTIFICATION CARD A form provided to insureds that identifies them as members of a particular insurance plan and may provide basic information about their coverage. Although such cards do not guarantee eligibility for medical care benefits at any given time, they provide procedures for providers to follow to verify that a patient has health coverage.

INCONTESTABLE CAUSE The provision in a group life and/or health insurance policy that prevents the insurance company from disputing the validity of certain coverage under specific insurance conditions after the policy has been in effect for a certain time (usually two years).

INCURRED BUT NOT PAID CLAIMS Claims that have not been paid as of some specified date (may include both reported and unreported claims).

INCURRED BUT NOT REPORTED (IBNR) CLAIMS Claims that have not been reported to the insurer as of some specified date.

INCURRED CLAIMS An amount equal to the claims paid during the policy year plus the change of the claim reserves as of the end of the policy year. The change in reserves represents the difference between the end of the year and beginning of the year claim reserves.

INDEMNITY A benefit paid by an insurance policy for an insured loss.

INDIVIDUAL INSURANCE Policies that provide protection to the policyholder and/or his or her family. Sometimes called personal insurance as distinct from group insurance.

INELIGIBLE EXPENSES A term describing the various types of expenses not eligible under the policy.

IN FORCE The total volume of insurance on the lives of covered employees at any given time (measured in terms of cases, lives, amount [volume] of insurance, or premium).

INITIAL RATE A premium rate that is charged on the effective date of a new group policy.

INSURABILITY Refers to the physical, moral, occupational, and financial status of a risk and its acceptability to the insurer.

MEDICAL EXPENSE INSURANCE

INSURABLE RISK   The conditions that make a risk insurable are the following: (a) the peril insured against must produce a definite loss not under the control of the insured; (b) there must be a large number of homogeneous exposures subject to the same perils; (c) the loss must be calculable and the cost of insuring it must be economically feasible; (d) the peril must be unlikely to affect all insureds simultaneously; and (e) the loss produced by a risk must be definite and have a potential to be financially serious.

INSURANCE   A plan of risk management that, for a price, offers the insured an opportunity to share the costs of possible economic loss through an entity called an insurer.

INSURANCE COMPANY   Any corporation primarily engaged in the business of furnishing insurance protection to the public.

INSURED   The person and dependent(s) who are covered for insurance under a policy and to whom, or on behalf of whom, the insurer agrees to pay benefits.

INSURER   The party to the insurance contract that promises to pay losses or benefits. Also, any corporation primarily engaged in the business of furnishing insurance protection to the public.

INSURING CLAUSE   The clause in a policy that names the parties to a contract and states what is covered by the policy.

INTEGRATED DEDUCTIBLE   A high fixed amount (e.g., $1,000) or the sum of the benefits paid under a base medical care plan, whichever is greater, that must be exceeded before supplemental major medical benefits are payable.

INTENSIVE CARE BENEFIT   An extra benefit, in addition to the hospital daily benefit, which is payable for each day a patient is confined to an intensive care, critical care, or cardiac care unit.

L

LAPSED COVERAGE   Termination of coverage provided in an insurance contract because of the nonpayment of a premium within the time period.

LAPSE RATE   A measure of the number of policies voluntarily canceled to the total number of policies issued.

LATE APPLICANT   An eligible person who applies for insurance after the normal 31-day open enrollment period.

LIMITATION   A provision that sets a cap on specific coverage.

LOADING FACTOR The amount added to the net premium rate determined for a group insurance plan to cover the possibility that losses will be greater than statistically expected because of older average age, hazardous industry, large percentage of unskilled employees, or adverse experience.

LOSS (1) The amount of insurance or benefit for which the insurer becomes liable when the event insured against occurs; (2) the happening of the event insured against.

LOSS RATIO The ratio of incurred claims to premiums (incurred claims divided by earned premiums).

M

MAJOR MEDICAL EXPENSE INSURANCE A form of health insurance that provides benefits for most types of medical expense up to a high maximum benefit. Such contracts may contain internal limits and usually are subject to deductibles and coinsurance.

MANAGED CARE The term used to describe the coordination of financing and provision of health care to produce high-quality health care on a cost-effective basis.

MANDATED BENEFITS Certain coverages required by state law to be included in health insurance contracts.

MANUAL PREMIUM The premium developed for a group's coverage from the insurer's standard rate tables.

MANUAL RATE The premium rate developed for a group's coverage from the insurer's standard rate tables, usually contained in its rate manual or underwriting manual.

MARKETING The sum total of all corporate functions and activities directly or indirectly involved in the selling of products to the consumer.

MATERIAL MISREPRESENTATION A false or misleading statement of fact on an application for an insurance policy, that influences the insurer's decision as to the prospective insured's insurability. Such statements may serve as a basis for voiding the policy. (See "Rescission.")

MATERNITY BENEFIT Benefits for a normal pregnancy are paid under this provision of the hospital or medical policy rather than the regular provisions that apply to sickness, since maternity is not normally considered a sickness.

MAXIMUM BENEFIT PERIOD The maximum length of time for which benefits are payable during any one period.

MAXIMUM DAILY HOSPITAL BENEFIT The maximum amount payable for hospital room and board per day of hospital confinement.

MEDICAL EXPENSE INSURANCE A form of health insurance that provides benefits for various expenses incurred for medical care. Benefits for prevention and diagnosis, as well as for treatment, are sometimes included.

MEDICALLY NECESSARY Term used by insurers to describe medical treatment that is appropriate and rendered in accordance with generally accepted standards of medical practice.

MEDICARE Government program that provides hospital benefits (Medicare Part A) and medical benefits (Medicare Part B) to persons aged 65 and older, and to some others. (Medicare covers short-term acute medical conditions rather than long-term, chronic conditions that require custodial care.) Medicare is administered by the Social Security Administration.

MEDIGAP Private insurance that can be purchased to supplement Medicare.

MINIMUM GROUP The fewest number of employees permitted under a state law to constitute a group for insurance purposes; the purpose of minimum group is to maintain a distinction between individual and group insurance.

MINIMUM PREMIUM PLAN A combination approach to funding an insurance plan aimed primarily at premium tax savings. The employer self-funds a fixed percent (e.g., 90 percent) of the estimated monthly claims and the insurance company insures the excess.

MORBIDITY The frequency and severity of sicknesses and accidents in a well-defined class or classes of persons.

MORTALITY The death rate in a group of people as determined from prior experience.

MULTIPLE EMPLOYER GROUP Employees of two or more employers, such as trade associations of employers in the same industry or union members who work for more than one employer, covered under one master contract.

MULTIPLE EMPLOYER TRUST (MET) A legal trust established by a plan sponsor that brings together a number of small, unrelated employers for the purpose of providing group medical care coverage on an insured or a self-funded basis.

N

NATIONAL ASSOCIATION OF INSURANCE COMMISSIONERS (NAIC) A national organization of state officials who are charged with the regulation of insurance. It was formed to promote national uniformity in the regulation of insurance. It has no official power but wields tremendous influence.

NEGOTIATED TRUSTEESHIPS A policy issued to the trustees of a fund established by a formal agreement concerning employees subject to collective bargaining, or employees of two employers who have signed the trust agreement. An example of a negotiated trusteeship is a Taft-Hartley health and welfare trust plan.

NET COST In group insurance it equals claims plus reserves plus expenses.

NET PREMIUM Amount paid or earned premium after discounts.

NONCANCELLABLE POLICY A contract the insured can continue in force by the timely payment of the set premium until at least age 50 or, in the case of a policy issued after age 44, for at least five years from its date of issue. The insurer may not unilaterally change any contract provision of the in-force policy, including premium rates.

NONCONTRIBUTORY PLAN A group insurance plan under which the employer does not require employees to share in its cost.

NONDUPLICATION CLAUSE A policy provision that results in a stricter application of coordination of benefits principles. When an individual is covered by two or more policies, this provision excludes expenses incurred that are covered by another policy.

NONRENEWABLE FOR STATED-REASONS-ONLY POLICY A contract of health insurance under which the insurer has the right to terminate the coverage for only those reasons specified in the contract.

NONRENEWABLE POLICY A policy issued for a single term that is designed to cover the insured during a period of short-term risk.

NOTICE OF CLAIM A written notice to the insurer by an insured claiming a covered loss.

O

OCCUPATIONAL HAZARDS Dangers inherent in the insured's occupation that expose him or her to greater than normal physical danger by their very nature.

OPTIONALLY RENEWABLE POLICY A contract of health insurance under which the insurer has the right to terminate the coverage at any policy anniversary or, in some cases, at any premium due date.

OUT-OF-POCKET EXPENSE Those medical expenses that an insured must pay that are not covered under the group contract.

OVERHEAD EXPENSE INSURANCE A form of health insurance for business owners designed to help offset continuing business expenses during an insured's total disability.

P

PARTICIPATION The number of insureds covered under the group plan in relation to the total number eligible to be covered, usually expressed as a percentage.

PENDING CLAIM A claim that has been reported but on which final action has not been taken.

PER CAUSE DEDUCTIBLE The flat amount that the insured must pay toward the eligible medical expenses resulting from each illness before the insurance company will make any benefit payments.

PERSISTENCY The degree to which policies stay in force through the continued payment of renewal premiums.

PHYSICIAN'S EXPENSE Insurance coverage that provides benefits toward the cost of such services as doctors' fees—for surgical care in the hospital, at home, or in a physician's office—and X-rays or laboratory tests performed outside of a hospital. (Also called regular medical expense insurance.)

POINT-OF-SERVICE (POS) PROGRAM Health care delivery method offered as an option of an employer's indemnity program. Under such a program, employees coordinate their health care needs through a primary care physician.

POLICY The document that sets forth the contract of insurance.

POLICY ANNIVERSARY The manual date that separates the experience under a group policy for dividend and retroactive rate purposes. The period is normally 12 consecutive months.

POLICYHOLDER The legal entity to whom an insurer issues a contract.

POLICYHOLDER ADMINISTRATION (SELF-ADMINISTRATION) Situation whereby the group policyholder maintains all records and assumes responsibility regarding insureds covered under its insurance plan, including preparing the premium statement for each payment date and submitting it with a check to the insurer. Under this method the insurance company, in most instances, has the contractual prerogative to audit the policyholder's records.

POLICY ISSUE   The transmittal of a policy to an insured by an insurer.

POLICY NUMBER   That number assigned to a group contract that contains both the account number of the policy and the policy code number.

POLICY YEAR   The time that elapses between policy anniversaries, as specified in the policy.

PREADMISSION TESTING   The practice of having a patient undergo laboratory, radiology, and other prescreening tests and examinations prior to being admitted to a medical facility as an inpatient.

PRECERTIFICATION   A utilization management program that requires the individual or the provider to notify the insurer prior to a hospitalization or surgical procedure. The notification allows the insurer to authorize payment, as well as to recommend alternate courses of action.

PRE-EXISTING CONDITION   A mental or physical problem suffered by an insured prior to the effective date of insurance coverage.

PRE-EXISTING CONDITIONS PROVISION   A restriction on payments for those charges directly resulting from an accident or illness for which the insured received care or treatment within a specified period of time (e.g., three months) prior to the date of insurance.

PREFERRED PROVIDER ORGANIZATION (PPO)   A managed care arrangement consisting of a group of hospitals, physicians, and other providers who have contracts with an insurer, employer, third-party administrator, or other sponsoring group to provide health care services to covered persons.

PREMIUM   The amount paid an insurer for specific insurance protection.

PREMIUM NOTICE (BILLING)   The statement requesting the policyholder to pay a premium on a particular due date. The insurer may enclose a premium remittance card that should be returned with the policyholder's check.

PREMIUM RATE   The price of a unit of coverage or benefit.

PREMIUM TAX   An assessment levied by a federal or state government usually on the net premium income collected in a particular jurisdiction by an insurer.

PRIMARY SURGICAL PROCEDURE   For operative sessions involving more than one surgical procedure, the term used to describe the one procedure of most importance or highest complexity.

MEDICAL EXPENSE INSURANCE

PROBATIONARY PERIOD   A period from the policy's effective date to a specified time, usually 15 to 30 days thereafter, during which no sickness coverage is provided.

PROVISION   A part of a group insurance contract that describes or explains a feature, benefit, condition, or requirement of the insurance protection afforded by the contract.

R

RATING   Determining the cost of a given unit of insurance for a given year.

REASONABLE AND CUSTOMARY CHARGE   A charge for health care that is consistent with the average rate or charge for identical or similar services in a certain geographic area.

REIMBURSEMENT   An amount paid to an insured for expenses actually incurred as a result of an accident or sickness. Payment will not exceed the amount specified in the policy.

REINSURANCE   Acceptance by one insurer (the reinsurer) of all or part of the risk of loss underwritten by another insurer (the ceding insurer).

RENEWAL   Continuance of coverage under a policy beyond its original term by the insurer's acceptance of the premium for a new policy term.

RENEWAL UNDERWRITING   The review of the financial experience of a group case and the establishment of the renewal premium rates and terms under which the insurance may be continued.

RESCISSION   Voiding of an insurance contract from its date of issue by the insurer because of material misrepresentation on the application for insurance. The policy is treated as never having been issued and the sum of all premiums paid plus interest, less any claims paid, is refunded.

RESERVE   A sum set aside by an insurance company as a liability to fulfill future obligations.

RETENTION   That portion of the premium kept by the insurer for expenses, contingencies, and contributions to surplus (profit).

RIDER   A document that modifies or amends the insurance contract.

RISK   The probable amount of loss foreseen by an insurer in issuing a contract. The term sometimes also applies to the person insured or to the hazard insured against.

S

SCHEDULE A listing of amounts payable for specified occurrences (e.g., surgical operations, laboratory tests, X-ray services, and such).

SECONDARY SURGICAL PROCEDURES For operative sessions involving more than one surgical procedure, the term used to describe the procedures of secondary importance, which usually are of lesser complexity.

SELF-ADMINISTRATION Maintenance of all records and assumption of responsibility, by a group policyholder, for insureds covered under its insurance plan, including preparing the premium statement for each payment date and submitting it with a check to the insurer. The insurance company, in most instances, has the contractual prerogative to audit the policyholder's records.

SELF-FUNDING A medical benefit plan established by an employer or employee group (or a combination of the two) that directly assumes the functions, responsibilities, and liabilities of an insurer.

SELF-INSURANCE A program for providing group insurance with benefits financed entirely through the internal means of the policyholder, in place of purchasing coverage from commercial carriers.

SERVICES The term used to describe what is being done in terms of providing medical care (e.g., emergency room services).

SEVERITY A measure of the magnitude of a claim.

SOCIETY OF ACTUARIES A professional organization of life, health insurance, and pension insurance mathematicians.

STANDARD RISK A person who, according to an insurer's underwriting standards, is entitled to purchase insurance protection without extra premium or special restriction.

STATE INSURANCE DEPARTMENT An administrative agency that implements state insurance laws and supervises (within the scope of these laws) the activities of insurers operating within the state.

STATE OF ISSUE (SITUS) The jurisdiction in which the group insurance contract is delivered or issued for delivery.

STOP-LOSS INSURANCE Protection purchased by self-funded buyers against the risk of large losses or severe adverse claim experience.

SUBROGATION The substitution of the insurer in place of an insured who claims medical expenses from a third party.

MEDICAL EXPENSE INSURANCE

SUPPLEMENTAL MAJOR MEDICAL INSURANCE A form of health insurance that augments a plan that provides basic hospital-surgical coverage.

SURGICAL EXPENSE BENEFIT Benefit for the physician's or surgeon's operating fees. The benefit may consist of scheduled amounts for each surgical procedure.

SURGICAL SCHEDULE A list of cash or unit allowances up to a maximum amount an insurer will reimburse [for various types of surgery], based on the severity of the operation.

SURPLUS The amount by which the value of an insurer's assets exceeds its liabilities.

T

TEN-DAY "FREE LOOK" A right of the insured to examine a policy for ten days and return it for a refund of premium if not satisfied with it. A notice of this right is required to appear on the first page of health insurance policies.

THERAPEUTIC SURGERY Reparative or reconstructive surgery done to restore the patient's appearance to preinjury or presickness status, or to alleviate a severe condition that makes it impossible for the patient to function in school or business.

THIRD-PARTY ADMINISTRATION That method by which an outside person or firm, not a party to a contract, maintains all records regarding the persons covered under the group insurance plan and may also pay claims using the draft book system.

THIRD-PARTY PAYER Any organization, public or private, that pays or insures health or medical expenses on behalf of beneficiaries or recipients.

TIME LIMIT ON CERTAIN DEFENSES The two- or three-year period after which the insurer cannot deny a claim or void a policy because of pre-existing conditions or misstatements in the application.

TREND The rate of growth of the premium needed to cover claims plus expenses.

U

UNDERWRITER The term generally applies to (a) a company that receives the premiums and accepts responsibility for the fulfillment of the policy contract; (b) the company employee who decides whether the company should assume a particular risk; or (c) the agent who sells the policy.

UNDERWRITING The process by which an insurer determines whether and on what basis it will accept an application for insurance.

UTILIZATION Patterns of usage for a single medical service or type of service (hospital care, prescription drugs, physician visits). Measurement of utilization of all medical services in combination usually is done in terms of dollar expenditures. Use is expressed in rates per unit of population at risk for a given period, such as number of annual admissions to a hospital per 1,000 persons over age 65.

UTILIZATION REVIEW A program with various approaches designed to reduce unnecessary hospital admissions and to control inpatient lengths of stay through use of preliminary evaluations, concurrent inpatient evaluations, or discharge planning.

W

WAITING PERIOD The time a person must wait from the date of entry into an eligible class or application for coverage to the date the insurance is effective.

WORKERS' COMPENSATION Liability insurance requiring certain employers to pay benefits and furnish medical care to employees for on-the job injuries, and to pay benefits to dependents of employees killed by occupational accidents.

WORKERS' COMPENSATION LAW A statute imposing liability on employers to pay benefits and furnish care to employees injured and to pay benefits to dependents of employees killed in the course of and because of their employment.

INDEX

Abuse, 207-208
  see also Fraud
Accident and sickness insurance policy, 264
Accounting statement, 150
Acquisition expense, 56, 114
Actuary, 53, 60, 63, 277
Administration, 277
  card, 135
  manual, 135, 277
  materials, 135-136
  requirements, 114
  simplification, 208-209, 235-236
Administrative services only (ASO), 74, 153-154, 161, 277
Administrator, 277
Adverse selection, 103, 277
  underwriting, 125
Advertisement
  benefits payable, 265-267
  defined, 263
  form and content, 265
  losses covered, 265-267
  premiums payable, 265-267
  rules governing accident and sickness insurance, 261-275
Affiliation period, 216
Age
  at entry rates, 71
  -banded rates, 67
  classes, 70-71
  distribution, 108
  maximum, 3
  policyholder base, 59
  public employers, 124
  rates, 61

Agency sales management hierarchy, 45
Agent, 38-39, 45-46, 145, 277
  commissions, 114
  information, 134
Aggregate stop-loss insurance, 75
Alcohol addiction, 16
  see also Substance abuse
All cause deductible, 8, 277
Allocated benefit, 277
Allowable expense, 240-241, 250-251
Ambulance benefit, 29
Ambulatory care, 277
Ancillary charge, 21-22, 278
Annual report, ERISA, 155
Antiselection, 65
Applicability, 199-200, 213
Application, 278
Area rating factors, 71
Associations
  sales, 49
  underwriting, 122-123
Attained age rate, 71
Audit, 150, 187
  trade associations, 147-148
Authorization, claims and investigations, 180-182
Automated voice response system (AVRS), 142
Availability, HIPAA, 201-202
Avocation, underwriting, 118

Banks, 49, 192
Base plan, 278
Base rate structure, 71
Basic coverage, 278

297

Beneficiary incentive provisions, 233-234
Benefit, 278
  assignment, 180
  change, 120, 129-130
  design, nonstandard, underwriting, 125
  determination, 20-29
  information, 134
  maximum, 12, 21, 22, 164-165, 278, 288
  payable, 93-94
  paying, 150
  payment summary, 84-85
  period, 278
  provision, 93, 99, 278
  reserve, 256
  rider, pregnancy, 26
  structure, 110, 112
  waiting period, 278
Billing, 291
Blending, 72
Blue Cross, 278
Blue Shield, 278
Body distortion, 16
Body manipulation, 16
Breach of contract, 182
Broker, 38-39, 45, 46, 145
  commission, 114
  information, 134

Canada, 50
Cancellable contract, 278
Capitation, 41, 279
Card-only approach, 158-159
Carrier, 279
Case, 279
Cash flow, 73-74
Catastrophic loss, 115
Cede, 279
Ceding company, 130-131

Ceding insurer, 279
Certificate, 264
  holder, 279
  issue, 149
  of insurance, 81, 88, 91, 279
Certification method, 158
Charge, 279
Claim, 241, 279
  adjudication, automated, 184-185
  administration, 57, 157-188
  cost estimating, 59-65
  costs, 53-55, 59, 62, 73, 75
  denial, 184
  determination period, 241, 251
  investigation principle, 180-182
  payment provision, 100
  procedure, 157-161
  processing, 162-179
  reserves, 55-56, 65-66, 279
  reserves estimation, 66, 67
  services only (CSO), 161
  submission, 158-159
Claim-kit approach, 158
Claimant, 279
Claims experience, 112-113
Claims stabilization reserve rider, 91
Class, 279
Classification of insureds and benefits, 85
Closed panel plan, 241, 251
Code of Ethical Practices, 150-151
Codes, claim processing, 165-172
Coinsurance, 10, 61-62, 125, 164, 177-178, 279
  maximum, 10-11
Combination rider, 90
Commission, 279
Common accident provision, 10
Communication, customer service and, 49-50
Company overhead expenses, 57
Compensatory damages, 183

Compliance, 279
Complication of pregnancy, 279
Comprehensive plans, 2, 37, 280
  reimbursement, 4
  underwriting, 125
Confidentiality, 144
Consideration, 97
Consolidated Omnibus Budget Reconciliation Act of 1985 (COBRA), 87, 222-223
Consumer explanatory booklet, COB, 254-256
Contestable period, 181, 280
Contingency margin, 54, 58
Continuance of insurance, 85, 86-87, 174, 246-247, 252-253, 259-260
Contract, 280
  development, 100-101
  provisions, 79-101
  rate, 280
Contribution, 280
Contributory insurance, 82, 280
Conversion, 100, 172, 280
Coordination of benefits (COB), 96, 241, 118, 172-178, 280
  administration, 174-175
  allowable expenses with coinsurance, 177-178
  contract provision, use of model, 244-245, 250-254
  examples, 175-178
  maintenance of benefits, 178
  model regulation, 239-256
  reimbursing at 100 percent of allowable expense, 176-177
  rules, 245-247
  with and without provisions, 175-176
Copayment, 280
Corporate commitment, 140
Corporate-owned life insurance (COLI), taxation, 236

Corridor deductible, 4-5, 280
Cosmetic treatment and surgery, 35, 280
Cost, 43
  average charges for inpatient services, 109
  benefits, 20
  management, 280
  sharing, 280
  shifting, 63
  trends, 193-196
Cost containment, 10, 11, 41, 62, 125, 185
  deductible, 11
  coinsurance, 11
Cover page, 80
Coverage, 12-14, 87-88, 94, 281
  COB, 174
  individual, 20-23
  length, 247
  limits, 94
  persons, 248, 281
  services, 12-14
  transferring from HMO to indemnity, 84
Credibility percentage, 72
Custodial parent, 242, 251
Customer, 37
  knowledgeable, 38-39
Customer service, 49-50, 139-145
  measuring performance, 140
  tailoring, 141
  training model, 139

Daily benefit, 20, 22, 28, 281
  maximums, 28
  pregnancy, 26
Death of insured, 99
Declination of issue, 119
Deductible, 7-8, 61-62, 125, 162, 281
  all cause, 8, 277

299

cost containment, 11
maximum, 10, 11
per family, 162-163
per year, 163-164
sliding, 8-9
timing of incurred charges, 9-10
Definitions, 98, 199-200, 240-244, 277-295
Delinquent premium, 281
Demand, price and, 43
Demographics
   marketing and, 44
   rates, 61
   see also Location
Dental conditions and treatments, 33-34
Dependent, 252, 281
   COB, 173-174
   eligible, 83-84
   termination of insurance, 86
Diagnostic tests, 23
Digital imaging, 137
Direct selling, 47-48
Direct writer, 45
Disclosure, 202, 265
   small employer, 226-227
Discontinuance and replacement (D&R) regulation, 113
   model regulation, 257-260
Disparaging comparisons and statements, 269-270
Distribution, 45-49, 281
   alternative, 46
   market and, 49
   systems, 192-193
Document scanning, 137
Documenting coverage, HIPAA compliance, 144
Domicile, 281
Double payment, prevention, 14-15
Drug addiction, 16
   see also Substance abuse

Duplicate coverage, 281
   inquiry (DCI), 175

Earnings, 108
Eastern Europe, 50
Effective date, 82, 249, 260, 281
   dependent, 83
   group insurance, 92
Electronic claim
   adjudication, 186-187
   processing, 184-187
Electronic data interchange (EDI), 185-186
   increased use, 186
   standards, 186
Electronic funds transfer (EFT), 187
Electronic on-line record, 137, 138
Eligibility, 77, 98, 110, 282
   claim submission, 158
   date, 81, 83, 282
   dependents, 83
   employees, 80-81, 282
   group, 92, 282
   guaranteed issue, 202-203
   mandates, 81
   medical expense, 282
   MSA, 205
   period, 282
   requirements, 282
   Taft-Hartley plans, 121-122, 149
   underwriting, 123-124
Elimination period, 282
Employee Retirement Income Security Act of 1974 (ERISA), 154-155, 190-191, 193, 282
   enforcement, 214
   punitive damages, 183
   reporting and disclosure, 222
Employee
   active or inactive, 174, 246, 252

benefit plan, 39, 44
certification, 147-148
class, 108, 130
information, 134-135
Employer
contribution, 2-3, 112, 282
multiple group, 122
new responsibilities, HIPAA, 215-223
-sponsored coverage, 2-3
subsidization, 43
Enforcement procedure, 273
Enrollment, late, 82
see also Special enrollment
Errors, 88
Errors and omissions (E&O) insurance, 46
Ethics, 150-151
Exception, 82, 264, 282
dependent, 83
Excess risk, 131
Exclusion, 14-15, 62, 77, 282
365-day, 30-31
common, 15
mandatory, 234-235
rider, 120
underwriting philosophy, 65
Exclusive provider organization (EPO), 282
plans, 95
Exception, 267
Existing contract, 249
Expected persistency, 114-115
Expense, 56-57, 283
covered, 94
loading, 282
not covered, 94
ratio, 116, 282
Experience
analysis, 73
prior claims, 112-113
rating, 71-73, 283

Explanation of benefits (EOB), 186-187
Extended care benefit, 27-28
Extension of benefits, 99-100, 113, 257-259
Extra premium, 120

Facility of payment, 89, 253-254
Family
classification, 67, 70
deductible, 162
underwriting, 119
Federal continuance, 87
Fee schedule, 283
Fee-for-service, 41, 283
Field agent, 105-106
Field office claim administration, 159-160
Financial institution, 49
Financial rider, 90-91
First-dollar coverage, 5, 6, 283
Fixed retention, 72
Foreign national, 50
Form 5500, 155
Franchise organization, 283
underwriting, 123
Fraternal organization, 283
underwriting, 124
Fraud, 207-208
criminal sanctions, 234
new federal provisions, HIPAA, 233-235
Frequency, 54, 283
Fully insured plan, 73-74
Functional organization, 104
Funding method, 73-75

Gender, *see* Sex
General rider, 89
Genetic information, HIPAA, 216
Geographic area, 61, 71

Government hospital, 31-32
Grace period, 88, 143, 283
Gross premium, 283
Group
  location, risk selection factors, 108-110, 111
  membership, 121, 144
  representative, 284
Group insurance, 1-17, 283
  composition, risk selection factors, 107-108
  contract, 80-96, 283
    insured, 91-96
    risk selection factors, 106-115
  COB model regulation, 239-256
  customer service, 141
  discontinuance and replacement model regulation, 257-260
  experience rating, 71-72
  HIPAA, 200-202, 224-228
  implications, 271
  information, 134
  insured and, 91-96
  manual rate, 59-60
  market, 37, 39
  medical expense account, 133-135
  new responsibilities, HIPAA, 215-223
  policyholder, 80-91, 284
  premium statement, 142-143
  previous, 113-114
  product design, 40
  rating structures, 67-69
  underwriting philosophy, 64, 65
Guaranteed access, 228-229
Guaranteed issue, 64, 77, 202, 203, 224-225
Guaranteed renewable policy, 63, 77, 225-226, 229-230, 284
A Guide for Employers and Health Insurers, HIPAA, 211-238

Handicaps, 3, 99
Health care delivery arrangements, 37
Health coverage, 199-200
Health Insurance Portability and Accountability Act of 1996 (HIPAA), 16, 63, 77, 88, 107, 110, 190, 191-192, 199-209, 284
  complying with, 211-238
  documenting coverage, 144
  EDI, 186
  eligibility, 81
  group insurance, 224-228
  individual market, 228-230
  pre-existing conditions, 30, 179
  structure and enforcement scheme, 213-214
  underwriting, 127
Health insurance, defined, 284
Health insurance purchasing cooperative (HIPC), 47, 193, 284
Health maintenance organization (HMO), 37, 40, 41, 284
  indemnity contracts and, 84
  underwriting, 126
Health status, 3
  HIPAA, 219-220
High deductible plan, HIPAA, 206, 232
High-technology medicine, 44, 64
Home health care, 27, 28-29, 284
Home office
  claim administration, 159
  policy administration, 284
Hospital daily benefit, 24, 284
Hospital indemnity insurance, 284
  benefits, 242
Hospital-surgical insurance, 285

Identification card, 285
Identification of plan or number of policies, 269

Illness prevention, 42
In force, 285
Incontestable cause, 285
Incurred but not paid claims, 285
Incurred but not reported (IBNR)
  claims, 285
  reserves, 65, 66
Incurred claims, 285
Indemnity, 41-42, 285
  HMO-related provision, 84-87
  with cost containment provision, 41
Individual insurance, 19-35, 285
  accounts, 138-139
  contract provision, 96-100
  excluded or limited expense, 29-35
  HIPAA, 202-204, 228-230
  market, 37, 39
  policyholder, 145
  product design, 40
  rating, 70-71, 76-77
  renewal rating, 73
  underwriting, 65, 115-120
Industry
  issues, 189-198
  rates, 61
  risk selection factors, 107
  size and growth, 1-2
Ineligible expense, 285
Inflation, 59, 62, 63-64
Information, accurate and up-to-date, customer service, 141-142
Initial rate, 285
Inpatient services
  average charge, 109
  utilization statistics, 111
Institutional advertisement, 264
Insurability, 285
  evidence of, 126
Insurable risk, 286
Insurance, 286
  company, 286
Insured, 286

Insurer, 264, 286
  identity, 270
Insuring clause, 93, 97, 286
Integrated deductible reimbursement, 5-6, 286
Intensive care, 21, 286
Intermittent nursing care, 28
Internal customers, 145
Internal Revenue code enforcement, 214
  see also Taxation
International Claim Association (ICA), 180-181
International Classification of Diseases (ICD), 166-168, 169
Internet, sales, 48
Introductory offers, 271-272
Invitation
  to contract, 264
  to inquire, 264
IRA withdrawals for medical expenses, 238
Issue options, underwriting, 119-120

Jaw disorders, 16
Jurisdictional licensing, 270

Labor unions, underwriting, 121-122
Laboratory test, 23
Lapse rate, 58-59, 286
Lapsed coverage, 286
Late applicant, 286
Lawsuit, 182-184
Lead-generating device, 264-265
Level rate, 71
Liability, 74
  public employer, 124
Life insurance, 103
  living benefits, 237
Limitation, 15-16, 62, 94, 264, 267, 286

Limited coverage for specified conditions, 120
Litigation, 181, 182-184
Loading factor, 287
Location, *see* Demographics
Long-term care, 204-205
 taxation, 237-238
Loss, 287
 ratio, 56, 76-77, 287
Low-deductible plan design, 43
Low persistency, public employer, 124

Major medical expense insurance, 287
 key features, 6-14
 exclusions, 14-15
 limitations, 15-16
 maximum benefit, 93-94, 127
Managed care, 41-42, 189, 287
 effectiveness, 194-195
 products, 41
Managed indemnity plans, 37, 94-95, 99
Mandated benefits, 44, 287
Manual
 premium, 287
 rate, 287
Market
 changing, 50
 distribution driven, 49
 research, 48
Marketing, 37-51, 287
 mix, 38
Material misrepresentation, 287
Maternity benefit, 25-26, 287
Maximum benefit, 12, 21, 22, 164-165, 278
 daily hospital, 288
 period, 288
 see also Benefits

Medical expense insurance, defined, 288
Medical history, underwriting, 116-117
Medical inflation, 63, 193-194
Medically necessary, 288
Medical savings account, 192, 205-207
 demonstration project, 230-233
 effects, 206
 taxation, 206, 232-233
Medical spending trends, future, 195-196
Medicare, 288
 HMO sanctions, 235
 integrity program, 233
 reform, 196-197
Medigap, 197, 288
Mental health coverage, 16, 34, 221
MEWA, *see* Multiple employer welfare arrangement
Mexico, 50
Microfiche and microfilm, 137
Military duty, 31-32
Military hospital, 31-32
 nonservice-related injuries, 32
Minimum group, 288
Minimum premium plan, 74, 288
 rider, 90
Miscellaneous hospital expense, 21-23
Misrepresentation, 181
Modified issue, 119-120
Moral hazard, underwriting, 118
Morbidity, 53, 103, 107, 108, 288
 tables, 59-60
Mortality, 58, 103, 288
Mothers, HIPAA, 220-221
MSA, *see* Medical savings account
Multigroup plans, policy administration, 146-152
Multiple coverage claims, 174-175

Multiple employer group, 122, 288
Multiple employer trust (MET), 122, 151-152, 288
Multiple employer welfare arrangement (MEWA), 191, 193, 214
Multiyear deductible, 8

Name certificates, 81
National Association of Insurance Commissioners (NAIC), 190, 289
   guidelines, 76
Negotiated trusteeships, 149-151, 289
Nervous conditions, 16, 34
Net cost, 289
Net premium, 289
New accounts, policy administration, 133-139
Newborns, HIPAA, 220-221
New class additions, 130
New medical technologies, 44, 64
No-name certificates, 81
Noncancellable policy, 63, 289
Noncontributory insurance, 82, 289
Nondependent, 173, 252
Nondiscrimination requirements, 3, 200
Nondomestic market, 50
Nonduplication clause, 289
Nonrenewable policy, 289
   for stated reasons only, 63, 289
Nonrenewal, 129
Notice of claim, 289
Nursing care, 21
Nursing homes, *see* Extended care

Occupation
   rate, 61
   underwriting, 117-118
Occupational hazard, 289
Open-end plans, R&C, 168-169
Optionally renewable, 63, 290

Order of benefit determination (OBD), 96, 173-174, 245-246, 251-253
Out-of-pocket expense, 4-5, 20, 112, 194, 290
   maximum, 11
Outpatient
   expenses, 22-23
   tests, 23
Overdue premium collection, 143-144
Overhead expense insurance, 290
Overinsurance, 118
Overutilization, underwriting, 125

Paper file, 136-137
Partial experience rating, 72
Participation, 290
Payroll deduction program, 48-49
Pending claim, 290
Pending reserves, 65-66
Per cause deductible, 8, 290
Performance-based management, 50
Persistency, 58, 290
   public employers, 124
Person, 264
Personal identification number (PIN), 142
Physician inhospital expense benefit, 27
Physician's expense, 290
Physicians' Current Procedural Terminology (CPT), 165-166
Pilot Life Insurance Company vs. Dedeaux, 183
Pilot project, HIPAA, 206
Plan, 242-243, 250
   administration, 123
   design, 61-62, 110, 112
   options for issuers, HIPAA, 229
   types, 125-126
Point-of-service (POS) plan, 40, 41, 164, 290

Policy, 290
  administration, 57, 133–156
  anniversary, 290
  application, 89
  issue, 138–139, 291
  number, 291
  provisions, 162–179, 267
  riders, 89–91
  schedule, 97–98
  termination, 143–144
  year, 291
Policyholder, 19, 290
  administration, 290–291
  approach, 159
Pooling charge, 72
Pre-existing conditions, 3, 15, 29–30, 65, 77, 82, 178–179, 267, 291
  HIPAA, 200–201, 215–217
  specified, common, 30–31
Preadmission testing, 291
Precertification, 291
Preferred provider organization (PPO) plan, 40, 41, 95, 164, 291
Pregnancy, 3
  complications, 26–27
Premium, 39, 48, 66, 194, 291
  group, 142–143
  levels, 59
  notice, 291
  overdue, 143–144
  provisions, 87, 100
  rate, 53–59, 148, 291
  rate change, 87
  taxation, 57
Premium Rates and Renewability of Coverage for Health Insurance Sold to Small Groups Model Act, 76
Presurgical tests, 23
Prevailing Healthcare Charges System (PHCS), 170–172
Price, 39, 53–78

  demand and, 43
  demography and, 44
  high-tech medicine, 44
  marketing concept, 42–44
  regulation and, 44
Primary care physician (PCP), 43, 126
Primary plan, 243, 250, 254–255
Primary surgical procedure, 291
Prior claims experience, 112–113
Prior coverage, HIPAA, 201
Prior review, filing for, 273
Probationary period, 292
Product-line organization, 105
Products, 39–42
Professional association, 49
  policy administration, 148–149
Profit margin, 58
Promotion, 46
Provider-sponsored network plan (PSN), 197
Provision, 292
Public employer, eligibility, 124
Punitive damages, 182, 183–184
Purchasing group, 192–193

Quality control, 142
Quota share, 131

Rate
  guarantee, 62–63
  increase, 59
  stabilization reserve, 72
Rate manual, 53, 59–60
  trend, 63–64
  variation from, 60–65
Rating, 127, 292
  appropriate, 53
  classes, 66, 70–71
  structures, 66–71
Reasonable and customary (R&C), 12, 13–14, 23–24, 168–172, 292

Rebuttal actions, 172
Recordkeeping, 136-137
Reduction, 264, 267
Regional issues and environment, 59, 75-77, 190-192
 organization, 105
 price and, 44
Reimbursement, 292
 comprehensive plan, 4
 methods, 4-6, 7
 supplemental plans, 4-5
 variations, 5-6, 7
Reinstatement, major medical plan maximums, 127
Reinsurance, 130-131, 292
Reinsurer, 130-131
Relative Values for Physicians, 172
Release of information, 180
Renewability, 59, 62-63
 HIPAA, 202, 204
Renewal, 292
 premiums, 129
 provision, 97
 rating, 73
 underwriting, 128-129, 292
Reporting, HIPAA, 217-218
Rescission, 292
Reserve, 292
 bank, 122
 trade associations, 147
 see also Taft-Hartley health and welfare trust
Resolicitations, 127-128
Resource Based Relative Value Scale (RBRVS), 172
Retention, 72, 292
Retirees, employer-sponsored coverage, 3
Retroactive rate-reduction-dividend provision, 88
Retrospective premium arrangements, 74

rider, 90
Rider, 292
Right
 of recovery, 254
 to examine policy, 97
 to receive and release information, 253
Risk, 292
 bearer, 39
 employer-assumed, 153-154
 pools, 44
 selection factors, 106-120
 transfer, 42
Room and board, 20-21
Russia, 50

Sales, 37-51, 45-49
 commissions, 56
Schedule, 84-85, 91-92, 293
 referencing, 85
Secondary plan, 244, 250, 254-255
 procedures, 247-248
Secondary surgical procedures, 293
Self-administration, 135, 141, 142, 146, 290-291, 293
Self-employment, 19
 taxation, 204, 236
Self-funding, 115, 293
 cases requesting an insured contract, 115
 group, TPA, 161
Self-insurance, 74-75, 153, 189, 191, 192-193, 293
Services, 293
Severability provision, 273
Severity, 54, 293
Sex
 classification, 70
 distribution, 108
 rates, 61
Size, risk selection factors, 107

Skull disorders, 16
Sliding deductible, 8-9
Small Employer Health Insurance Availability Model Act, 76
Small group laws, 76
Social organizations, underwriting, 124
Society of Actuaries, 293
Solicitation, 148
Special enrollment periods, 82, 201, 218-219
Specific stop-loss insurance, 75
Spine, subluxation, 16
Spouse, 3
Standard issue, 119
Standard risk, 293
State
   alternative mechanisms, HIPAA, 203, 229
   authority, erosion, 190-191
   continuance, 87
   enforcement, HIPAA, 214-215
   flexibility and preemption, HIPAA, 227-228
   insurance department, 293
   mandates, 75-76, 125
   of issue (SITUS), 293
   regulation, 190
   reinsurance pools, 44
   restrictions and requirements, 148-149
Statements about an insurer, 273
Statistics
   advertisements, 269
   compiling, 138
Stop-loss insurance, 76, 293
   application, 115
   specific, 75
Strategic marketing, 38-39
Subrogation, 293
Substance abuse, 16, 119
Suicide, attempted, 31

Summary annual report (SAR), 155
Summary plan description (SPD), ERISA, 154-155
Summary report, 151
Supplemental major medical, 2, 4-5, 294
   underwriting, 125-126
Surgical expense benefit, 23-24, 294
   maximum, 25
Surgical procedures, multiple, 24-25
Surgical schedule, 24, 294
Surplus, 294

Table of contents, 97
Taft-Hartley health and welfare trust plans
   administration, 149-151
   underwriting, 121-122
Taxation, 2, 57, 236-238
   MSA, 206
   self-employment, 204, 236
   see also Internal Revenue code enforcement
Technologies, new, 44, 64
Ten-day "free look," 294
Termination
   by insurer, 88
   by policyholder, 88
   of benefit, 184
   of coverage, 83, 84, 98-99
   of employment, 3, 144
   of policy, 58, 87-88, 96
Therapeutic surgery, 35, 294
Third-party
   administration, 152, 160-161, 294
   payer, 294
   testimonial or endorsement, 268-269
This plan, 244
Three-month carryover provision, 9-10

Time limit on certain defenses, 294
Timing of incurred charges, 9-10
Tobacco classes, 70
Toll-free numbers, 142
Tracking, 217-218
Trade associations, 49
   policy administration, 146-148
   special problems, 147
Transferred risk, 130
Transplant coverage, 44
Trend, 294
   analysis, 63-64

Ukraine, 50
Underwriter, 105-106, 294
Underwriting, 103-132, 295
   classes, 70
   department, 104-106
   issues, 124-129
   management, 129-130
   other groups, 121-124
   over time, 65
   philosophy, 64-65

Unemployment, 110
Uniformed Services Employment and Reemployment Rights Act of 1993, 87
Uninsured persons, 189
Unscheduled plans, R&C, 168-169
Utilization, 295
   control of, 112
   inpatient statistics, 111
   patterns, 63
   review, 94-95, 295

Variable deductible, 8-9
Veteran's continuance, 87
Veterans Administration (VA) hospital, 32
Viatical insurance, taxation, 237

Waiting period, 295
Waivers, 120
War, 32
Welcome letter, 136
Workers' compensation, 33, 295
   law, 295